Praise for *Platform Engineering*

Platform Engineering distills an enormous amount of actionable and nuanced advice into a well organized and readable guide. Everyone who's building systems at scale needs to read it.

—*Adrian Cockcroft, Technology Consultant at Orionx.net,*
previously Cloud Architect at Netflix and AWS VP Architecture Strategy

The authors cut through the platform engineering hype and get right to the reality of building and managing internal platforms. They draw on their direct experience as they share techniques for avoiding common failure modes and creating platforms that are trusted, and even loved.

—*Tanya Reilly, author of* The Staff Engineer's Path

Platform engineering is a team sport. This is your playbook.

—*Kelsey Hightower, former Google Distinguished Engineer*
and coauthor of Kubernetes: Up & Running

This book makes a compelling case for the platform as a product, for organizations of all sizes. It highlights the role of the platform as an enabler of success, rather than a constraint on how things can be done.

—*Sam Newman, technologist and author*

Platform engineering is challenging to get right: initiatives can take months or years of effort to pay off, and it's difficult to link those initiatives directly to business outcomes. Camille and Ian have the hard-won experience of building great platform engineering groups, and it shines through this fantastic book. They show how to build good teams, pick the right initiatives, navigate organizational politics, and how to know whether you are succeeding.

—*Sarah Wells, independent consultant and author*

Camille Fournier and Ian Nowland, both figuratively and literally, wrote the book on platform engineering. Their book is the definitive reference on understanding and building platform engineering. I highly recommend it.

—*James Turnbull, CTO and author*

A must-read for any leader who is embarking on their platform engineering journey. This book is a detailed map for navigating technical, organizational and systemic challenges, and building high leverage platforms through the lens of deep expertise, humble experiences and cognitive empathy.

—*Smruti Patel, VP of Engineering at Apollo GraphQL*

Platform Engineering

*A Guide for Technical, Product,
and People Leaders*

Camille Fournier and Ian Nowland

Beijing · Boston · Farnham · Sebastopol · Tokyo

Platform Engineering

by Camille Fournier and Ian Nowland

Published by O'Reilly Media, Inc., 1005 Gravenstein Highway North, Sebastopol, CA 95472.

O'Reilly books may be purchased for educational, business, or sales promotional use. Online editions are also available for most titles (*http://oreilly.com*). For more information, contact our corporate/institutional sales department: 800-998-9938 or *corporate@oreilly.com*.

Acquisitions Editor: David Michelson	**Proofreader:** Piper Editorial Consulting, LLC
Development Editor: Virginia Wilson	**Indexer:** WordCo Indexing Services, Inc.
Production Editor: Kristen Brown	**Interior Designer:** David Futato
Copyeditor: Rachel Head	**Cover Designer:** Karen Montgomery

October 2024:   First Edition

Revision History for the First Edition

2024-10-08:   First Release

See *http://oreilly.com/catalog/errata.csp?isbn=9781098153649* for release details.

978-1-098-15364-9

[LSI]

Table of Contents

Part II.   Platform Engineering Practices

Part III.   What Does Success Look Like?

Foreword

In my career, I've had the privilege of working with hundreds of organizations and leaders to help them deliver value to their customers through software. It all began with the DORA research program, which set the standard for measuring software delivery performance in the industry.

Over the years, I've also researched how we can improve the developer experience to fuel innovation in complex software environments. In the midst of technological transformations, I've seen companies struggle with the complexities, often pinning their hopes on a shift to the cloud as a cure-all solution, only to find that more groundwork is needed.

This is where platform engineering plays a vital role, providing a crucial foundation for boosting agility, speeding up time to market, and enhancing overall product quality and user experience. By standardizing tools, infrastructure, and workflows, platform engineering streamlines development, fosters collaboration, and amps up efficiency among teams. It's the backbone that ensures scalability, reliability, and security, empowering organizations to keep pace with evolving needs while maintaining top-notch performance.

Yet, despite its significance, there's a glaring lack of resources guiding organizations through platform engineering work. This book steps in to fill that void, offering practical advice that extends beyond the developer experience to thinking about your infrastructure holistically and planning for what happens beyond putting your code into production—that is, explicitly including a systems focus in the work.

As you dive into these pages, you'll find insights into key questions like when to kick off a platform project, how to structure your platform team, and what sets platform planning apart from other initiatives. As well as addressing the overarching challenges and motivations, Camille and Ian provide clear, actionable advice—from defining team roles to nailing stakeholder management—that you can put into practice right away.

Chapter 4 presents a breakdown of key roles and responsibilities within a platform engineering team, alongside interview strategies and tips for structuring engineering ladders for success. Chapter 5 does the not-obvious-until-it-is work of telling us why platforms should be treated like products, complete with product discovery and evolution, roadmaps, customer support, and migration plans, each adapted to internal applications and stakeholders. Those who are familiar with my work will know I'm a sucker for an effective set of metrics; I'm fond of them because good data helps me understand context and diagnose problems. The authors step in here with the power-interest grid introduced in Chapter 10, which serves as a powerful tool for evaluating workplace dynamics, offering clear guidance for informed decision making.

So as you embark on your own platform engineering journey, I encourage you not only to absorb the knowledge inside but also to roll up your sleeves and apply it in your own context. Let this book be your guide as you navigate the complexities of platform engineering, guiding you toward success in your organization's tech endeavors.

— Nicole Forsgren, PhD
March 2024
Partner Research Manager, Microsoft
Lead author, Accelerate

Preface

A Note from Camille

In 2017, right as my first book was being published, I took a new job as head of platform engineering. This is where I first met Ian, newly moved to NYC from Seattle, where he had spent several years at Amazon and AWS. We were fast allies: two people who found themselves in the situation of helping a group of brilliant engineers turn around their organizational reputation from one of "a team that builds what they think is fun without enough concern for customer needs or stability" to a mature, well-operated, customer-focused platform team.

Over the next couple of years, we laid the groundwork for that turnaround. Ian taught me the value of everything he had learned in his time at Amazon: from writing six-pagers for design and planning to hiring systems engineers to establishing stronger operational practices (as well as injecting a heavy dose of skepticism about user-level networking). I brought in a focus on product management, decisive leadership, goal setting, and general willingness to change things that needed to be changed in pursuit of organizational excellence. Together with the technical, product, management, and operational expertise of the other platform leads, we succeeded in changing the culture of our teams and implementing a lot of the practices you will read about throughout this book.

When Ian left a couple of years later to tackle this challenge in the growth startup world, we stayed in close touch. Ian was (unsurprisingly) a very successful startup executive, and as we continued to evolve as leaders of platform teams, we supported one another through the peaks and chasms of career growth.

Fast-forward to early 2023, and I had a nagging idea: given the increasing popularity of "platform engineering," what if I wrote a book on it? I was working a big job and didn't think I could trust myself to tackle such a project alone, but I realized that I knew the perfect coauthor—someone who was a good writer, a clear thinker, and had strong opinions on the topic: Ian! One text message and a video chat later, we were pitching O'Reilly, and now here we are.

That trip down memory lane is all to say that we are writing this book because platform engineering has been our passion and profession for many years. While the term may be a recent technology buzzword, we've been in the trenches trying to figure out how to do it well for much longer than the latest hype cycle.

The truth is that most platform engineering teams we hear about have that same reputation the organization I mentioned earlier started with: building tech for the fun of it, without care for who needs it, and often without even the operational maturity that such critical work deserves. And this is because doing platform engineering is hard! When you strip away the hype, what we think you'll find is an evolution of organizational maturity. Now that we know about product management, we have no excuse to keep bumbling around building things just because they seem fun to build. We can't keep hiding behind the challenges of planning to excuse our inability to execute well. If we want to be trusted to provide critical systems to other engineers, we need to care about the operational stability of those systems.

This book is about all that and more. All of the hard lessons we've learned over the years of doing this have been the baseline for writing this book. And to make sure we've got enough data, we've asked several other experts in various areas of platforms from across the industry to contribute their advice and stories.

Who This Book Is For

This book is focused on the technical, product, and people leaders in organizations that engineer and operate software platforms: senior engineers; architects; product, program, and engineering managers. Most of these readers understand intuitively that platforms are not just about building automation for the cloud and open source systems, but they lack both a clearer definition of what they should be doing and the practices to do it well.

We also hope to reach the broader technology leadership community: the CTOs, SVPs, and "product engineering" leadership team. These leaders have a tendency to ask questions like "Why is the platform organization so big when we also have AWS?" "Why does our platform have all this headcount but still move so slowly?" and "Why didn't our recent adoption of [public cloud/SRE/developer experience] solve this?" The first two chapters of the book should start to answer these basic questions, and many of the techniques we spell out in the later chapters will be useful to product organizations as well (and may even provoke some introspection by these leaders!).

Finally, this book is really for anyone interested in learning how to make platform engineering work beyond the technical implementation details. Whether you are at a startup wondering when to start, a big company thinking about moving from infrastructure engineering to platform engineering, or anywhere in between, this book is for you.

How to Read This Book

The book is divided into three parts.

Part I, "The What and Why of Platform Engineering", introduces the basics of platform engineering: what it is, why to do it, and its core pillars. These two brief chapters are intended to ground you in what *we* mean when we talk about platform engineering.

Part II, "Platform Engineering Practices", is the meat of the book: eight chapters full of detailed advice on different common challenges in the platform space. We expect these chapters to provide an overview of important leadership and execution concepts and practices. There is an occasional bit of more technical content, but this book is not intended to teach you about the underpinning technologies of platforms. Rather, it focuses on the organizational practices that are needed to succeed in this space. Some of these chapters can only provide a high-level overview to what could be an entire book's content (for example, the chapter on platform as a product is long and still barely scratches the surface); we hope that those of you who read this and have more ideas will share them with the tech community in blog posts, talks, and books of your own.

Finally, Part III, "What Does Success Look Like?", pulls it all together. This is where we share more stories of success—or, in many cases, partial success—and give you an idea of what it might look like if you start to apply the practices from Part II.

O'Reilly Online Learning

 For more than 40 years, *O'Reilly Media* has provided technology and business training, knowledge, and insight to help companies succeed.

Our unique network of experts and innovators share their knowledge and expertise through books, articles, and our online learning platform. O'Reilly's online learning platform gives you on-demand access to live training courses, in-depth learning paths, interactive coding environments, and a vast collection of text and video from O'Reilly and 200+ other publishers. For more information, visit *https://oreilly.com*.

How to Contact Us

Please address comments and questions concerning this book to the publisher:

O'Reilly Media, Inc.
1005 Gravenstein Highway North
Sebastopol, CA 95472
800-889-8969 (in the United States or Canada)
707-827-7019 (international or local)
707-829-0104 (fax)
support@oreilly.com
https://oreilly.com/about/contact.html

We have a web page for this book, where we list errata, examples, and any additional information. You can access this page at *https://oreil.ly/platformEngineering*.

For news and information about our books and courses, visit *https://oreilly.com*.

Find us on LinkedIn: *https://linkedin.com/company/oreilly-media*.

Watch us on YouTube: *https://youtube.com/oreillymedia*.

Acknowledgments

From Camille

The list of people to thank for their help with this book is longer than my arm.

Thank you to my buddies: Ben, Leif, Kelly, Renee, Scott, Nicole, Jordan, Coda, Ale, Tim, Pete, James, Greg, Kyle, Juan, Caitie, Tasha, Ines, Alex, Lita, Nathan, Zach, Maggie, Silvia, Marco, Kellan, André, Brad, Alexis, Adam, Laura, Jason, Selena, Daniel, Chris, David, Carla, Bea, Danielle, Fiona, Dan, Peter. You've all made contributions major and minor to this book, and I couldn't have done it without your collective wisdom.

Thank you to all of my many colleagues who have taught me so much over the years, and special thanks to Alfred Spector for giving me the chance to become a leader in this space.

Thanks to my husband, Chris, for taking on most of the parenting duties while I spent hours writing, and for occasionally deigning to help me think through a particularly tricky section. I would not be the writer I am today without you.

And finally, the biggest thank you to Ian, for being a fantastic collaborator and putting up with my occasional need to completely rework things (not always for the better). I always learn things from you, and I'm grateful you agreed to be my partner in this endeavor.

From Ian

I would like to start by thanking my wife Sam, who over the years has had to listen to many frustrated complaints about colleagues "doing the wrong things" by the platforms my teams were trying to build. Those complaints eventually subsided as I learned the lessons that make up much of the material in this book.

I also want to thank a lot of my colleagues, from whom I directly and indirectly picked up the techniques and perspectives included here. In particular, Peter Desantis, James Hamilton, and Curt Ohrt at AWS were the three who helped me make the transition to seeing engineering leadership as a discipline. I also learned a lot from those who reported up to me along the way: Ashley Miller, Ivo Dmitrov, Johan Anderson, Sesh Nalla, Rob Boll, Remi Hakim, Conor Branagan, Joel Barciauskas, Makoto Nozaki, Andrew Kochut, Chris Fortier, Brian Barrett, Jack Bomkamp, Daniel Podwall, Tim Flowers, and Tim O'Hare.

Finally, my thanks to Camille for asking me to write this book with her. I was between jobs and able to spend five hours a day writing, but Camille had a full-time job and so for months spent her evenings and weekends writing. We got there in the end.

From Both of Us

We would both like to thank the team at O'Reilly for all their edits and other help: Virginia Wilson, David Michelson, Sarah Grey, and Melissa Duffield. They also coordinated a great team of technical reviewers we need to thank: Tanya Reilly, Cian Synnott, Raju Gandhi, Matt Holford, Diego Quiroga, Jordan West, James Turnbull, Sarah Wells, Niall Murphy, and Smruti Patel—with a big callout to Diego, Jordan, James, and Smruti for their substantial contributions, as well as Kelly Shortridge, Leif Walsh, and Nicole Forsgren for theirs.

The What and Why of Platform Engineering

Innovation is not born from the dream, innovation is born from the struggle.
—Simon Sinek, *Start with Why*

If you're reading this book because you are already working in platform engineering and looking for tips on how to do it better, you might be tempted to skip these first couple of chapters. After all, they will hopefully tell you what you already know: why you should be building platforms, and the core pillars that make up the "what" of platform engineering. However, we encourage you to stick with us, because many people don't get it like you do. These chapters will support you in explaining platform engineering to your colleagues, your boss, and your team, when you're faced with questions like: What is the motivation for doing it? What are the problems we could be solving with platform engineering? And what does our team need to focus on to do it well?

We start this book with the "why" not only to lay out the reasons we think you should care about building platforms but also to share our motivation for writing the book. We are passionate about solving these problems, and we want to see more of you inspired to solve them as well. Platforms are born from the struggles of modern scaled software engineering: the incredible demands we place on teams to manage a vast ecosystem undergoing rapid change, without sacrificing the availability and performance of their applications. This doesn't mean that platform engineering can solve all of our problems, but we explain why it is the right approach in the face of this complexity, building on the lessons learned from software trends including Agile, DevOps, site reliability engineering, and product management.

Staying high-level, Chapter 2 describes our core pillars for a successful platform engineering approach. Platform engineering is a bigger shift than just putting some people on a team and giving them the responsibility of solving for the "why." These people also need to appreciate and operate within the foundations of platform engineering: product, software, breadth, and operations. The later chapters are written with the assumption that you have a platform engineering team in place that approaches the problem through these foundations.

CHAPTER 1

Why Platform Engineering Is Becoming Essential

She swallowed the cat to catch the bird, she swallowed the bird to catch the spider, she swallowed the spider to catch the fly; I don't know why she swallowed a fly—Perhaps she'll die!
—Nursery rhyme

Over the past 25 years, software organizations have experienced a problem: what to do with all of the code, tools, and infrastructure that is shared among multiple teams? In reaching for a solution, most have tried creating central teams to take responsibility for these shared demands. Unfortunately, in most cases this has not worked particularly well. Common criticisms have been that central teams provide offerings that are hard to use, they ignore customer needs in favor of their own priorities, their systems aren't stable enough, and sometimes all of the above.

Instead of fixing these central teams, some have tried getting rid of them entirely, giving each application team access to the cloud and their choice of open source software (OSS). However, this exposes those application teams to the operational and maintenance complexity of their choices, so instead of creating efficiencies and economies of scale, even small teams end up needing site reliability engineering and DevOps specialists. And even with these dedicated specialists, the cost of managing the complexity continues to threaten the productivity of the application teams.

Others, while embracing the best of the cloud and OSS, have not given up on central teams; they've stuck with the model, certain that the benefits outweigh the downsides. The best have succeeded by building platforms: developing shared offerings that other engineers can comfortably build on top of. They have become experts at managing the complexity of the cloud and OSS while presenting stability to their users, and they are willing to listen to and partner with the application teams to continually evolve and meet the company's needs. Whether or not they've called their efforts platform engineering, they embody the mindset, skills, and approach necessary for solving the problem of ever-growing complexity (the fly) without swallowing ever-larger animals in the process.

To set the stage, in this chapter we'll cover:

- What we mean by platforms, and a few other important terms we'll use throughout the book
- How system complexity has gotten worse in the era of cloud computing and OSS, leaving us in an "over-general swamp" of exposed complexity
- How platform engineering manages this complexity and so frees us from the swamp

This chapter has a slight emphasis on infrastructure and developer tooling, but don't worry, this book isn't just for people working on infrastructure or developer platforms! We'll use systems common to all developers to provide a tangible illustration of the current state of affairs, but the underlying challenge of managing complexity is common to all kinds of internal platform development.

Defining "Platform" and Other Important Terms

Before we get started, let's define several important terms we'll be using throughout this book, so we all have the same frame of reference:

Platform

We use Evan Bottcher's definition from 2018 (*https://oreil.ly/y2NfD*), with a couple of terms updated. A platform is a foundation of self-service APIs, tools, services, knowledge, and support that are arranged as a compelling internal product. Autonomous application teams[1] can make use of the platform to deliver product features at a higher pace, with reduced coordination.

A corollary here is to ask: what, then, isn't a platform? Well, for the purposes of this book, a platform requires you to be doing platform engineering. So, a wiki page isn't a platform, because there's no engineering to be done. "The cloud" also is not a platform by itself; you can bring cloud products together to create an internal platform, but on its own the cloud is an overwhelming array of offerings that is too large to be seen as a coherent platform.

---

1 We'll sometimes call these teams your "users" or "customers," if it makes more sense in the context.

Platform engineering

Platform engineering is the discipline of developing and operating platforms. The goal of this discipline is to manage overall system complexity in order to deliver leverage to the business. It does this by taking a curated product approach to developing platforms as software-based abstractions that serve a broad base of application developers, operating them as foundations of the business. We will elaborate on this in Chapter 2.

Leverage

Core to the value of platform engineering is the concept of leverage—meaning, the work of a few engineers on a platform team reduces the work of the greater organization. Platforms achieve leverage in two ways: making applications engineers more productive as they go about their jobs creating business value, and making the engineering organization more efficient by eliminating duplicate work across application engineering teams.

Product

We believe that it is essential to view a platform as a product. Developing platforms as compelling products means that we take a customer-centric approach when deciding on the features of a platform. This implies a core focus on the users, but it requires more than just performatively hiring product managers and calling it a day. With the word "product" we strive to achieve for platforms what Steve Jobs created with Apple products: against a broad range of demand for features the product is deliberately and tastefully curated, both through what it does and, more importantly, through what it leaves out.

The Over-General Swamp

There are many types of internal platforms, and the advice in this book is relevant to all of them. However, we see the most acute pain today in the infrastructure and developer tooling (DevTools) spaces, and we see this driving the most demand for platform engineering. That is because these systems are the ones most closely integrated with the public cloud and OSS. These two trends have driven a lot of industry change over the last 25 years, but rather than making things uniformly better, they are increasing the ownership costs of systems over time. They make applications easier to build but harder to maintain, and the more your system grows, the slower you get—like you're walking through a swamp.

This comes back to the economic realities of writing and maintaining software. You might believe that the major cost of software is associated with the act of writing it. In fact, most of the cost is related to its upkeep, support, and maintenance.[2] Estimates

---

2 For a good diagram of the software lifecycle, see *https://oreil.ly/iDM5u*.

suggest that at least 60–75% of the lifetime cost of software accrues after initial development, with about a quarter of that dedicated purely to migrations and other "adaptive" maintenance.[3] Between required upgrades for security patches, retesting of the software, migrations to new versions of underlying dependencies, and everything else, software costs a lot of engineering time in maintenance overhead.

Rather than reducing maintenance overhead, the cloud and OSS have amplified this problem, because they provide an ever-growing layer of *primitives*: general-purpose building blocks that provide broad capabilities but are not integrated with one another.[4] To function, they need "glue"—our term for the integration code, one-off automation, configuration, and management tools. While this glue holds everything together, it also creates stickiness, making future changes much harder.

The *over-general swamp* forms as the glue spreads. Each application team makes independent choices across the array of primitives, selecting those that allow them to quickly build their own applications with the desired cutting-edge capabilities. In their rush to deliver, they create whatever custom glue is needed to hold everything together, and they're rewarded with praise for shipping fast. As this repeats over time, the company ends up with the type of architecture seen in Figure 1-1.

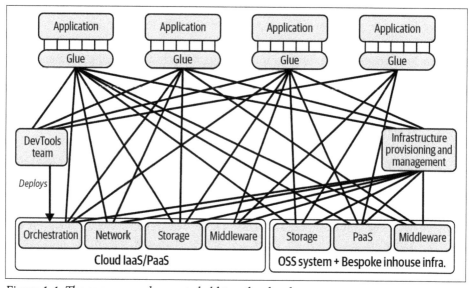

Figure 1-1. The over-general swamp, held together by glue

---

3 See Jussi Koskinen's paper on software maintenance costs at *https://oreil.ly/EFNZ6*.

4 This is literally what they were called in the 2003 AWS vision document (see *https://oreil.ly/n4ie_*).

The problem with the swamp isn't just the messy architecture diagram; it's how difficult it is to change that sticky mess over time. That's important because applications are constantly evolving, due to new features or operational requirements. Every OSS and cloud primitive also undergoes regular changes, and all of this requires updating the glue that binds them. With the glue smeared everywhere, seemingly trivial updates to primitives (say, a security patch) require extensive organization-wide engineering time for integration and then testing, creating a massive tax on organizational productivity.

The key to avoiding this situation is to constrain how much glue there is, which aligns with the old architectural principle of "more boxes, fewer lines." Platforms allow us to do this, and thus to extract ourselves from the swamp. By abstracting over a limited set of OSS and vendor choices in an opinionated manner, specific to your organizational needs, they enable separation of concerns. You end up with an architecture more like Figure 1-2.

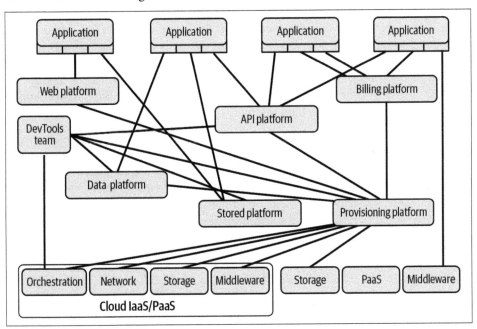

Figure 1-2. How platforms reduce the amount of glue

In sum, platforms constrain the amount of glue needed by implementing the concepts of abstraction and encapsulation and creating interfaces that protect users from underlying complexity (including the complexity of an implementation that needs to change). These concepts are about as old as computer science itself—but if they're so well known, why does the industry need platform engineering? To answer that question, we'll start with a look at how enterprise software engineering has changed over the last quarter century.

How We Got Stuck in the Over-General Swamp

The software industry has changed immensely over the past 25 years, kicking off with the widespread use of the internet. For those of you who have been in the industry for a while, we don't need to tell you how much this affected every aspect of software development, but for the relative newcomers, it's no exaggeration to say that the over-general swamp largely exists due to the internet itself and the pressure to ship more, faster, without failure. Let's look at the key changes that led to us getting stuck here, and the implications of that result.

Change #1: Explosion of Choice

The internet generated incredible demand for new software, and software has to run on hardware, no matter what the name "serverless" might imply. The initial wave was realized by provisioning a lot more hardware in data centers, and this led to the growth of infrastructure engineering. Every company was buying a lot more servers and network gear, negotiating with their data center providers, installing hardware in ever greater quantities all across the world—big I infrastructure doing big E engineering powering the big I internet.

We don't want to minimize the challenges that were overcome in this relatively short period of time. However, application developers interacting with infrastructure teams were constantly frustrated by the extent of hardware issues they had to deal with. They suffered from a limited but constantly changing menu of server choices, frequent data center capacity issues, and weird hardware-related operational problems that no one would help debug—the common response was "nothing in the system logs, must be your software."

It's no surprise that when the public cloud came along, frustrated application developers were eager to jump over to a world where they could call an API and seemingly control their own destiny. Despite reasonable concerns about the architectural complexity, security risks, reliability, and cost, even large, conservative companies were driven to some level of cloud adoption.

Unfortunately, those reasonable concerns have proven not just valid, but worse than feared. While the cloud promised platforms (PaaS) that would make applications independent of infrastructure, what has seen wide adoption is IaaS, which in many cases has tied applications to infrastructure even more than before. Reminding you of the difference:

- With *infrastructure as a service* (IaaS), the vendor's APIs are used to provision a virtualized computing environment with various other infrastructure primitives, which run an application more or less like it would be run on physical hosts.
- With *platform as a service* (PaaS), the vendor takes full ownership of operating the application's infrastructure, which means rather than offering primitives, they offer higher-level abstractions so that the application runs in a scalable sandbox.

Figure 1-3 shows a high-level comparison of the two approaches.

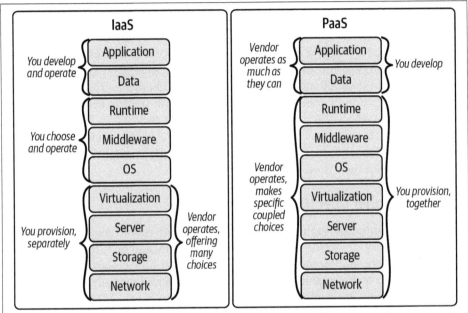

Figure 1-3. Comparison of IaaS and PaaS models in terms of vendor versus customer responsibility

Initially, it was hoped that application teams would embrace fully supported PaaS offerings—solutions as user-friendly as Heroku but capable of handling greater complexity.[5] Unfortunately, these platforms have struggled to support a wide range of applications and to integrate with existing applications and infrastructure. As a result, almost all companies doing in-house software development at scale embrace IaaS to run that software, preferring to accept the added complexity of provisioning and operating their infrastructure in order to get the flexibility of choice.

---

5 Other full service PaaSes that failed to see broad success were Force.com, AWS Elastic Beanstalk, and Google AppEngine. As a result, vendors often use the term *PaaS* for more flexible offerings, which means they need to be combined with other IaaS and so have similar problems around complexity.

The rise of the orchestration system Kubernetes is in many ways an admission that both PaaS and IaaS have failed to meet enterprise needs. It is an attempt to simplify the IaaS ecosystem by forcing applications to be "cloud native" and thus need less infrastructure-specific glue. However, for as much as it standardizes, Kubernetes has not been a complexity win. As an intermediary layer trying to support as many different types of compute configurations as possible, it is a classic "leaky" abstraction, requiring far too much detailed configuration to support each application correctly. Yes, applications have more YAML glue and less Terraform glue,[6] but as we've discussed, a goal of platform engineering is to reduce the total amount of glue.

Kubernetes is also an example of the second source of complexity we mentioned. Matching the rise of the cloud has been the rise of OSS ecosystems for all types of software. Where once you paid a vendor for your development tools and middleware, now there are thriving and evolving ecosystems for a wide array of development tools, libraries, and even full independent systems like Kubernetes. The problem with OSS is the proliferation of choice. Application teams with specific needs can usually find an OSS solution that is optimal for them but not necessarily for anyone else at the company. The bespoke choice that lets them quickly ship their initial launch eventually turns into a burden, as they must independently manage the maintenance costs that came with their "free, like a puppy"[7] OSS choice.

Change #2: Higher Operational Needs

In parallel with this explosion of infrastructure primitives and applications using them came the question of who was going to operate them, and how. If you went back to the 1990s, before the internet took off, and looked at how companies developed and operated their in-house software applications, you would typically find two roles, which in most cases were staffed in entirely separate teams:

Software developer
> Responsible for architecture, coding, testing, etc., leading to software applications being delivered as monolithic distributions, handed off to someone else to operate

Systems administrator
> Responsible for all aspects of the production operation of software (in-house applications as well as vendor software and OSS) on the company's computers

As the internet took off and in-house software became more important to companies' success, these roles started to mutate. The importance of 24/7 operational support

---

6 We will discuss what this looks like in Chapter 2.

7 As per former Sun Microsystems CEO Scott McNealy (*https://oreil.ly/1xi1F*), alluding to the long-term cost of adopting either OSS or puppies.

for an increasing number of applications initially led to the growth of *operations engineering* teams, which tended to be filled with a lot of early-career systems administrators—this was the proving ground they had to face before graduating into a less operational role.

You still see pockets of operations engineering in companies today, but the role is declining. As the 2000s progressed, software developers adopted the "Agile" model of regular releases of incremental functionality, as a better way to get feedback and so ship a better product. Agile brought a challenge to the operations engineering model: with one team taking on all the responsibility for making code changes and pushing for fast release cycles and the other team taking on all the frontline responsibilities when the code had problems, there was some tension. As anyone who lived through it knows, "some tension" is putting it mildly; particularly after an outage caused by something that had been "thrown over the fence," there was usually a large amount of finger-pointing about which side was to blame. The problem was that there was generally no clear answer, because Agile had blurred the lines of responsibility.

This led to the creation and broad adoption of what the industry now calls *DevOps*. DevOps was framed as a model to integrate application development and operations activities, and it became associated as much with a culture change as a set of specific technologies or roles to adopt. That being said, the operational work didn't go away, and on the ground teams implemented it in two different ways:

Split
> Keep the separation between operations and development teams, but have the operations team do some amount of development, particularly around creating glue for pushing code to production and integrating it with infrastructure. Thus, the old operations team with operations engineers was now the DevOps team with DevOps engineers.

Merged
> Merge the operations and development teams into one. With this approach, described as "you build it, you run it," everyone who works on a system is on the same team, with all of them sharing in the operational work (the most salient aspect being part of the on-call rotation). While many teams succeeded with 100% software developers, others were more cross-functional, with specialists to own the glue that pushed code to production and integrated with infrastructure. At some companies, these engineers were also called DevOps engineers.[8]

In an act of parallel evolution, in about 2004 Google moved away from operations engineering toward something they called *site reliability engineering* (SRE). In 2015, during the upswing of DevOps popularity, Google published a book on its practices,

---

8 In other companies, they were called systems engineers or systems development engineers.

Site Reliability Engineering: How Google Runs Production Systems (O'Reilly). This caused a lot of excitement, because while many companies had been adopting DevOps, plenty were struggling with the practical complexities of making it work. With its heavy emphasis on reliability-oriented processes and organizational responsibilities, some thought SRE was the silver bullet the industry needed to finally balance operational and development needs, enabling the creation of much more reliable systems.

We would argue that SRE, as it was originally sold, has not been a widespread success outside of Google. The processes were too heavyweight; their success relied too much on the specific cultural capital and organizational focus that came from Google being the world's biggest search company. This was well summarized by former director of SRE at Google, Dave O'Connor, who after a couple of stints outside Google wrote a post (*https://oreil.ly/FO2Zg*) in 2023 titled "6 Reasons You Don't Need an SRE Team" that concludes, "The next stage in removing our production training wheels as an industry is to tear down the fence between SRE and Product Engineering, and make rational investments in reliability as a mindset, based on specific needs."

There is no getting away from the needs of operating software. Every company that offers online software systems must have operational support for this software during applicable usage times (which may be working hours, 24/7, or somewhere in between). But how do you manage this in the most cost-effective yet sustainable way possible? You want to limit the places where you must have dedicated operations teams (or, using the terminology introduced earlier, "split" DevOps/SRE teams) and make it as easy as possible for the developers of the software to deploy and operate it themselves, achieving the initial vision of DevOps.

Result: Drowning in the Swamp

So you've got more application teams, making more choices, over a more complex set of underlying OSS and cloud primitives. Application teams get into this situation because they want to deliver quickly, and using the best systems of the day that fit the problem (or the systems they know best) will help them do that. Plus, if they've gotta own all the operational responsibility for this system themselves, they might as well pick their own poison!

Add to this that application engineers with new features are not the only ones wanting to ship as quickly as possible. The increasing surface of internet-accessible systems has led to an escalation of cyberattacks and vulnerability discoveries, which in turn means that infrastructure and OSS are changing faster to address these risks. We've seen upgrade cycles for systems and components move from years to months, and these changes mean work for application teams who must update their glue and retest or even migrate their software in response.

The pressure for change has created a swampy mess of glue mixed with the long-term consequences of individual team decisions. Every new greenfield project adds more choices and glue to this bog of complexity, and over time your developers get stuck in the mire. It's hard to navigate, slow to move through, and full of hungry operational alligators (or worse, crocs!). How do you extract yourself from this morass? It's no surprise that we think the answer is platform engineering, and next we will cover the ways in which it helps you do just that.

How Platform Engineering Clears the Swamp

If you've been stuck in the over-general swamp, you can appreciate the intellectual appeal of platform engineering. You're hiring more people in roles like infrastructure, DevTools, DevOps, and SRE engineer, but you never seem able to keep up with the new complexity arising from OSS and cloud systems. Your applications grow more complex, your application developers become less productive, and you need a way out. Building platforms to manage this complexity sounds great.

But building platforms takes significant investment. This includes the costs to build and support them, as well as the overhead associated with limiting application teams' choices of OSS and cloud primitives. Additionally, establishing a platform engineering team can incur organizational costs through reorganizations, role changes, and the overhead of rolling out a new focus area for the company. In this section, we explain how platforms and platform engineering will justify these investments and deliver long-term value.

Limiting Primitives While Minimizing Overhead

The explosion of choice wasn't all bad: greenfield applications can ship much faster now than in the past, and application developers feel more autonomy and ownership when they have systems they enjoy using. These benefits often get forgotten when companies start to focus on reducing the support burden and long-term costs that arise from the diversity of choices. In this situation, the first instinct of leadership is to prescribe a set of standards using appeals to authority. "Because I am the expert in databases," they say, "I will choose which databases you, the application teams, can use." Or, "I am the architect, so I decide on all of the software tools and packages." Or, "I am the CTO, so I decide everything." Inevitably, these experts will struggle to understand the business needs well enough to make optimal choices, and application teams will suffer. Standardization via authority isn't enough.

Platform engineering recognizes that modern engineering teams should have systems that they enjoy using, provided by teams that are responsive to them as customers and not just focused on cost reduction or their own support burden. Instead of prescribing a set of standards based on appeals to authority, platform engineering takes a customer-focused product approach that curates a small set of primitives able to meet a broad range of requirements. This requires compromises in light of business realities, incremental delivery of good platform architecture, and a willingness to partner directly with application teams and listen to what they need. When done well, you can point to the demonstrated leverage of partnering to use the platform-provided offerings instead of appealing to the authority of the architect, database administrator, CTO, or platform VP. In this way, you can reduce the number of OSS and cloud primitives used, without the worst consequences of top-down mandates.

Reducing Per-Application Glue

On top of reducing the number of primitives in use, platform engineering aims to go one step further and reduce the coupling "glue" to those that remain. This removes most of the application-level glue, by abstracting the primitives into systemic platform capabilities that are able to meet broader needs. To illustrate this, we'll dive into the common challenge of managing Terraform.

OSS and cloud offerings are complex in a lot of ways, with one of the most costly ways being their configuration—the endless lists of parameters that, if not specified correctly, will eventually lead to issues in production. Nowhere is this more of a problem than in cloud configuration, for which the 2024 state-of-the-art tool is an OSS infrastructure as code (IaC) system called Terraform that provides a perfect illustration of how platform engineering addresses the downsides of glue.

When application engineering teams all started pushing hard for the smorgasbord of the IaaS cloud, most companies decided that the path of least friction was to give each team the power and responsibility to provision their own individual cloud infrastructure with their own configuration. In practice, that meant they became part-time cloud engineering teams, versed in configuration management and infrastructure provisioning. If you want infrastructure that is repeatable, rebuildable, and can be secured and validated, you need a configuration management and provisioning template like Terraform. So, the common approach was to have application development teams learn Terraform. In our experience, this led to the following progression:

1. Most engineers don't want to learn a whole new toolset for infrequent tasks. Infrastructure setup and provisioning are not an everyday core focus—not even for teams doing mature resiliency testing and regularly rebuilding the system from scratch. So, over time the work would get shunted either to unsuspecting new hires, or to the rare engineers who were interested in DevOps. In the best case this would lead to one or two people evolving into infrastructure provisioning experts who could write Terraform and own all of this for the team. However, most of the time these engineers didn't stick around on application teams for long, which pushed the work back onto new hires, who usually made a mess of it.

2. The shortage, combined with people cobbling together their own Terraform all over the company, often led leadership to centralize the work across multiple teams (or even the whole company). But rather than centralizing with the goal of building a platform, all the Terraform engineers were just pulled into a team that provided Terraform-writing services.

3. These centralized Terraform-writing teams became trapped in a feature shop mindset, taking in work requests and pumping them out. This meant no strong developers (the type that can change the structure of the Terraform to provide better abstractions) wanted to be part of it. Over time, the codebase devolved into a spaghetti mess, which slowed down application teams who wanted something slightly out of the norm and eventually created a security nightmare.

A better path is to realize that you need to do something more coherent than offer centralized Terraform-writing support, and think about how to evolve this group of experts from a "glue" maintenance center into an engineering center that builds things—namely, a platform. This will require you to go one level deeper in understanding your customers' needs, to develop opinions about which solutions to offer rather than just trying to make it easier for people to get access to whatever they want, and to think about what you can build that takes you beyond just the provisioning step.

As you move into new models for providing underlying infrastructure, it is important to centralize expertise and create efficiencies. Instead of each engineering team hiring their own DevOps and SRE engineers to support the infrastructure, a platform team can pool these experts and expand their remit to identifying broader solutions for the company. This not only supports the one-off changes but permits their expertise to be leveraged to create platforms that abstract the underlying complexity. This is where the magic starts to happen.

Centralizing the Cost of Migrations

We will mention migrations often in this book, as we believe managing migrations is an important part of a platform's value. Applications and primitives have long but independent lifetimes, during which they each undergo many changes. The combination of these changes creates high maintenance costs. Platform engineering reduces these costs by:

Reducing the diversity of OSS and cloud systems in use
The fewer primitives you have, the less likely it is that you'll need to do a migration because of one.

Encapsulating OSS and vendor systems with APIs
> While platform APIs are often imperfect at encapsulating all aspects of the OSS and vendor systems they leverage, even "good enough" APIs that abstract a lot of their implementation will allow the platform to protect its applications from needing to change when the underlying systems change.

Creating observability of platform usage
> Platforms can provide various mechanisms to standardize collection of metadata around both their own use and that of underlying OSS and vendor systems. This visibility into the dependency state of the applications using your platform should allow you to ease the burden of upgrades when those dependencies need to change.

Giving ownership of OSS and cloud systems to teams with software developers
> When APIs are later shown to be imperfect, unlike traditional infrastructure organizations, platform teams have software developers who can write the non-trivial migration tooling that makes the migration transparent to most application teams.

Allowing Application Developers to Operate What They Develop

The goal of mature DevOps was to simplify accountability through a "you build it, you own it" approach. Despite this having been a popular idea for over a decade, many companies have not managed to execute on this model. We believe that, for those that have succeeded, a major contributor to this success is the leverage that their platforms provide through abstracting the operational complexity of underlying dependencies.

No one loves being on call. But when teams are only on call for issues caused by their own applications, we have found that a surprising number are willing to take on operational responsibility. After all, why wouldn't they stand behind the business-critical systems they spend their days creating? For too many companies, however, the operational problems caused by the infrastructure, OSS, and its glue completely dominate the problems in the application code itself.

An example of this can be seen as applications seeking higher resiliency are deployed across multiple availability zones, cloud regions, or data centers. This leaves application teams exposed to intermittent cloud provider issues such as networking problems, and the 2 a.m. alerts that inevitably follow. Platform engineering addresses this by building resilient abstractions that can handle application failover on behalf of the application teams, reducing the number of late-night wakeup calls they receive.

When most of the underlying systems' operational complexity is hidden behind platform abstractions, this complexity can be owned and operated by your platform team. This requires you to limit the options that you support, so that you can push the abstraction boundary upward into a core set of offerings, each handling a broad set of application use cases. It also requires that you have high operational standards within your platform team, so that application teams are comfortable relying on them.

Yes, building and operating platforms that handle these issues is hard, especially when it comes to getting application teams to accept limitations on their choices. But the only alternatives are either directly exposing your entire organization to these issues or perpetuating your use of operations teams (by any name), and so in turn perpetuating the accountability problems, negative impact on agile development, and finger-pointing.

Empowering Teams to Focus on Building Platforms

If you want to leverage OSS and vendor primitives but reduce the complexity that slows progress later, you need teams that can build platforms to manage those primitives and their complexity. There are four platform-adjacent approaches that are popular today, all of which bring valuable skills to the organization, but none of which are set up to have the combination of focus and skills needed for building platforms. Table 1-1 summarizes these approaches and why they are not adapted to this task.

Table 1-1. Platform-adjacent approaches and why they struggle to build platforms

Approach	Focus	Why they struggle to build platforms
Infrastructure	Robust operation of underlying infrastructure	Little focus on abstracting infrastructure to simplify applications, particularly across multiple infrastructure components
DevTools	Developer productivity up to production delivery	Little focus on solving developer productivity challenges related to systems in production running on complex infrastructure
DevOps	Application delivery to production	Little focus on ensuring their automation/tools help the widest possible audience
SRE	System reliability	Little focus on systemic issues other than reliability, often delivering impact through organizational practices instead of developing better systems

Individuals from each of these backgrounds might assert that they personally want to build more platforms rather than glue, but their organization won't let them. We empathize; we are not describing individuals, but rather how these approaches have evolved within organizations and how organizations typically define the respective teams' missions. However, the problem remains—individuals' roles are limited by the mission of their team, and changing a team's mission is not easy when the greater organization expects it to just do what it always has done.

Platform engineering asks each of these groups of engineers to come out of their silos and work in teams with a broader mission to create platforms that provide balance. This involves:

- *For infrastructure teams*, balancing infrastructure capabilities with developer-centered simplicity
- *For DevTools teams*, balancing development experience with production support experience
- *For DevOps teams*, balancing optimal per-application glue with more general software to support a lot more applications
- *For SRE teams*, balancing reliability with other system attributes like feature agility, cost efficiency, security, and performance

As a deliberate reset of organizational expectations, platform engineering gives you the ability to create teams that focus on building the technologies to finally clear the swamp.

Do Platforms Support Innovation?

As you're hopefully starting to see, platforms can cure all kinds of developer pain points, make your systems faster and more secure, make your developers more productive, deal with migrations automatically, and shorten the feedback loops for getting things done. And while we recognize that it can take quite some time to achieve all of these outcomes, we believe that this is an ideal worth striving for.

But what about the other good things that a platform might do? We're engineers, after all, so it's natural to expect our platforms to also support innovation and experimentation, because we know that innovation is the growth engine of our companies. Indeed, they can, but we want to clarify what this means, because platforms can get in the way of innovation and experimentation as much as they can support it.

If we are speaking purely of business innovation that can be developed within the context of the existing technology offerings, yes, platforms support that innovation. After all, by making application developers more productive, and in particular enabling them to push new features to production safely (such as through the use of feature flags and A/B testing), platforms allow them to build more faster, and thus support rapid experimentation with business ideas using the existing technology.

However, there will always be innovations that the platform by its nature does not support, and even fights against. Most significant innovation involving technology is going to require tools that don't exist yet in the company to be brought to bear on a problem. The data space is a great example, because it moves so quickly. You may have an excellent platform that supports easy access to relational databases and enables most of the engineers at the company to do their jobs well. But if a team

---

realizes they need a storage option with very different performance characteristics than your relational database offering in order to power a new, innovative business opportunity, they are going to leave your platform, at least partially, to build out this idea. If and when it comes to fruition, you may find that the new storage system is a good thing to pull into the platform offerings—but the innovation here is not enabled by the platform! That doesn't mean you should try to cram every new idea into the platform; rather, the best path is often to let these ideas develop independently, then merge in only those that are successful and have widespread demand.

It's tempting for platform teams to seek to quash innovation and experimentation that would take people off the platform. Much of the time, these ideas are a waste of engineering effort, driven by the "not invented here" bias that drives software engineers everywhere to build and create their own solutions to problems. But in some cases, these teams are right that they need to do something outside of the norm. If the platform team fights against all exceptions to using their offerings, or insists that they be the ones to build all new offerings that the teams might need, they not only push their systems to be too general but also risk inhibiting healthy innovation along the way.

So, yes, your platform should support easy experimentation and innovation within the bounds of the known, by making developers more productive and focused on the application layer. But you will not be the be-all, end-all support of innovation, and in fact, if you want to support innovation, you'll need to let some teams go their own way for a while to prove out new ideas. Making smart choices about when to push people toward central offerings and when to let them spin out their own alternative "shadow platforms"[9] is a key skill for platform engineering leaders, and one we will discuss more in Chapter 10.

Wrapping Up

We're on a complexity collision course, and many of us are already hitting the wall. Whether it's with the challenge of making DevOps effective, dealing with a million snowflake decisions, managing the increasing complexity of infrastructure as code, or simply dealing with the required upgrades and migrations that come with all software products, we need help. This is the reason that we believe platform engineering is becoming more and more important for the industry. By combining a product mindset with software and systems engineering expertise, you can build platforms that give you the leverage to manage this complexity for your company.

---

9 This is the platform equivalent of "shadow IT"—systems deployed by departments other than the central department, to fill gaps or bypass limitations and restrictions that have been imposed by central systems.

CHAPTER 2

The Pillars of Platform Engineering

The carrying power of a bridge is not the average strength of the pillars, but the strength of the weakest pillar.

—Zygmunt Bauman

Now that we've talked about the "why" of platform engineering, let's talk about the "what." Remember the initial definition we gave in Chapter 1:

> Platform engineering is the discipline of developing and operating platforms. The goal of this discipline is to manage overall system complexity in order to deliver leverage to the business. It does this by taking a curated product approach to developing platforms as software-based abstractions that serve a broad base of application developers, operating them as foundations of the business.

From this definition, we can identify the four pillars of platform engineering practice:

Product
  Taking a curated product approach

Development
  Developing software-based abstractions

Breadth
  Serving a broad base of application developers

Operations
  Operating as foundations for the business

These four pillars are critical to platform engineering success. Without them, you end up pushing the complexity around, but not actually managing it. Approaches that have come before have not managed to square this circle. This is not surprising, because building good platforms is hard! That's precisely why we wrote this book. In this chapter, we'll outline why we view these as the pillars of platform engineering, and what they look like in terms of underpinnings.

Taking a Curated Product Approach

The first pillar of platform engineering is the curated product approach that balances the concerns of the other three. By *product* approach, we mean getting out of a purely technical mindset and refocusing on what your customers need from your systems, and their experience using these systems. By *curated* approach, we mean not just that there are specific interaction patterns and usage conventions, but that you have an opinion about what is and is not in scope for this platform and curate the offering accordingly.

This is why we say *curated product approach*, rather than just curated approach or product approach—because either of these applied without the other is insufficient to create successful platform teams. A product approach without curation leads to great customer responsiveness but no coherent strategy, turning your teams into service centers. And curation imposed without a product mindset creates rigid offerings for application teams that may not meet their actual needs.

A successful curated product approach leads to two distinct types of platform products:

Paved paths

> The most common type of curated platform layers multiple offerings together into easy-to-use workflows, sometimes described as "paved paths" (see Figure 2-1). These platforms build on top of the work that good infrastructure organizations do in curation of offerings to make these offerings work well together. Product success comes from hiding most of the complexity of these common multisystem workflows from your application teams. This is a coverage play with a usability angle—you want to be opinionated enough to cover (and encourage) common uses, perhaps following the Pareto principle to identify the 20% of use cases that will cover 80% of needs, and focus on making these work extremely well. This also means saying no to outliers; this is a paved path, not a forced offering, and those with outlier needs can step off it at will.

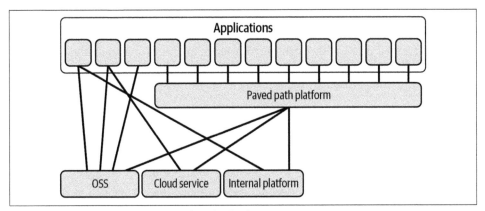

Figure 2-1. Architecture of a paved path platform

Railways

The second type of curated platform looks very different from the paved path type. In this case, you have discovered a meaningful gap that is not covered by any existing product but that would fill a need for many application teams. These platforms are the result of a product discovery process that looks for patterns of need across application teams and then investigates how teams are working around this missing platform.

They're often based on prototypes application teams have built to meet their specific needs, which are then generalized to create a more broadly useful offering. But the goal of creating this type of platform isn't just to smooth out common processes, and it often involves a major infrastructure investment to bring a specific piece of functionality into the company. We call these platforms "railways" (see Figure 2-2). Some railways we've built include a batch job platform, a notifications system, and a global application configuration platform.

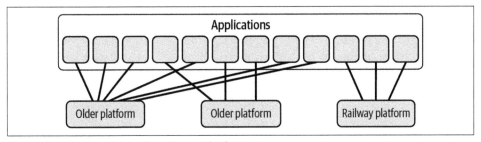

Figure 2-2. Architecture of a railway platform

That said, taking a product approach to building platforms involves much more than thinking about the user experience and identifying obvious gaps. It requires adopting a customer-focused mindset throughout your team, in everything you build. It means thinking deeply about what would make your customers' lives better, and going beyond making things easier by considering what work you can take off their hands entirely.

Developing Software-Based Abstractions

If you aren't building software, you aren't doing platform engineering.

The most common form of platform engineering today doesn't happen at the infrastructure or developer tooling level; it happens within larger software organizations that have multiple product lines. These product lines typically have core capabilities that are built in-house and that should be shared across all of them: billing systems are a common example. The natural thing to do is to pull these out and offer them as a platform, so that a single team can support them across multiple product lines. Obviously, this team will include software engineers, as the platform's components will have been built in-house as the company grew; software engineers created these systems, and they are core to keeping them going. The platform may evolve to integrate SaaS products with the in-house logic, but the idea that you would run such a team without any software development capability is silly.

We believe that this is true of all platform engineering teams, and not just the ones responsible for platforms that were spun out of bespoke in-house systems. As a corollary, if you don't need to write software yet, you may not be ready to embark on "platform engineering." If a wiki with pointers to the approved cloud provider offerings and instructions on how to onboard is a sufficient platform investment for your engineering team today, that's great! It's not what we consider "platform engineering," but for your company, or for the particular problem at hand, it might not be time to invest in a platform engineering team to solve these problems.

If you are starting a platform engineering initiative, be careful about doing so without involving software engineers from the get-go. Whether you're offering an internal billing platform or an infrastructure-level compute platform, platform engineering creates leverage by using software logic developed in-house to abstract underlying systems. Put another way: without that abstraction, you are not creating platforms that manage complexity; you are vending infrastructure and passing all the complexity on to users.

To provide pointers to what these engineers might build, we'll walk through some of the abstractions you are likely to need as part of your platform. This includes the platform service and its APIs, as well as thick clients, OSS customizations, and integrations with metadata services.

The Major Abstractions: Platform Service and Its APIs

Yes, this is straight from microservices or service-oriented architecture (SOA), which we assume you, like everyone in the industry, are familiar with in 2024. To cover the basics, the service is a major component of a platform; it implements the logic to coordinate the behavior of underlying OSS, vendor, and in-house systems, presenting abstract APIs for application systems to use (see Figure 2-3). To add some detail, a single platform may split its implementation into multiple service components. Further, the "API" need not be a traditional synchronous request/response; there may be queueing on either side, or the platform service may send messages to applications that are completely removed from a specific request.

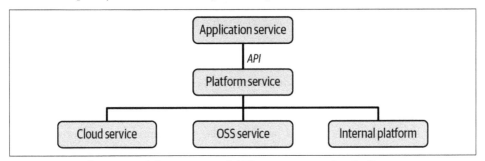

Figure 2-3. Architecture of the service and API components of a platform

The service and its APIs are an important part of platforms, and they're the reason it's essential to have software engineers involved from the start. Without them, it is very hard to create the abstractions over complexity that make things simpler for the applications and their engineers.

As important as APIs are, we do have a warning, particularly for infrastructure platforms. Those coming from a purely software background tend to believe an API and its service need to *encapsulate* the underlying OSS, vendor, and in-house systems. For example, we have seen platform teams propose that when the core of their platform is an OSS system such as PostgreSQL, the only way they can control their fate with regard to changes and migrations is by creating an API layer that fully encapsulates it, so that clients now need to send API requests, rather than SQL.

The key test of whether full encapsulation is the right level of abstraction is to look at it through the eyes of the application engineers—by reducing the surface area and divorcing them from resources associated with the underlying OSS and vendor systems (including things like their public documentation), have you made their productivity higher, or have you just made things easier for the platform team to manage? Until you are sure of the former, it's better to allow direct access to the underlying systems and learn from them, rather than imposing an API where your users are divorced from the wider ecosystem. Figure 2-4 shows an architecture where most platform dependencies have been encapsulated, but one has been left exposed.

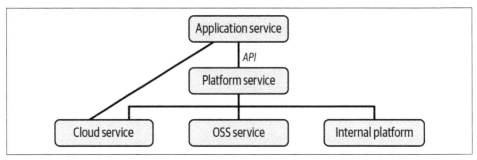

Figure 2-4. Architecture of a platform that avoids full encapsulation

Thick Clients

A follow-on to the previous section is that applications are often best served by client-side code being more complex than the "thin shims" of pure service architectures. This can take the form of thick client libraries (as in Figure 2-5) or actual executable binaries, which used to be called "daemons" and are often now called "sidecars." There are sometimes significant benefits to having rich logic in the client, such as reliability and performance enhancements around sharding, local caching, and load balancing. This is particularly the case when supporting legacy applications; for example, we have seen any number of storage platforms have to implement FUSE[1] mounts as a way of presenting themselves as a normal filesystem for legacy users.

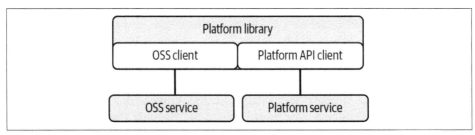

Figure 2-5. Architecture of the thick client component of a platform

---

1 A userspace filesystem mounted by a non-privileged (non-root) user.

As platform software now runs within the customer's application, thick clients come with significant costs related to observability, debugging, and the upgrade cycle not being controlled by the platform team. Thus, when it comes to complex logic, such as coordinating multiple underlying services, we much prefer putting it in the service. But we have also seen too many teams dismiss the possibility of a thicker client for reasons of architectural or operational purity, without considering the trade-offs and whether it is the best abstraction for their platform's users.

OSS Customizations

In some cases, OSS is very close to providing the abstractions that application engineers need, and it just requires some amount of customization to the specific problems your company faces. Sometimes these take the form of plug-ins to the OSS, and the platform team builds those plug-ins and operates the overall system. Other times, the platform team is forced to customize the OSS in order to meet a specific business demand. You may end up becoming contributors to or leaders of the OSS project itself as part of this customization, or you may just create a fork for your company. The ability to work within and modify the OSS code itself is part of the value-add of platform engineering.

Integrating Metadata Registries

We want to focus on this particular integration as it is a constant topic in discussions around platform engineering, to the point that some insist it is the core of platform engineering. As we've mentioned, one of the opportunities platform engineering affords is the ability to deal with problems and changes in the underlying OSS and cloud primitives on behalf of your users. However, to do this you need to have metadata about each primitive that makes it possible to reason about what each one is being used for, and by whom. Some examples of the questions platform teams might need to answer are:

Ownership
Who owns this service?

Access control
Does this service need to have such broad access to this blob store bucket?

Cost efficiency
Which organization should be charged for this blob store use?

Migrations
What teams are using the blob store in a nonstandard way, and who will we have to talk to about how we shim them as we migrate to a different vendor?

We're seeing a few different types of systems emerge to keep track of this information. These include:

Tag management systems
All major cloud providers and observability platforms now provide ways to "tag" individual resources with metadata. They are also starting to provide management tools that allow platform teams to enforce schemas and run rich exploration queries.

API/schema registries
These are focused on collating compile-time information about platform and application APIs, gathering the relevant information into one place for management, governance, and exploration.

Internal developer portals (IDPs)
These take registries one step further, offering a centralized catalog for not just API and resource metadata, but platform configuration as well. A key aspect is a programmable UI that allows each platform team to "plug in" their offering, creating a consistent, centralized user experience across all platforms.

There are some companies claiming great success with each approach, but it's early to say how this will all play out. We've seen registries struggle to get off the ground when the teams that created them thought of them as something users would manually populate, or that they would "just" need to clean up after machine scraping. We're confident that broad success will depend on how well platforms can integrate into these registries to automatically capture and label the metadata on an ongoing basis. There is nothing engineers like less than being curators.

Is an IDP a Required Component of a Platform Engineering Offering?

As we write this in 2024, there is a fair bit of noise about internal developer portals, with many claiming not only that they are a core component of a platform (sometimes in this context called internal developer platforms, with a common acronym that confuses), but also that they are the most important component of the strategy, to the point of being required.

We are not opposed to such systems. Having one place that ties together ownership of platform resources with all your platform's self-service UIs and documentation may well be exactly the high-leverage thing your customers need today. Equally, it may not be. Integrating the majority of platform use cases that would make it worthwhile is going to be a lot of work, and arguing "look at what the shiny UI could do someday" is not going to reduce that work.

If your customers are saying that one of their biggest problems is figuring out where to go to find the right UI or documentation to use the platform, then yes, bring in an IDP. However, if that's further down on their list of asks, then we're happy to tell you that you can ignore standing up an IDP for now, and instead just use tools like wikis for your documentation and links to APIs. An IDP is not a requirement for building a great platform.

Serving a Broad Base of Application Developers

The target audience for platforms is application developers—and not just one or two teams, but a broad base of teams. Sometimes application teams struggle with the usability overheads of central platforms. If you're used to having direct access to a machine to install whatever you want, having to go through a central platform that abstracts all of that from you can seem like a burden. While the purpose of a platform isn't to make every single action as easy as it could be for expert users who want direct access to primitives, platform teams need to invest in the things that offer the best development and operational experience to all of its users.

That's why we use the indefinite team "broad base." In modern microservices/SOA systems, a large number of teams build software with abstractions and APIs that are called by multiple other teams. We don't think calling all such systems "platforms" is useful. However, as usage broadens in terms of users and use cases, you need to move from just developing features to also developing capabilities that make the system cheaper, safer, and easier to use. These include:

Self-service interfaces

To scalably support a large set of customers, self-service is a key part of a platform offering. If every new customer onboarding requires the platform team to do manual work, or worse, requires multiple parts of the team to do manual and coordinated work, you will lose your leverage. This means it's essential to offer self-service access, provisioning, and configuration. These may be set up as graphical/web-based user interfaces or command-line tools, and they often integrate into continuous integration/continuous delivery (CI/CD) platforms (see Figure 2-6). The best platform offerings will have an easy-to-use set of defaults for novice users but will also provide the ability for power users to access the building blocks themselves when needed for more advanced activities.

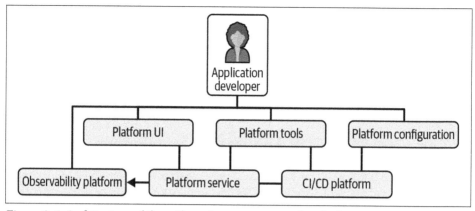

Figure 2-6. Architecture of the self-service components of a platform

User observability

A particular type of self-service that is less talked about but crucial for platforms is user observability. This requires building the telemetry to help developers debug their own problems throughout the full lifecycle of developing and operating applications that use the platform. Tanya Reilly, senior principal engineer and author of *The Staff Engineer's Path* (O'Reilly), told us: "One of the goals we ask our platform teams to aim for is that a user of the platform should be able to tell whether they're doing something wrong or the platform is doing something wrong. Obviously that's an ideal you can never entirely reach, but it's a good mindset."

Guardrails

When serving a broad base of users, you cannot expect them all to be experts in the underlying systems—particularly when they cross into details like security, compliance, reliability, and cost controls. In all these cases, a simple misconfiguration can turn out to be costly. Thus, an important part of building a platform is implementing guardrails, the protections and default limits that help ensure such expensive misconfigurations are highly unlikely. Because the exact requirements vary so much from company to company and over a company's lifetime, having an in-house platform that can react to the changing demands in this space can provide a major advantage for application developer productivity over time.

Multitenancy

A core aspect of broadly used platforms is that they are efficient only if they are built to be multitenant—that is, they can support different applications within the same runtime components. In the case of a hyperscaler cloud provider, this approach is used to support efficient economics (*https://oreil.ly/dqwJF*) with respect to the underlying hardware. For your platforms, the aim of multitenancy is more likely to be to support efficient economics of engineering time—that is, instead of operating one system per application, you can have a central team that provides shared systems that support many applications (see Figure 2-7).

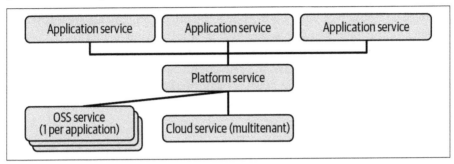

Figure 2-7. Architecture of a platform with hybrid multitenancy

A lot of hard engineering problems crop up when you start to offer multitenancy. This is another reason why you need software and system engineers on your platform teams. You may decide there are certain components (or certain customers) for which it is better not to be multitenant and choose a hybrid approach, but if you don't intermingle applications and/or users in at least some of the components or deployments of your platform, it's probably not a platform.

Operating as Foundations

The last pillar of platform engineering practice is that platforms need to be operated as foundations—something rock-solid stable that application engineers can trust their business on. When your platform is flaky, either due to the underlying components or to your own code, you force your customers to become experts in the platform's operation. Not only is that not providing leverage, it is doing it in the worst way possible, as the only way customers will become experts is through the reactive experience of the platform causing new operational issues.

Some companies approach platform engineering through a strong developer experience focus, but then struggle with the operational side of things. As a foundation supporting a growing number of different application needs, all on top of external OSS and vendor systems beyond your complete control, it takes a lot of work to avoid "operational hell," where you are not able to operate your platform at the quality level the business needs.

There are three major aspects to a platform being a foundation: taking operational responsibility for the full platform, ensuring the platform is supported, and being disciplined in operational practices. Let's look at each of these in turn.

Responsibility for the Full Platform

Platform engineering teams must operate the full platform, not just the software developed in-house (see Figure 2-8). When the other components are pushed off to customers to operate themselves, you give up a lot of your platform's leverage. You may have built something that makes it easy for an application team to get started, but as soon as they run into issues in production, they will need to become experts in the underlying primitives and in how the platform services are tying them together.

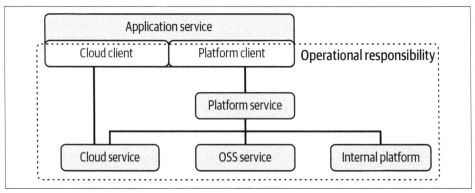

Figure 2-8. Architecture demonstrating how platform teams take full operational responsibility for all components and dependencies

We have seen teams dodge operational responsibility around vendor and OSS software, shipping their platforms in a few patterns that create development-time leverage but give no operational-time leverage. These include:

Provisioning platforms
> The platform provisions new instances of the OSS/vendor systems, and the application team takes over operational responsibility after provisioning.

Framework platforms
> The platform collates OSS and vendor library versions, perhaps with some in-house logic, but the application team owns all operational responsibility.

Tools platforms
> The platform provides tools and UIs that make it easier to manipulate OSS and vendor systems, but the application team still owns all operation responsibility for those systems.

We are all for provisioning, frameworks, and tools being part of a platform engineering team's remit, and there are certainly cases where it makes no sense to invest beyond them at the time. However, because they expose so much operational complexity to users, these narrow approaches scale badly, and these efforts should not rightly be thought of as platform engineering.

Supporting the Platform

For many application teams, user support escalations are a rare problem. If the application is for external customers, they usually have large support engineering organizations and only see escalations that can be handled as operational issues. If it's an internal service that's not a platform, whether because it has a limited number of users, breadth of use, and/or complexity, those same characteristics usually mean that it won't generate many support cases either.

The situation is very different for platform teams. As we discussed earlier, they should build in features like self-service interfaces, user observability, guardrails, and multitenancy. But against a broad base of use cases, rarely can these be implemented so well that the team can avoid a constant stream of customer questions. These questions tend to be about a combination of edge cases during onboarding and application-specific production issues, whether caused by changes in or problems with the application, the platform, or the underlying systems. Rarely are internal platform teams large enough that they can justify hiring dedicated support specialists.

All of this means that user support is an important part of platform engineering, not just in terms of support practices but also in terms of creating a customer empathy culture across the entire team.

Operational Discipline

Operational discipline, by which we mean a focus on carrying out operational practices on a routine basis, is an area that it's easy for those with an application software development background to overlook (or worse, roll their eyes at). Some folks think the only reason systems people have to focus so hard on operational practices is that they didn't build their APIs right in the first place.

Now, it may be true that the APIs could have been better (although, as we covered earlier in the chapter, there are costs to that). However, the bigger issue is that it is difficult to operate a system whose major functionality predominantly comes from someone else's code—be it an OSS or vendor system, or some other in-house system. This adds a level of complexity in that unknown operational problems (the "unknown unknowns") are a constant threat, and the only way to manage that threat is with a discipline that seeks to understand and address all anomalies early, before they cause acute pain.

A large part of why infrastructure engineering–style cultures have continued even at companies that would be better served by platforms is that the software developers who would build such platforms don't want to engage with the practices needed to operate other peoples' systems well. Platform engineering teams need to be proactive in their use of operational practices, understanding that they are a major part of ensuring that those platforms are a foundation the company can rely on.

What Does Generative AI Mean for Platform Engineering?

If platform engineering has grown in popularity thanks to the combined forces of DevOps/SRE, OSS, and the cloud, what might the latest iteration of generative AI mean for this world? While neither of us is an expert in generative AI, there are some areas that platform developers will probably want to think about as this technology becomes more widespread:

The tooling around the model experience will matter.
> *Machine learning operations*, or *MLOps*, is the industry term for the operations of building, training, deploying, and operating models. This process is not dissimilar to the SDLC processes that developers need to use to deliver software, with the exception that the users are often not engineers but rather researchers or, perhaps increasingly, other nontechnical people.
>
> This customer base will need a set of coherent tooling that works within their desired context. In the same way that good developer tooling supports developers staying within their integrated development environment of choice, on the command line, or in a well-connected set of dashboards, thinking about how you can keep researchers within their notebooks and other familiar contexts rather than forcing them to jump from platform to platform to do their jobs will be key to supporting their productivity.

Platforms that help optimize for underlying infrastructure efficiency will become a focus.
> The cost of training these models is high, and there will be a race to drive efficiencies in the underlying compute and storage resources, optimize the placement of workloads, and minimize network costs in a way that is transparent to the researcher. Many people are using APIs from major providers like OpenAI, but as the cost scales with usage, it is possible that, in time, in-house platforms will be developed for the most valuable and intensive use cases. We expect that significant R&D will be applied to the underlying distributed systems and infrastructure in this space.

The platforms developed for machine learning using company data will require special focus on controls and data entitlements.
> We expect that changing regulations and consumer demands will increase the need for a solid understanding of data provenance, being able to explain the outcomes of a model, and knowing who has access to what data. These are all tricky problems to solve on their own, and solving them in a holistic way across the ML systems in a company will demand platform solutions that support meeting these controls without forcing everyone into an inflexible workflow and out of their desired working context.

AI will help you operate better, but only if and where you have the data.

Machine learning requires data to make decisions, and specifically for your own platforms, the only way it will help you is if you have the instrumentation that can produce the needed data. For many modern systems this might be easy enough, but for those of you with legacy applications and platforms, if you want to be able to apply machine learning to improve your operations you'll need to get on top of the telemetry.

Platforms will be built that curate the ecosystem of large language model (LLM) tooling for your company and ensure all of the components work together well.

This is, if anything, an opportunity for platform engineers to expand their expertise and value to companies. To date, the world of tooling to support research and model generation has largely been the domain of either massive companies like Google or understaffed data engineering teams that haven't properly invested in the usability and operability of their platforms due to a lack of funding and/or attention. Many of the companies building out in-house AI infrastructure are hitting the same problems that we have always seen when dealing with large-scale distributed infrastructure: handling software and hardware failures, orchestrating the work efficiently, and debugging when things go wrong.

Wrapping Up

In this chapter, we described the four pillars of successful platform engineering and gave some examples of what they mean in practice. To summarize, platform engineering teams should:

1. Take a curated product approach, building paved paths and railways as they identify common customer needs.

2. Develop software-based abstractions. These may include services, APIs, libraries, OSS customizations, and metadata integrations.

3. Serve a broad base of application developers. The platform should support multiple tenants, and each tenant should have self-service capabilities, with appropriate guardrails to prevent the mistakes that come at scale.

4. Operate foundational offerings, meaning applying high operational discipline and providing support for the full platform.

If you're doing all of these things, then you're doing platform engineering. There are cases where it will make sense to do less, but beware of the long-term consequences. Without opinions about what's in scope, you'll fail to manage the overall complexity, and without a customer-centric product approach, you'll probably build the wrong systems. If you're not doing any software engineering, you're just doing operations with a high level of customer empathy. If you are building for only a small set of application teams, you're not really building a scaled platform. And without operational maturity, no one will trust your offerings.

Now that we've told you why you should care about platforms, and what specifically we mean when we talk about platform engineering, we'll turn to the hard stuff: how do you actually pull this off?

PART II

Platform Engineering Practices

It may be hard for an egg to turn into a bird: it would be a jolly sight harder for a bird to learn to fly while remaining an egg.
—C.S. Lewis

In Part I, we talked about the "why" and the "what" of platform engineering, and we hope to have convinced most of you of the value of doing more of it in your company. But we're sure that some of you are still skeptical, wondering whether this isn't just a rebranding of infrastructure engineering, DevOps, and SRE, where the team promises to develop customer-focused products but really just doubles down on operating a bunch of disjoint OSS and vendor systems. Or you might be skeptical for other reasons; perhaps you've had the experience of new leaders coming in from an application/product engineering background who think they can solve all the hard problems of scaled platforms with new software, but who have no deep appreciation of what's involved in operating critical and complex systems.

We've lived through these experiences as well, and our goal for Part II is to teach you how to avoid these outcomes, and so break out of the egg, eventually to fly. To do this, we're going to spend the next eight chapters—the bulk of the book—talking about the "how" of great platform engineering organizations. We'll start by discussing getting started, choosing the right people, adopting a product mindset, and operating your platform successfully. Then we'll move on to the more complex work of planning, rearchitecting, migrations, and stakeholder engagement.

This part of the book will walk you through and help you tackle the main failure cases that we have seen—namely:

- You start too early or underestimate the amount of change needed when it's time
- You don't have the right blend of people
- You don't think your platforms need product management
- You don't operate your platform well
- You struggle to plan and deliver new value on a continuous basis
- You are stuck with naive architectures
- You burn goodwill with costly migrations
- You fail to communicate your value to peer leaders (aka stakeholders)

Let's take a quick look at each of these in turn, before diving in.

You start too early or underestimate the amount of change needed when it's time

As we discussed in Part I, platform engineering comes with costs. Not only are there the direct costs of engineering time invested but also cooperative development with customers, which often flows freely when a platform is small, becomes difficult as a platform scales, and so more formal management mechanisms are needed.

In Chapter 3, "How and When to Get Started", we'll first look at what you should be doing at a small scale, when cooperation is working, and how to mature slowly into a platform approach. Then, we'll look at what you need to consider when a common problem gets big enough to warrant replacing cooperation with a formal platform team. Finally, we'll consider a different getting-started problem: when you need to change the culture of a traditional infrastructure-focused organization.

You don't have the right blend of people

It's easy to imagine that you can just throw together a group of motivated engineers and end up with a successful platform engineering team, but getting the mix of skills needed for a good team right is a novel undertaking for many. You want a team that has software engineers who are prepared to develop lots of code, but those engineers need to have some interest in lower-level systems, a willingness to not build everything from scratch, and the ability to work on longer-running projects. As you will usually be building on top of OSS and vendor systems, you also need people who have a deep understanding of those technologies and are ready to tackle the underlying complexity that comes with infrastructure. But you don't want everyone on your team to have this background, because building platforms is about more than operating, scaling, and supporting other people's software.

Building a great team and a great team culture is often a challenge, because whoever's putting the team together will likely come from one of these backgrounds, and although they'll know in principle that they need to hire the others, in practice they may find it hard to manage people with significantly different strengths than their own. Thus, in Chapter 4, "Building Great Platform Teams", we provide some guidance: we lay out the different kinds of people who should be on every platform team, what they are great at, and how to build a culture where they all feel appreciated.

You don't think your platforms need product management

We all go into platform building with good intentions and great ideas—and then reality sinks in. All the edge cases that you didn't factor into your planning come back to haunt you as a never-ending backlog of problems your customers are asking you to fix (yesterday, if possible). Everyone is mad, and stuck. The platform is slowing your customers down, and no matter how hard you try to get your team to fix the pile of problems, they never seem able to keep up with the demand. What do you do?

A key thing to note is that the struggle of balancing "what is" versus "what if" is just a usual part of growth on the way to success, and this is no different for platform teams than for any SaaS business. Successful SaaS businesses use product management techniques to manage these trade-offs and find balance. This allows their engineering teams to be strategic in balancing their systems' operational needs and their customers' requests, and to build great products that manage complexity rather than passing it through. In Chapter 5, "Platform as a Product", we talk about how to adopt a product mindset and use it to define what your platforms need to be.

You don't operate your platform well

There's more to great platforms than stability, but without stability you will have a hard time getting your colleagues to trust your systems. Why would they want to be held accountable for the operational problems of a component? Most platforms critically depend on OSS and vendor systems. Operating these is something that infrastructure, SRE, and DevOps teams do well. However, they don't usually do it while also owning responsibility for developing software abstractions that will be used by many application teams and engineers across the company.

To balance platform feature development with its operation, a modified approach is needed. In Chapter 6, "Operating Platforms", we cover various practices that need to be handled with disciplined routine, from providing on-call coverage to user support and operational feedback.

You struggle to plan and deliver new value on a continuous basis

It takes time to deliver features in the platform systems that are the foundation of a business. The best roadmaps are meaningless if delivering on them takes so much time that some customers decide they are better off standing up their own shadow platforms. Things can go off the rails in many ways. We've seen insufficient planning at the project level, with teams going for "big bang" changes that take too long to implement. We've seen teams not factoring operational load into their roadmaps, then disappointing everyone when heavily sold new features get reactively deprioritized in favor of "keeping the business running" activities. Finally, we've seen teams fail in terms of communication, doing all the right things but not finding the balance between burying their customers in detail versus being too quiet and leaving everyone wondering why their engineers aren't doing more valuable work.

In Chapter 7, "Planning and Delivery", we cover each of these failure modes and describe strategies that you can put in place to ensure they don't happen in your team.

You are stuck with naive architectures

A product-led approach to building new platforms means they are often under-architected for the scale that comes with ongoing success. It's easy for them to end up frozen in time—the type of platform that, while foundational to the business, requires substantial operational work just to meet business expectations, with no engineering time available for (or tolerance for the risk of) adding new features.

Avoiding this outcome requires an ongoing investment in system rearchitecture, taking care to avoid the "big bang" flaws we covered in Chapter 7. In Chapter 8, "Rearchitecting Platforms", we lay out a framework that will allow you to enable rearchitectures by ensuring they continuously deliver incremental business value.

You burn goodwill with costly migrations

No matter how well you plan rearchitectures and other big projects, at some point some workloads are going to need some customer work to facilitate migrating between systems. Mandated org-wide migrations are often a massive tax on application engineering teams, both in terms of the time spent not delivering top-line features and in terms of morale, creating a feeling that application engineers are there to serve the platform's goals, rather than vice versa.

We covered how platform teams can build platforms that take away most of this cost in Chapter 1. In Chapter 9, "Migrations and Sunsetting of Platforms", we talk about the mechanics of how to do it.

You fail to communicate your value to peer leaders (aka stakeholders)

Finally, you can be doing everything else right and fall victim to what is sometimes called politics. No matter what "globally right" optimization you achieve, for certain leaders of application teams, if you haven't delivered exactly what their teams need, you've done a bad job. Particularly when you are early in your leadership career, it's easy to think of such people as bad actors who need to be brought in line by the CTO. Unfortunately, the world is not so simple. These team leaders are not always wrong; they just have a strongly differing opinion about the value of their part of the business relative to whatever you are using to make your decisions, and sometimes not even your "leader in common" will want to make the hard calls that enable you to make easy decisions. Instead, it's on you to communicate, and sometimes compromise.

Thus, in Chapter 10, "Managing Stakeholder Relationships", we round out this part of the book by covering some methods that, while we can't promise they will win everyone to your side, should buy you the goodwill to continue executing on your mission.

CHAPTER 3

How and When to Get Started

Once upon a time, there were three little pigs. One pig built a house of straw, while the second pig built his house with sticks. They built their houses very quickly and then sang and danced all day because they were lazy. The third little pig worked hard all day and built his house with bricks.

—"The Three Little Pigs"

This chapter is targeted at those leaders whose teams are not doing platform engineering yet. (Those who are doing it already can skip straight to Chapter 4). We focus on three specific starting points:

- In the first section, we talk about what it means to do platform engineering at a small startup, where it's usually best to start by building cooperation around your shared code.

- In the second section, we cover how to handle the transition to a formal platform engineering organization when those initial cooperative mechanisms start to fail.

- In the final section, we cover a different problem that's typically encountered in older and larger companies: transitioning a traditional infrastructure engineering team into a platform engineering culture.

Sometimes it's OK to build your platform quickly from straw and sticks and use the extra time to build more important things for the business.[1] But it's good to know when you need to start laying bricks and how to start renovating your old stone castle into something more modern.

---

1 Which, we are loath to admit, is harder than just "singing and dancing," and not at all "lazy," in the negative sense of the word.

Fostering Platform Cooperation at Small Scale

While we have a lot of experience running platform teams, most of it has been at either scaled startups or even larger companies. But we know that those of you at small startups have some big questions on this topic: Should you be doing platform engineering? When should you start? How should you approach it? To answer these questions, we turned to our friend James Turnbull. James has been a leader in the DevOps space since its inception, authoring books on Puppet, Docker, Prometheus, and other popular technologies, as well as writing *The Art of Monitoring* in 2014. He has also been a startup executive for most of his career, with a focus on leadership of early-stage startup teams. Through this experience, James has learned many lessons on starting and growing startup teams, and in particular how fostering a culture of cooperation through lightweight processes, sensible automation, and collaborative decision making helps to maintain cohesion and productivity in teams as they scale. What follows is from James.

PLATFORM PERSPECTIVES

When you read about the outcomes of platform engineering, what probably springs to mind is a mature and efficient platform that enables engineers to code, build, test, and deploy with the least amount of friction. The presence of a platform team suggests a level of maturity and stability.

These two concepts are a long way off for early-stage companies. But all these platforms, and their teams, didn't just spring into life fully grown. They emerged from embryonic beginnings, dragging themselves out of a primordial soup of automation and process. If you're at an early-stage company or startup, how do you start this evolution and avoid as many pitfalls as possible?

Bad news first. You're going to get things wrong. A lot. This process usually isn't the story of an elegant evolution from sensible choices of stacks and tooling into a fully mature platform. You'll both underscale and prematurely optimize. There will be evolutionary dead ends, backtracks, and disasters. What's important here is learning from these detours and setbacks. Try not to make the same mistake twice; try to make new mistakes.

To understand this journey, we will do some Software Engineering™ and use a maturity model to track our progress. (Apologies to the CMM/CMMI (*https://oreil.ly/JwZjQ*), which I have shamelessly adapted into the abbreviated elements of my quick-and-dirty maturity model.) We'll look at the first two stages of evolution for platforms, broadly up until an organization has (nominally) about 50 engineers:[2]

---

2 Based roughly on Dunbar's model, discussed later in this chapter, which says we can have about 50 "friends."

- Stage 1: Ad hoc—whatever works right now
- Stage 2: Somewhat managed—we've started to take a more principled approach

There are later stages of development as the organization or startup grows, but this model focuses on the early stages in smaller and startup organizations.

Stage 1: Ad Hoc, Just Crawled from the Water and Learned to Breathe

Most initial startup engineering teams are a few folks sitting around a table (or on a video call) building a product and probing for product-market fit. The focus is on short iterations, a minimum viable product, and the quickest possible cycle time between the code being written and the product being used.

This focus usually results in no formal processes or tooling. The stack and tools (and what few processes there might be) are selected based on individual developer preferences. Code is written fast. Sometimes tests are present, but often not; code is merged quickly with limited review and is frequently deployed manually. Most diagnostics and observability metrics are eyeballed, and problem solving is reactive and localized. Knowledge is shared organically because the team is small and close-knit; no documentation or knowledge-sharing processes exist.

In this world, you don't need a platform team; you need to start with the bare basics and move fast. The focus is on removing friction between the code being written and deployed. That focus is the foundation for what might be a platform team someday, but today it's about getting sh*t done as you look for product-market fit.

You can make decisions based on your preferences, but you should share your choices and the basics of what drives them. These basics are the initial content of the README file in your repository. A few specific recommendations for Stage 1 follow.

Source control

Always use source control. It might appear redundant in the world of GitHub and GitLab to remind people of this, but many startups start using source control later than you might imagine.

Automated continuous deployment

The easiest lever you have to reduce friction and get users' eyes on your product fast is the automated continuous deployment of code. Take advantage of off-the-shelf deployment tools and stacks that require little or no configuration. Does your app need Kubernetes from day one? No, it does not. Seriously, no. Don't overthink your future scaling needs; focus on simple, cost-effective solutions that work for now. If, at some point, you go from tens of users to hundreds of thousands of users, it's a great problem to have and that'll be the right time to think more deeply about scaling.

Many platforms support building an artifact when code is merged to main and deploying that artifact with little to no human intervention. These range from the venerable PaaS Heroku, to tools the cloud providers and content delivery networks provide, to hosted application platforms like Netlify, Vercel, Cloudplane, and North-flank. Selecting a platform is very situational. Try to balance:

- Complexity
- Cost
- Scale
- Lifespan

You can automate the deployment and management of these via code with tools like Terraform. This automation allows you to build the basis for a future of automated and managed infrastructure. At this stage, you're always asking yourself, "Is this tool business-differentiating or core business for me?" If it's not, outsource; get a platform or service to do it for you.

Lightweight processes

You should frame a lightweight process for recording and tracking work. When deciding what kind of process to implement, I like Kevin Stewart's adaptation (*https://oreil.ly/120Ja*) of Michael Pollan's food laws:

> Use a process.
> Not too much.
> Mostly agile.

Start with a simple ticket-based system for tracking work. Don't be overly concerned with estimates, sprints, or the more formal aspects of (A|a)gile. Consider tracking the ratio of new feature development to support/technical debt as a signal of how much velocity your product has and the lowest level of granularity you initially need. If your team is small, you're either shipping product or not.

And that's it. Don't overthink things. Don't rush to create a team to do platforms. You not only likely do not have the resources to dedicate people to this mission, but you'll also risk slowing down the rapid iteration you need. Cooperative part-time efforts are much better. Get everyone involved in solving these issues—your engineers are the best people to solve the problem because they live it.

Stage 2: Somewhat Managed, or Hunting and Gathering

As your startup finds product-market fit, your team grows, and your product gains users, pressures on your engineering tools and processes increase. A larger team means more complex communication requirements, and more people interacting with your codebase means more complexity in writing, reviewing, merging, and deploying.

In this stage, your platform's components emerge, and your environment becomes managed. That doesn't mean you launch a platform team. Your team likely includes a small group focusing on infrastructure and automation, some dedicated but others with additional responsibilities. These folks may form the nucleus of a future platform team, but for now, platform engineering is still a shared responsibility.

This stage is also where you will outgrow some initial tool choices. To support growth, you may need to replace tools that worked fine for 5–25 developers with others that offer better performance, capabilities, or optimized pricing. You may also need to rethink some tooling and stack choices that were based on individual developer preferences and require niche knowledge or skills shared by only some of the engineers on your team.

The underlying focus of the tooling and solution choices you will make in this stage will remain: "Is this core business?" If it is not, outsource it to a platform, service, or tool that takes care of it for you.

Additionally, this is generally the only time you can entertain the phrase "Let's rewrite it in…" Usually, those words should elicit cries of "Not ever, absolutely never under any circumstances." Early on, though, this might be the one window where the urge to rewrite is less toxic. Here are some specific recommendations for Stage 2.

Local development

In this stage, you should begin to automate your local development environment. This development will probably start simply: a shell script wrapper around a container tool is a typical first pattern. However, this pattern breaks down quickly; it's hard to manage, configuration drift occurs as your team grows, and it is frequently fragile during upgrades and updates.

There are some steps you can take to mitigate this. Colocate your development environment setup in the repository with your source code. Publish container images containing the elements of your local development stack when you build the artifacts you deploy into your production environment. Your wrapper script can then become as simple as installing a container tool and downloading and launching the required images. Git hooks can prompt or update the development environment as part of developers' regular workflow of pulling and pushing commits, greatly increasing the likelihood of these environments staying in sync with production and across your team. This pattern is much easier to manage and is helpful for keeping up to date with changes.

All the world's a stage

Consider more robust testing and deployment processes for your product. Prior to this stage, most development was done locally and then pushed, hopefully automatically, into production or a build. As the team grows and more complexity emerges, going directly into production can be riskier.

There are at least three complementary areas or branches of evolution to consider here that will help you mitigate the risk of increased change and cross-traffic in your development environment:

More robust tests and continuous integration
> Start to measure test coverage as a metric and ensure coverage grows by only merging code once there is sufficient test coverage and the tests are green. Test coverage is not perfect as a metric; it doesn't consider the criticality of the code, for example, and doesn't distinguish between the coverage of the platform that bills your customers and something that has a lower impact if it breaks. But at this early stage, when you're just getting some tests in place and setting the muscle memory of "no tests, no merge," it's a good driver. Solidify this foundation by looking at your environment as a form of "heat map": identify where bugs, especially customer-impacting ones, pop up most frequently. These are likely the areas that need that larger investment in testing.

Branch-based deployments
> Build solutions that allow engineers to build and deploy from branches. This growth might be part of local development, or it may expand to branch deployments for on-demand or ephemeral environments.

Feature flagging
> Hide features you are building behind flags that allow you to limit the damage if they are buggy or unstable. Remember, a feature-flagging system is very, very likely not core business for you. Follow the maxim: if it isn't core business, leverage someone else's solution.

Observability

You should have basic observability for your platform and workflows by now. You want to know that builds complete successfully, alert on failures, and be aware of your environment's status and performance. To achieve this, you'll need metrics and exception and application logging for your platform and workflows. If you don't have these, you should start building them. There's hopefully a shortcut here: you likely have observability around your product already (if you don't, why not?). You can extend your existing tooling to include your platform and workflows.

Have the right technology

Local development, branch deployments, ephemeral environments, feature flagging, enhancements to observability, and CI/CD will require that your infrastructure be automated. You should have the basis for this from your initial work in Stage 1 on automating your infrastructure for deployment. Build on this to fully manage your production environment. Then, take advantage of and extend this work to manage continuous integration and capabilities like ephemeral environments for development and testing.

Socialize change and decision making

Now is the time to consider a more formal process for managing change in your environment's stack and architecture. Changes now have a much wider impact, and individual developer choices must be considered in the context of the organization's larger needs. Choose a framework to help you make decisions and review changes. A good starting point is a Request for Comments (RFC)–like process, like that used by open source projects such as React, Swift, and Rust. Another option is using architectural design records (ADRs). Keep it lightweight, but any approach that considers the pros and cons of solutions, including technology, logistical, operational, and budgetary considerations, can be appropriate.

Knowing When to Move Up

Moving between stages is, unfortunately, hard to plan and predict. Often, the first time you know a tool or process is at breaking point is when it breaks. One failure frequently triggers a cascade of failures. This isn't entirely a bad thing, as it shows you what you need to invest in and when, but it can make for a chaotic and stressful environment. Accept that, no matter where you are, things will never be entirely a smooth ride.

While they may not perfectly correspond to your experience, a general understanding of these initial stages of evolution should give you a sense of the landscape and journey and help you identify areas of risk and where to focus your development. When you need to advance, either in response to pain points or an actual failure, review the current state and determine how much change you need. Is your existing tool or process a total loss, or can you expand or adapt it? Plan the changes you want to make and, most importantly, get buy-in from your fellow engineers. Platforms at this point are cooperative endeavors. Engineers often choose individual tools due to personal preferences or prior experience, and you need to ensure you get them on board if you want to make changes to your shared platform.

Finally, be patient. This process will take time and compromise, and results may not appear immediately or consistently.

Creating the Platform Teams That Replace Cooperation

As organizations grow, their practices must evolve and grow as well. That low-overhead, ad hoc cooperation around common code and tools that served everyone so well when there were 20 people using them often starts causing problems when there are significantly more. Like all straws that break the camel's back, the actual event that forces people to confront the shortcomings is often minor. It could be a slow buildup of technical debt that causes reliability or developer productivity problems. Or it could be a sudden business change that exposes the underlying unmanageable complexity—for example, an acquisition, or a migration to another vendor. No matter the event, it becomes clear that the right thing didn't happen, and that there is no owner accountable for making sure the right thing happens in the future. And so a platform is born.

A useful number to keep in mind is Dunbar's number (*https://oreil.ly/trcji*): when you have a cooperative group of between 50 and 250 people, it's no longer possible for everyone to know all the other members. This is the point at which you need more formal processes that define owners and assign accountability. Because the rule applies to the size of each cooperative group in the company, this can happen at different times; it usually happens early for infrastructure and backend developer platforms that must work for everyone in engineering, but later for data, frontend, and external customer APIs.

Even at companies that already have platforms, each new platform team usually struggles out of the gate. That's because the cooperative mechanisms, despite their flaws, were in place and functional for a long time, and there is no way a centralized team will displace them immediately. Worse, a centralized team creates new conflicts: engineers who used to cooperate to solve problems now argue about whether the platform team needs to do the work to fix the platform, or the customer team needs to do work to fix how they use the platform.

In the rest of this section, we lay out what you need to consider when you supplant cooperation with a formal platform and formal platform engineering.

Are the Benefits of Centralizing Ownership Worth the Costs?

When you see application teams building similar software, it's natural to think it would be more efficient to have a centralized, common platform. However, each centralized offering creates a new coordination point for application teams, and the more coordination points they have to work through to get their products shipped, the harder their jobs become. This means your reasoning for creating a new platform offering needs to be about leverage rather than just efficiency. The argument that "we could have two engineers building a common platform where instead we have five engineers working on similar code some of the time" is insufficient.

Sometimes there is a big leverage cost to having too many ways of solving a common problem. In the case of a billing platform, for example, you probably want your customers to get billed in a consistent manner rather than it being ad hoc depending on the business they are working with. But sometimes companies insist on a level of standardization that doesn't bring meaningful value and slows application teams down. Do you really have to have only one caching solution? Does every team need to use the same standardized web framework? Make sure a standard platform will bring leverage—outsized value that is hard to replicate.

You might want to do a quick total cost of ownership estimate: if this system requires a large team to build and maintain, and it can support multiple teams without significant configuration or logic changes for each team, it's a good candidate for solving once. But if it has a small cost to build and maintain, and especially if each application wants to configure or extend its logic, it's probably not a great candidate for centralizing.

Realize the Collective Dynamic Is Gone

This sounds obvious (you wouldn't be making the change if this weren't the case!), but in practice there is a human dimension that makes it hard for everyone to realize that it's past time for a change. So, you'll have customers with rose-colored glasses remembering when they could open pull requests on the platform codebase at will, and insisting that any process is just "big company ideas" brought in by problematic newcomers or "process for process's sake." This can be well-intentioned, but in our experience, some of them will never stop complaining about change, even when their own management begs them to cool it. Handling such criticism is one of the reasons we emphasize "customer empathy" as a platform team hiring requirement later in the book.

It's not just customer engineers who make this mistake, though; often it's the platform teams themselves. They think back to a major change that was done in a month across a shared codebase that served 50 users and assume that they can make a similar change, in a similar way, for a platform serving 500. Yes they know they have more users, but shouldn't it be easier now with a dedicated platform team? They can't see that the growth of the platform also impacts the way they need to approach major changes. The breadth of use cases has increased, and the number of people implementing and consuming the use cases has also increased. "Five good engineers in a room" can no longer represent all perspectives, which means a lot more opinions and a lot more conflict in getting to a decision. All of this means that change is now going to be much slower.

Focus on Solving Problems, Not New Technology or Architecture

Given that you have delayed forming a platform team until its leverage clearly outweighs the costs of coordination, the state of the initial system will often not resemble anything like a platform. APIs and service boundaries will be poor, if they exist at all—lots of platforms start as common code, in libraries or monoliths. There will often be duplicate implementations coming from different application teams. Now that you have a centralized team, there will be demands from customers to make this all more "engineered" and so easier for them to use.

Given that they have inherited a disparate mess, it is tempting for the new platform team to want to step back and bring in a new architecture or technology that allows them to do just that. However, as we just discussed, change is going to be much slower now! At this point, a full migration of an established platform to a new technology may take years to fully complete. That means new technologies or architectures won't help your in-production application teams with pressing problems. In fact, they take potential resources away from solving the problems via faster changes to the current systems.

At this point your team hasn't built any trust, only goodwill. You have just created a new organizational silo, and your goal should be to figure out how to maintain as much collaboration with the rest of engineering as possible. You need to deliver value quickly to develop trust, and even if you make architectural decisions that turn out in hindsight to be fully correct, your users will be skeptical until they start seeing value. So early on, look to the most pressing problems in the messy common code, such as libraries and monoliths, and look for solutions that deliver value as fast as you can. Think of your job now as detangling more than rearchitecting, and make sure you are delivering incremental value throughout.

Beware of New Engineers Coming from Much Bigger Companies

In Chapter 4 we'll go into detail about the strategies for staffing a platform team, but for now we offer you a caution: when you are creating your platform engineering team, be careful about hiring senior engineers and engineering managers from very big tech companies. It's tempting to hire such people because they have seen the next order of magnitude of scale. But while they may have experience with equivalent platforms at greater scale, they probably didn't work on the equivalent to your platform at the scale you are at today. As a result, you can end up with people who are very confident that they know the solution to your problems, when all they really know is what the fully delivered solution looked like at a company with a different culture that may have faced somewhat similar problems some time ago.

We're not saying you should never hire these sorts of engineers—some of the strongest engineers on our teams came from big company backgrounds and wanted to go somewhere where they could make a bigger impact. Just be careful. Interview them for their skills and attitude, rather than thinking their big company knowledge has inherent value. The "design" slot of interviews can be a good place to detect this bias. If they always jump to "BigCo X technology Y" as the solution to any problem posed in the interview, without being able to consider its pros and cons, then they likely won't be able to extend their situational reasoning within the role either.

Be Slow to Hire Product Managers (and Avoid Project Managers)

A final word that follows from the last: you need to have a fully staffed and working model of a platform engineering team before you start hiring product managers (PMs), and you need to wait even longer before hiring project managers.

We have three reasons for this recommendation:

- The optics of hiring non-engineers before you've shown your ability to deliver as a small engineering team are often negative for customers. It suggests that you are so bad at communicating with them that you need a specialist.

- Often the work to be done in the first year or two of a platform is straightforward problem solving through technology build-out, and the number of customer teams is small enough that your engineers and engineering managers can do lightweight informal requirements gathering.

- Your early senior engineers and engineering managers need to set the tone for communicating with customers with product focus that the team needs to keep as it grows. If you bring in a product manager too soon, this will be offloaded to them, and your engineers will never have firsthand customer empathy.

You will eventually need product and project managers, but the number you hire will depend on your culture and your problems. Our rule of thumb is that the number of product managers for a mature organization should sit somewhere between the number of team-level managers and managers-of-managers. The ratio for project managers should be significantly higher—there should be about 50 people on your platform team before it needs its first project manager, and ideally you'll never go above that 1:50 ratio. Thinking you need more or need them sooner is usually a signal to do a lot more definition of your platform's abstractions to avoid its changes requiring so much work of its users.

Finally, as we will talk about in Chapter 4, be careful to interview for "process fit" at this point, because many product and project managers who are great working within the established guardrails of bigger companies can't get things done without them. You need to hire people who can work without strict guardrails or well-established processes and who won't just spend their first year trying to re-create those processes.

Bonus Problems for Integration/Shared Services Platforms

To round out this section, we want to touch on the special problems of a different type of platform team that pops up at scaled companies—the platform team that horizontally supports multiple (external) products. Examples include:

- Billing
- User login, identity, and access management
- Mobile and web application platforms
- Revenue systems
- Shared application services (notifications, search, analytics, messaging)

These are trickier than pure "infrastructure" and "developer" platforms as they end up with some surface area directly visible to the external customer. As you consider whether to create such a team, it's worth asking a couple of questions:

How will you partner with external product management?

When you build products with business-facing surface area, business-facing product managers come with the territory. So, in these cases we advise hiring a PM much earlier—maybe as soon as the team is formed. However, you need to avoid the mistake of thinking every successful business-focused PM can successfully transition to internal platforms. They'll be accustomed to being evaluated based on whether they can deliver the company revenue and profits, so they'll be focused on business and customer needs. This likely means that not only will they want to leave platform aspects like "reliability" and "developer productivity" to their engineering manager counterparts to scope and prioritize, but they will also demand that such concerns take secondary priority unless they have visible customer impact, at which point it's usually far too late to solve them with cheap or easy fixes.

Furthermore, there is an aspect of "the bike shed and the nuclear plant"[3] in the business-focused decisions—meaning that small aspects of, say, UI design (the bike shed) become massive areas of investment because they are much more visible in the product than the underlying code and architecture (the nuclear plant), despite the latter providing the greatest leverage to the business. For some platforms, this makes every customer-visible platform decision of interest to executives like the CEO and head of project management. With the wrong product manager, this can leave engineers spending too much time "pleasing the CEO" by working on small details in the UI design and other end user interfaces while the core technology is neglected. This eventually leads not just to reliability problems, but to internal customer usability being neglected as well.

Of course, some business-focused product managers can make the transition; they just need to embrace a different role with a broader set of success criteria. We offer specific hiring advice in Chapter 4.

How will everyone find your offerings?

A major element that is underconsidered in building integration platforms is the challenge of discoverability. The bigger the company, the harder it is for people to realize that your team has offerings that they might need, particularly when these are semioptional systems that aren't needed by everyone. You may not want to mandate that every product in the company use your search service, for example, but it can start to cause friction when some external customers

---

3 See *https://bikeshed.com*.

experience different search behaviors as they move across your business's product portfolio. When application teams are trying to quickly spin something up, they may not bother taking the time to see what's out there and instead use their own preferred combination of vendor, OSS, and team-built systems. This allows them to ship quickly, until they need to integrate with the bigger picture—and then suddenly everything gets very messy indeed.

It's easy for an integration platform's semioptional offerings to get lost in the shuffle until someone notices that product X didn't bother to use the platform offering and now everyone is up in arms. Engineers get in their own way here by giving their internal platforms cutesy names that don't clearly describe what they do: naming your billing platform "Glengarry" instead of "Billing Platform" does not help your discoverability problem. Be sure you make a plan for how you will deliver awareness across the company for your offering. Start with a name that makes sense. Write documentation that is searchable on the company intranet. Send out email announcements, run learning sessions, or speak at company meetings to drive knowledge and awareness of your platform. It doesn't matter how you decide to do it; it just matters that you do it. Without a plan for getting the word out, you're likely to get lost in the shuffle.

Being Stuck in the Middle

It's worth pointing out that integration platform teams are inherently stuck in the middle. They usually aren't part of the core/infrastructure platform organization, which manages the underlying compute, storage, networking, and often security and identity offerings. They may not have the superuser access that these core teams have, because they are seen as application-layer offerings, which can make building shared platforms challenging. Sitting between applications and the underlying core platforms also means that they are subject to errors on both sides of the stack, and this can make debugging and operations that much trickier.

Because of those technical details, it is important to keep integration platform teams aligned to the core platforms, even if they don't sit under the same organization chart as the core/infrastructure platform team. Especially when initiatives span the two (a classic here is the API gateway, visible to customers' API calls, but also core networking infrastructure), beware of conflict between the teams, which is inherent because they have different alignments around assessing value. You can mitigate this by building camaraderie at the engineering level, through social team building events and common conferences and by having engineers from each side work together on projects whenever possible.

Transforming a Traditional Infrastructure Organization

Finally, we come to companies that have been around for a while, where the move to platform engineering is a transformation program that seeks to add product management and software sensibilities to an existing infrastructure engineering organization. This requires not only a skill set change in the makeup of the organization but also a major cultural change, moving from what is usually a siloed, process- and tech-focused mindset to a portfolio-, usability-, and customer-focused mindset. This is a hard transformation, and it's easy for people who have spent their whole careers building infrastructure to misunderstand what "product" and "platform" really mean.

Your Whole Engineering Culture Has to Change

Yes, seriously.

Infrastructure organizations tend to be good at many things. They're good at cost management, vendor negotiations, and running systems at scale. They have specialists who know about the murky depths of databases, the nuances of networking, and how to debug nasty kernel issues. They may even be good at triaging bug requests from tens or hundreds of teams, planning large-scale failure tests, and coordinating massive migrations.

Unfortunately, they are not usually very good at thinking about the people who will use their systems, taking their preferences into account, and treating them like customers whom they are trying to keep. (Why should they? The people who use their systems are often a captive audience![4]) You may or may not want to move away from designating this team as the preferred provider for core technology, but either way, a shift needs to happen if you want to adopt that curated product approach we discussed in Part I.

A culture that focuses on cost, scale, and process over people and usability is very hard to root out. And you don't want to lose all those rare skills in the process. So what do you do?

Identify the Most Promising Areas to Start

You don't have to change your whole team all at once! Trying to force this transformation upon the most conservative parts of your organization will distract you from making it successful with the teams that are ready and eager for the change.

---

4 We find that even when there is no formal mandate that all application teams use what infrastructure provides, in practice, most engineering leadership will default to requiring that their teams adopt these offerings to minimize their own risk and overhead for building their own shadow infrastructure.

You'll have better luck if you start with the areas that are already close to "platform engineering," learn what works, and expand from there.

Seek out teams that are delivering modern offerings, as these are most likely to have many of the elements you need to kick off this transition. Some of the characteristics that make for a promising team include a concentration of software engineers and bespoke software (versus packaged vendor systems or physical hardware) with a high rate of change and delivery of new features. You can also look for places where there is a large pent-up demand for modernization, such as moving from physical infrastructure or virtual machines to elastic container–based compute offerings. As we will discuss in Chapter 4, successful platform teams are made up of a blend of software engineers and systems engineers; where you have this mix, or are in the process of creating it, you are primed to make the transition.

Recognize That You Can't Just Rub Product Managers on It and Call It a Day

As tempting as it might be, just hiring product managers won't guarantee success. Even if you could find enough good product managers who want this type of job, they're useful only when they're paired with willing engineering teams. If the engineering teams don't feel a sense of ownership for delivering a great product to their customers, PMs are unlikely to close that gap, and more likely to turn into glorified backlog groomers than true product leaders.

Look for the areas that are already more customer-centric and start to introduce some product-oriented approaches to these areas.

Change the Way You Support Your Products

The ticket system black hole is a great way to make your customers feel more like a burden than a focus. We understand that it's hard to manage all the incoming requests for your teams, but keeping a close eye on how you provide support, what your response time is for questions, and how you triage incoming issues is critical to this transition. Your engineers should spend time supporting their products. If they are not regularly answering questions, they are missing a chance to appreciate the pain that customers are facing when trying to use their systems.

Be careful about making this optional or leaving it to junior engineers. Your senior folks will not build the kinds of humane products that you need if they are incapable of interacting with the users in a polite and helpful way, no matter how brilliant they might seem. If you have someone you can't trust to engage productively to support, enable, and help other engineers, watch out, because this person is probably not building products that are easy to use. Over time, you may find yourself redoing a lot of their work because it's hard to support and drives a high volume of complaints. We will offer more strategies for handling this in Chapter 6.

Update Your Interview Process

In the next chapter, we will discuss in depth the kinds of people you need in platform engineering teams—but to get you started on this transformation, we recommend adding what we call "customer empathy screening" to all of your interviews. This doesn't have to be deep; it can be as simple as asking the interviewees how they think about writing code so that other developers can understand it, or what their approach is to answering questions about the systems they have built. The idea is to set the tone that you expect your developers to think not just about how to build the systems, but also about the people who are going to use them or work with them.

Update Your Systems of Recognition and Reward

If you only promote people who solve big technical problems, you're going to have a hard time retaining the people who do the work to smooth out the usability edges, actively listen to the customer teams, and adjust their work priorities to fix the stuff that is causing the most pain. So, look closely at what you are celebrating, compensating, and promoting, and make sure you are including work that makes the product better, whatever that looks like, even if it isn't the hardest technical bits. You may even want to reevaluate your engineering ladder to make sure the expectations at each level reflect all of the skills you now demand. Remember, this is a cultural change, and cultural changes that don't involve changes to what is valued (as seen by what you recognize and reward) are destined to fail.

Don't Have Too Many Project Managers

There may always be some need for project managers, but infrastructure organizations that rely too heavily on project managers can lack up-front technical planning around one of the most common infrastructure team tasks: migrations. If your migrations are so painful that both your team and your customer teams need project managers to understand where all the dependencies lie and track what's happening, you are not taking ownership of the user experience of your software. Yes, migrations are part of your UX! If your organization is in the habit of offering new systems that are not compatible with the systems they are replacing, and you expect customers to do all the work to migrate to those new systems on your timeline, which doesn't take into account their other obligations, you have a lot of work to do here.

As part of moving to a platform model, you have to own much more of the migration process than you have up until now. The platform value add must include lowering the migration pain for customers. By limiting the number of project managers now, you force platform engineers to take on project management work they would otherwise avoid. And the good ones will realize that if they create automation to support the migration (whether it's detection of dependencies, compatibility-bridging libraries, or abstractions that allow them to change the internals without changing the client libraries), they won't have to do so much of that tedious project management work. By saving themselves time, they will save their customers time. So, limiting project managers is a good forcing function—just make sure you're giving engineers time to do this work.

Accept That Your Team Will Spend More Time Talking to Customers and Less Time Writing Code

There's no way to shortcut the product mindset transition for your engineering team. As we explained earlier, you can't just add a product manager or a customer advisory board meeting once a quarter and call it a day. The team needs to spend more time with the customers, and more time strategically planning for how to address holistic concerns, rather than just triaging the latest set of customer complaints. There will be an up-front cost as you change the way people work. They may complete fewer tickets or experience slowdowns in other process-oriented measures of productivity, and the pace of work might look slower than it did when they were just churning through a never-ending backlog of tickets. But over time, the work produced should be better, as measured by customer surveys, adoption, migration timelines, and, eventually, engineering productivity.

Do the Necessary Restructuring

With all of the changes we're proposing, inevitably some folks in your organization will fail to make the jump from the past ways of working to the new culture and processes. Leaders, including senior individual contributors, who don't get on board with the changes can sink the transition, and you may need to replace these leaders to support the new culture. Don't be afraid to restructure as needed to set your team up for success.

Keep It Fun!

By the time companies go through this transition, there's often a deeply ingrained us-versus-them mentality between the infrastructure organization and the other application engineering teams. It never feels good to have an antagonistic relationship with your users and colleagues. So, while this transition is going to be tricky, why not try and make it fun too? Get feedback from your users about what they love about the product. Share kudos as they come in and take the time to celebrate improvements in your customer satisfaction metrics. Make sure your teams are part of the celebrations when their work enables an application team to do something they couldn't do before. This is an exciting opportunity: a chance to learn, to modernize your approaches to work, and to create a more positive culture. Leading with a positive attitude will make all the difference in how fun it is for everyone.

In many ways, this cultural shift echoes the changes that happened during the DevOps/SRE transformation. Engineers in SRE/DevOps organizations do not build code that they carelessly throw over the wall to an operations team. In the same way, engineers in a product-focused platform organization do not build infrastructure without considering its users. These transformations ask more of the engineering teams, but they deliver higher-quality outcomes as a result. It's expensive and takes time, but we promise you, it's worth it.

Wrapping Up

In this chapter, we have covered the three main scenarios that might lead you to consider platform engineering. At an early-stage startup, you probably don't want formal platform engineering, but that doesn't mean there is nothing platform-related for you to work on. Instead, make sure you're investing in some baseline activities to keep the team moving fast.

Once you've grown enough that you are hitting problems in the shared code that are too big to handle through volunteer efforts, you can introduce your first platform team. Make sure that this team doesn't immediately turn itself into a silo; you want to deliver value fast and maintain a strong connection with the rest of engineering. As you continue reading this book, you will hear about all kinds of things that a mature platform engineering team will have to deal with: scaled customer support models, developing platforms as products, and strategies for rearchitecting legacy systems. But right now, it's important not to overdo any of this. If you try to immediately set up the kind of platform that only a scaled company needs, with the trappings of maturity like project managers, big company engineers, and cutting-edge technology, you're more likely to build the wrong thing. There's no need to rush this complexity; focus on solving today's problems, not the problems that might crop up years from now.

This is also the point at which some companies spin off integration platforms—that is, platforms that sit higher in the stack than infrastructure or developer tooling and serve shared product needs. With these, you have to do all the same things as with a developer-only platform, but you also have to deal with the hard problems of defining your mandate, getting the word out to engineers who may be inclined to work around you, and partnering with external product managers. It's a tough gig!

Finally, there are those at big companies who need to make the transition from more traditional infrastructure engineering teams to platform engineering. In this case, you have a big change management challenge ahead of you within your own organization, and you're going to want to be thoughtful about how you ease into that change. You don't have to do it all at once, and you probably don't want to try! Find your most platform-ready teams and get them going while updating your processes for support, hiring, and promotions. Slowly add in product managers and ease the culture away from what might have been a cost- and throughput-focused model to one that has room for everyone to talk to customers. You may have to make some personnel changes in the process, but keep top of mind that your goal is to make life better for *all* of the technologists at your company, including the ones on your own team, and focus on the positive as much as possible.

CHAPTER 4

Building Great Platform Teams

It's not DNS.
There's no way it's DNS.
It was DNS.
        —SSBroski

We start with a quote about DNS because it's a fundamental system most platforms depend on, and at close to 40 years old it seems it should be well understood by now. Yet, the point of the quote is that DNS still causes complex failures regularly, and it takes expertise not just to debug them, but also to avoid more DNS issues in the future.[1] This is also the challenge with staffing platform teams: by developing abstractions over complex systems, these teams enable productivity for your users, but if they aren't staffed with experts who understand those systems, they will create operational problems down the road.

We laid out the systems engineer (administrator) versus software engineer (developer) dichotomy in Chapter 1, as we think it is essential to understanding the challenges of not just building a platform engineering team, but creating the right team culture. It's tempting to insist that building a good team is just a matter of finding people who are skilled at both. And yes, as much as possible, you should seek out engineers who are strong software developers as well as capable of understanding complex systems they didn't develop. But no one is good at everything, so the way you build great platform teams is by hiring people with diverse strengths and creating a culture where each is enabled to succeed.

In this chapter, we give you the tools to do so. First, we'll explore the behaviors and challenges of teams that are focused on only one side of the systems versus

---

1 See for instance Laurent Bernaille and Elijah Andrews's 2022 talk on this (*https://oreil.ly/HhYuR*).

software divide. Then we'll introduce the four major roles for engineers on a platform team and cover how you build processes for hiring and recognition to accommodate all four roles. We'll look at the characteristics of great platform-engineering managers and at some special-purpose roles that collaborate closely with platform teams. Finally, we'll finish with some guidance on how to use all this to create a great team culture.

Getting your team set up right is as important as getting DNS configured correctly; while one bad hire probably won't take down your entire platform, you need to spend time implementing this foundation in order to achieve long-term success.

The Risks of Single-Focus Platform Teams

As we covered in Chapter 1, when the responsibility for platforms is assigned to teams with a narrow focus or skill set, the result for a company tends to be that not enough platforms get created, leading to the "over-general swamp." Before we present a solution, we want to paint a better picture of the problem. The types of teams we describe here embody outcomes at the extreme; we're not talking about all engineers or teams, but showing the consequences of how staffing around a single focus leads to a culture that doesn't deliver great platforms, and will also struggle to change.

Too Much Systems Focus

In this scenario, you have a team that is heavily populated by people who came up through infrastructure, DevOps, SRE, and systems engineering roles. Your team members usually have computer science or software engineering degrees, but few have written significant amounts of code within large software systems.

What they do well

These teams are great operationally. They know that the platform powers the business and take pride in that. They know the operation of their systems inside and out, including the underlying systems. When the Asia region experiences downtime at 2 a.m., not only is the US-based team on top of it, but their leadership team is awake and ready to help too.

The next day, not only will they be done with the incident review, but they will have a quick mitigation in production already and will be planning more hands-on work to make the longer-term fixes. They'll grumble and blame leadership for letting the "wrong" thing get built, but they'll still get it done. You can set your clock by them: they are reliable and hardworking, and they pay great attention to operational detail.

What they do badly

The code this team actively develops is mostly automation, templating, and one-off tools. They aren't doing much to build better platform abstractions to manage complexity, or working on a better architecture to solve operational problems for good.

Faced with the flaws of a system they can't change, they reach for rules and processes, often cataloged in meticulous wikis. Of course, users constantly run afoul of these rules, to the eternal frustration of both sides. To make any progress, the team management heavily leverages project managers, harassing customers' engineers to do one-off work that the platform team is incapable of streamlining.

Why they are stuck

Among both the leadership and the engineers, these teams tend to have a strong bias toward hiring experienced systems people who are already strong operators, steeped in directly relevant system knowledge. Their interviews, especially for senior-level candidates, emphasize the kinds of details found deep in books and manual pages. They might as well hang a sign over the interview room door saying "no software engineers need apply."

They justify this by arguing "that's what we need operationally," "we can't afford to train anyone with this workload," and sometimes, "what type of software engineer would be happy on this team?" The problem is that their technical filter becomes a cultural filter, and generalist senior software engineers—the type who could build better abstractions to shift the burden of operational load—stay away. Often the only software engineers such a team can hire are recent graduates, who tend to move on after a year or two due to a lack of mentorship. This personnel churn reinforces the team's belief that their culture isn't the problem; the problem is that their systems are just not appealing to software engineers.

Too Much Development Focus

In this scenario, the team is full of people who have spent their careers as software engineers and software engineering managers. They like to write code—lots of code. They probably have degrees in computer science and have been writing software for a long time, but usually very little of that experience involved developing platforms or infrastructure.

What they do well

These teams are builders. They nerd out on their platform architectures and technologies and think big about what comes next. They love to talk about "golden paths," "vNext," and "next-gen" platforms that will surely fix all the flaws of the current platform. And they're not wrong—at least, not in a reality where they had infinite time to deliver it.

What they do badly

This type of team reflects an adage among software engineers: that technical debt is any code some other engineers wrote. They get frustrated by any work that isn't building a newer, better system, and they view any effort expended on improving the old system as "throwaway" work, as it distracts from building the new system faster. What they overlook is the frustration and hampered productivity of the current system's users. This is made worse when, like most software engineers, they are too optimistic in their project estimates.

In the meantime, they treat the current in-product platform as what systems consultant Carla Geisser calls "haunted graveyards" (*https://oreil.ly/SrvDg*): curiosities to be carefully poked, not systems to be understood. This leads to operational problems, eventually causing a negative business impact. That 2 a.m. downtime issue? You'll probably have to page the on-call engineer a couple of times before they respond, and if you try the manager, they'll likely be upset that you thought waking them would solve any problem.

Why they are stuck

In the last 20 years, the industry has come to view delivering new code as the most valuable thing software engineers can spend time on, and has heavily tied it to compensation and promotions. This bias has spread to software engineering managers, since they got where they are by writing lots of code. So, for instance, they cannot imagine hiring anyone with the title "software engineer" who can't solve toy algorithm problems on a whiteboard in 30 minutes, regardless of their other, more practical abilities.

Some managers may grant that such an engineer does actually have value, but even in that case, they'll probably find it hard to believe they should be on the same team as their "real" software engineers. They will insist that there must be some other title for the work, some other team they should be on where they aren't distracting those undertaking the important work of developing software. In fact, ideally they would just be doing whatever is possible to make that software development go faster—per the split SRE/DevOps model, "taking on all the operations load, support, toil, and automation grunt work that distracts my software engineers from creating code." The problem is that unless the platform is massive, nobody wants that job.

The Different Roles of Platform Engineers

To unstick teams that are too focused on software or systems, you need to equally value both types of work, which usually means adding new roles to the team. This requires understanding what value each role brings. That's our goal in this section: even if you're not a manager, we want to help you better appreciate how your role relates to those of your coworkers.

The first step is realizing that the old software versus systems split, which does a good job of explaining how individuals' focuses may differ, does a poor job of illustrating how their roles relate. On the software side, the problem is that the term "software engineer" is used to describe a broad variety of roles outside of platform teams, and so misses the fact that various aspects of this role are different on a platform team— and these are differences you need to be aware of, hire for, and recognize.

Things are more complex on the systems side, where there are a plethora of roles and titles. While a lot of the work between them is duplicative, there are also specializations not just in skill set but also in culture. To simplify, we believe that three major systems-focused roles are needed in a platform team:

Systems engineer
> A true systems generalist, which many would call a DevOps engineer, although many other names are used across the industry

Reliability engineer
> Someone who has deeply focused their role on reliability, ignoring other facets of systems engineering

Systems specialist
> This could encompass many specific roles based on specific deep expertise—for example, Linux engineer, performance engineer, network development engineer

We show how these all relate in terms of team composition in Figure 4-1. In the following subsections, we'll take a closer look at each of these four roles in turn.

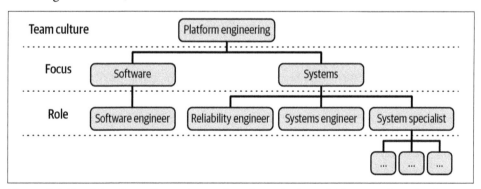

Figure 4-1. Breaking down the major engineering roles in a platform engineering team

Software Engineers

Your software engineers are going to be people who can and will write a lot of code. On most platform teams, these will be "backend" engineers—people who are used to writing server-side code—although you may have some "frontend" engineers as well. In successful platform teams, most of the software engineers, particularly the more senior ones, are a bit different from the generalist "backend" software engineers found in application teams:

They are drawn to understanding systems.

They have a strong desire to understand the interaction of their code and the systems the code runs on top of. They're not just interested in completing a feature for an end user, but think carefully about how their code fits into the ecosystem of software, hardware, and networking that it runs within, seeking a deeper understanding of the browser, the operating system, distributed systems, databases/storage, or whatever else is relevant.

You can spot these engineers because they're the ones who want to read the code for the libraries they depend on, and who are curious about the failure patterns that happen at the edges of applications. They want to think about the system more broadly than the feature they are implementing, and they are willing to figure out not only how to code the system but how to operate it and support it, because how can they know if the code makes sense if they don't understand how it actually runs in production?

They are comfortable being on call for business-critical systems.

This matters because, as we will cover in Chapter 6, most platforms are staffed at a level where they need every expert to be part of an on-call rotation, handling events of business-critical impact with ambiguous causes. None of us loves being on call, but the important thing here is not just a willingness to do it, but also the ability to be on call and respond effectively. We have found that many software engineers love to pore over the details of systems, but as an intellectual matter at design and coding time, not as something they need to draw on practically at 2 a.m. In our experience, there are a variety of causes for this—not strong on Unix skills, not strong on communication, uncomfortable working under time pressure—but whatever the reason, those people are going to struggle on most platform teams.

Within your company, you will find the people you're looking for by watching what happens during incidents: even when they're not paged, they will engage and make the incident remediation much faster. In the behavioral interview, you should ask about the largest incident the candidate has been involved in remediating and probe to be sure they were a significant part of it being resolved.

They are comfortable shipping at a deliberate pace.

You can find plenty of brilliant people who love system details and want free rein to write code to fix user problems ASAP. But while your platform software engineers will be writing code, they will also spend time on operations, integrations, and experimentation. Furthermore, there are large costs to mistakes in platforms, both in terms of operational risk and the risk of getting stuck supporting features that are much more expensive to maintain than they were to create.

An engineer who is strongly motivated by novelty and fast-turnaround feature building likely will not be a great fit for a mature platform team. (In Chapter 8, we will talk about how such "pioneers" are a much better fit in early-stage platforms, when your platform team needs to partner with product teams and iterate quickly.)

Systems Engineers

Roles around "systems" can be specialized in terms of breadth or depth. We'll cover the depth form in the following sections, on reliability engineers and systems specialists. In our experience, however, a broad systems engineer is the more common role on successful platform teams, so we'll start with that.

Almost all platforms benefit from the presence on the team of someone who, while more focused on understanding systems than writing software, uses that focus broadly, to understand more than one speciality. True, they won't be world experts in performance, Linux, or networking. But because of their motivation to understand the intricacies of how different types of systems work and come together, they will know a lot more than most of your software engineers, and they'll be a lot more motivated to do work that involves manipulating systems despite those intricacies.

But what *do* they do? Well, mainly stuff covered in the SRE and DevOps literature: lots of automation, particularly for infrastructure integration, scaling, reliability, and observability configuration. But it doesn't stop at automation and configuration. Their broad systems knowledge can be put to use for building platform features as well—specifically, those arcane aspects that take a lot of knowledge to get right. This is why, even though there is a lot of crossover, we prefer not to use the name "DevOps engineer" or "SRE engineer" for this role. When you have adopted a platform engineering culture, everyone on the team should be thinking of their work in terms of features of the platform product, not just its automation or reliability.

Where systems engineers tend to shine the most is in using their knowledge to resolve deep systems issues that involve both the platform codebase and the underlying dependencies. A lot of these issues are operational—we have seen cases where software engineers left issues languishing for months (*https://oreil.ly/6gtnh*), lacking the knowledge to make progress, until a systems engineer came along to help. However, focusing on operational debugging is seeing the value of the role too narrowly. We've also seen a systems engineer rescue a launch deadline by spotting an easy optimization in OSS configuration, whereas our software engineers were telling us that fixing the issue would take months of rewriting code.

Why recognize and hire for a broad systems engineer role rather than pushing for specialists in particular elements of the system (say, the OSS or cloud vendor you're using)? There are three reasons:

- Specialization tends to take a long time to achieve, making it hard to hire systems engineers who aren't already at "senior" levels of experience.
- Strong systems engineers will feel the need to specialize in order to get promoted, and the team will lose the breadth that is so important to their contributions.
- You don't want too many specialists, but you *need* broad systems engineers.

While systems engineers' expertise should increase in depth over time in certain areas, based on what they have worked on, it is a mistake to push them into that specialization as a career unless your company really needs that. So, with that in mind, let's turn to the specialists.

Reliability Engineers

Given its popularity in some parts of the industry today, we expect some readers to believe the "SRE" role captures all the systems work that is not feature-based "software development." There are a few problems with that thinking. First, Google itself split the SRE job into two (*https://oreil.ly/llZlW*), differentiating between software engineers and systems engineers, with both sharing the same culture but filling different roles. Second, as we highlighted in Chapter 1, the role of "DevOps engineer" covers a lot of the same skills, although with a very different culture. This comes back to the fact that naming matters. A lot of people, including some SREs, think that "reliability" is *all* the job should be about, whereas the general systems engineer role also encompasses support, efficiency, security, performance, and even adding features.

So, when we use the term "reliability engineer," we mean those who want their role to be focused on that, versus more general responsibilities. Now, that's not to say the role is unimportant. Many great SRE practices work much better when led by passionate practicing engineers. These engineers excel at high-impact incident management, consulting on service level objectives (SLOs) and chaos engineering, and running game days, production readiness reviews, rigorous incident postmortems, and even weekly operational meetings. They have the technical depth to know what matters and the skill set to implement a lot of the technical stuff behind it, and so they drive reliability across the organization's systems.

In theory, other engineers could do all this on a part-time basis. But in our experience, few are willing. The type of people who are motivated to do this are *systems thinkers*, those for whom the social dimension of a solution makes it even more motivating. They tend to ask, "How do we make everyone a little bit better?"

Take, for example, incident management. In an organization with teams doing their own on-call rotations, SREs as incident managers can ensure that thematic issues don't fall through the cracks. An incident can span multiple systems, and even if your team owns all of those systems, it's very easy for each person or subteam to think only about their portion of the issue. You need someone to track incidents, alert senior management about unresolved challenges, and plan and implement ways to remediate those challenges. This is best done by someone who loves to focus on big broken things and has the patience to see a project through to completion.

People like this can often be found on platform engineering teams, working with highly complex technical systems. Usually they start doing this work part-time, for their own teams. If you want to scale their work up and give them a broader mandate, we have found they typically need to be in a focused team that stays close to the platform engineering team—something like a core reliability team. Coworkers sometimes see people in this role as "talkers who have never done it," which takes away from their impact. We recommend rotating reliability specialists in and out of platform teams to keep their skills current.

Systems Specialists

Cloud networking engineer. Kernel engineer. Performance engineer. Storage engineer. At a certain scale, an engineer with depth in any of these roles can be game-changing. The best specialist can level up an entire organization's practices around their speciality, educating even as they do hands-on work. But it's a mistake to think that your platform team can just be a combination of software engineers and systems specialists, and we encourage you to wait to hire them until the need is clear. When you do have a need, keep the bar high, and avoid hiring more than a few specialists until you can clearly see the positive impact of your first round of new hires.

It takes a fairly large organization to not just want to employ such specialists full time, but also to give them problems that fully interest and utilize them. If a big part of your platform's offering revolves around networking management, for example, all of your engineering team should understand the network. But it's easy to take this too far and end up with a bunch of people who are too focused on implementing the state-of-the-art ideas of their specialty and not focused enough on building the thing you need. We once witnessed a developer tools team made up of version control experts: instead of focusing on the lack of user-friendly tooling, they spent all their time refining interfaces to the version control system. Such work can be important, but when it isn't the current problem, an overspecialized team can end up ignoring the bigger picture of what's needed.

Another way we have seen this play out is specialists refusing more general work. Instead, they want a role we call "specialist as internal evangelist." They imagine spending their time contributing to open source projects of no immediate value to the company, speaking on the conference circuit, researching obscure new offerings, and perhaps running nice-to-have internal programs aligned with their speciality. We encourage these activities for all engineers *in moderation*, but evangelism is a full-time role for SaaS vendors—when an engineer tries to make a full-time role of it internally without having much to show for their expertise, they tend to struggle for credibility, and so usually undermine the ideas they are trying to spread.

Hiring and Recognizing Engineers in All Roles

We understand if you're feeling a little confused after the last section. Are you looking for one role, two roles, four roles, or even more? There is no single answer, because it depends not just on your needs as a platform engineering team, but also your company's job families and hiring processes—what they are today, and how much flexibility there is to change them.

These days, most of the tech industry's hiring and promotion processes greatly favor software engineers who ship a lot of new code to production—their impact on the organization is seen as easy to evaluate. Since their systems are slower to change, software engineers working on platforms can struggle to get recognized in company-wide processes, and the three other roles fare even worse. The organization generates an organ rejection of talented individuals, usually by hiring them into too-junior positions or refusing to promote them, all because their impact on the organization is not as easy to evaluate compared to shipping software.

We've had mixed success in dealing with this challenge, for reasons that involve company culture, our positions within the hierarchy, and the CTO's appetite for making and communicating process changes. What we've learned is that success is about *positive marginal change*—making a case for incremental changes based on individual cases, while building evidence for bigger changes in the long run.

With this experience in mind, the next sections lay out our best practices, which we summarize in Table 4-1.

Table 4-1. Engineering roles and best practices in platform engineering teams

Role	Title	Interview process	Job family/level matrix
Software engineer	Prefer "software engineer." Allow "platform software engineer" only if unavoidable.	Custom behavioral interview to cover fit with the platform engineering team.	Common to the company-wide role.
Systems engineer	Allow specialized, such as DevOps engineer.	Same as for software engineer, but more flexibility in the coding interview. Design questions should cover the candidate's systems breadth.	Common across the three roles. Net impact is the same as software engineer. Differences emphasize impact created less by writing code, and more by exercising distinct knowledge, skills and practices.
Reliability engineer	Allow specialized, such as SRE.	Same as for systems engineer, but design questions should cover the candidate's depth in SRE.	
Systems specialist (splits into many roles)	Allow specialized and per-role, such as kernel engineer, performance engineer, and storage engineer.	Same as for software engineer, but design questions should cover the candidate's depth in their system speciality.	

Allow Role-Specific Titles

The preceding table breaks out three different facets of a role: its title, its level matrix (usually called a "job family"), and its interview process. We have seen people with a systemizing bent want to systemically link these together, insisting that everyone in positions that use a certain level matrix must have the same interview process and must have the same job title. What could be more simple? And it's so rational!

The problem is that a job title indicates someone's specific role, both to fellow employees and to external stakeholders. There is a personal aspect to it, especially when someone has built their career around a specialization. Forcing, say, your first kernel engineer to be called an SRE because that's the level matrix you will use not only won't make sense to their peers but also demeans their depth of experience, all while introducing a feeling of bureaucratic rigidity.

While we believe it's fine to allow role-specific titles, we definitely don't embrace the other extreme of everyone getting to choose their own title, as that will confuse people too. Creating a new title should be done only for good reasons, in recognition of substantial differences in the new role. Crucially, this does not need to be coupled with immediately creating a new level matrix or interview process (we'll look at when this might be required in the following sections).

Avoid Creating a New Software Engineer Level Matrix

Standard software engineering job descriptions heavily emphasize creating new code, systems, and architectures. Platform software engineers are often ill-served by these definitions, both in the interview process and in the criteria used to evaluate their performance and readiness for promotion. They do all these things, but the business criticality of the mature systems they work on means they do them more slowly. Many organizations respond to this issue by seeking to create a "platform software engineer" level matrix, recognizing a platform as a substantially different type of system whose successful development requires different skills, and so whose practitioners should be evaluated differently.

However, this problem exists for other specialized software development roles as well. For example, data engineers, mobile engineers, and frontend engineers all write software and create new systems (just different types of systems). So, should they get their own set of job levels, too? It's tempting to say yes, but once you've written and launched a few job ladders, you realize that they are expensive to create and even more expensive to maintain. There's a technical analogy in the trade-offs of forking code to support a new use case versus generalizing it to support both. What looks cheap initially (forking the code/ladder) becomes a long-term maintenance burden, particularly in the presence of many similar forks.

Because all of these roles are primarily about software development, we have found the sanest path is keeping all of them together on a single ladder. To make this work, you will need to specify level criteria in terms of *outcomes achieved*, as opposed to overly relying on *methods used*. This can take time and iteration to get right.

In the meantime, what should you do when you have a great platform software engineer but can't get them promoted? We've found that you'll be much better off stretching *within* the system, by finding people outside of platform engineering, at the next level up, who can attest that "this person's impact is just as high as mine." In fact, bringing such cases forward usually spurs the organization to adjust its level criteria. To support a case for promotion, Diego Quiroga, principal software engineering manager at Microsoft, suggests providing evidence of some of the following:

- Tools, dashboards, or wikis the engineer has created (particularly those that are widely adopted within the team or organization)

- The quality of their customer interactions, including clarity, technical depth, and responsiveness

- Their contribution to handling and resolving tickets efficiently, considering volume and complexity

- Their involvement in postmortems, ability to coach other teams in analyzing incidents, and ability to propose solutions

Back up these and any other artifacts with feedback from those on the receiving end of the engineer's work products, and prompt for feedback that speaks to both the impact and the technical expertise needed to do the work well.

Have, at Most, One Level Matrix for the Systems Roles

In smaller companies, the practice we've outlined in the last few sections works well to hire and reward great software and systems platform engineers, without needing a second level matrix. However, at scale, because they don't write as much code, we have seen challenges in getting organizations to recognize the commensurate value of people in all the "systems" roles—reliability engineers, systems engineers, and all the variants of systems specialists.

A common example: we've seen a team interview a great systems engineer with 10 years of experience on planet-scale systems, then propose to hire them at a non-senior level "since they can't solve coding problems like a senior engineer does." Similarly, we've seen company-wide promotion committees struggle with how to evaluate senior-level engineers who had written only a thousand lines of code in the last year, or staff-level engineers who hadn't led the building of a new system. The panel was biased to think of leverage only in terms of new code and systems being created.

With that in mind, we believe most organizations should eventually create a second level matrix for the "systems" roles that don't churn out lots of code. The key is to create only *one*, rather than three, or else you'll again run into the problem of confusing everyone by codifying subtle differences in how to evaluate impact in similar roles. Since these job titles have seen so much renaming in recent years, we won't suggest a new name, but a couple of examples we've seen are Meta's production engineer level matrix and Amazon's systems development engineer level matrix.

Finally, if your company already has a level matrix for DevOps engineers or SREs, it's fine to use that. The name won't be a perfect match, since these are more specific roles, but as there's no such thing as a perfect name anyway it's OK to avoid the work around renaming—just make sure the level criteria accommodate all three roles, since otherwise you'll be limiting who can be successful on your platform teams.

If Needed, Create a New Software Engineer Interview Process

Assessing a candidate during an interview and evaluating an employee's job performance are totally different beasts. In the case of performance and promotion, the employee has been doing the job for thousands of hours, with clear business impact in deliverables and other specific role information that can put the evaluation in context. Interviews, on the other hand, provide only a few hours of information, none of which involves actually doing the job. Thus, "forking" the software engineering interview process may be the right thing to do.

Platform teams at companies that use "company-wide" software engineering pipelines can get stuck on evaluating an "application software engineer" profile and miss the differences we covered earlier in the chapter. For instance, we have seen coding questions that are less about practical coding skills (creating a solution with high attention to detail, particularly around assumptions and edge cases) and more about computer science knowledge that rarely comes up in day-to-day platform programming, such as data structure manipulation or first-order algorithms. We've also seen bias in design questions, which may be focused on choosing the right platforms to combine as part of an application, as opposed to designing platforms themselves. None of these map well to platform software engineering.

For platform engineering teams, we prefer an interview process that looks something like this:

- One traditional coding interview, typically with an algorithm that has a working naive/brute-force approach that can then be optimized through more advanced algorithms or data structures. The candidate is evaluated not only on whether they can find the optimized solution, but also on whether they can implement the "bookkeeping" details of the answer, including error handling and testing.

- One coding interview that shows the breadth of the candidate's understanding of systems detail. It may take them 20 minutes to get the code correct, but such questions should generate 30 minutes or more of discussion about the underlying assumptions. During this discussion, you can test their methodology and their assumptions around real-world factors like testing, observability, and scale-up; for example, you might ask how the candidate's answer would change if the inputs were larger than what a single computer could handle.

- One traditional design interview, but focused on designing a *platform*, as opposed to an application.

- One inverted design interview, in which you ask the candidate to dive deep into the technical trade-offs of something real they have designed and built.

- One behavioral/values interview, with a particular focus on operational experience, ability to lead in the face of conflict, and empathy with customers.

If any of these types of interviews are new to your company's process, you will need to be "hands on" in managing the rollout process to ensure your early interviewers are calibrated. You'll want to set up a small working group to create a set of standard questions to be covered, with a common rubric or a set of green and red flags. As the process is initially rolled out, you will need to collect interviewers' feedback on how well they think the question evaluated the candidate, and present any trends to the working group to make further corrections. In our experience, such a hands-on rollout can take six months before we are confident that the early interviewers are well calibrated.

Vary the Interview Only Slightly for Systems Roles

As indicated in Table 4-1, for systems roles, we like to use the same interview outline as for platform software engineers. However, we suggest three main changes. The first is more flexibility on the design question—the more you focus on the candidate's specialization, the more information you have to evaluate whether they pass the interview and what level they should be at. The second is, of course, in the inverted design interview: you want to dive into their depth of systems knowledge in their specific role, ideally having someone in that role asking the questions.

The third change is the largest point of contention: keeping the coding interviews. People with systems backgrounds often argue that "Whiteboard coding isn't real coding, so I shouldn't need to do it." Sometimes they follow that with "You should trust from my resume that I know how to code." Unfortunately, there are many people in the world who can't actually create code in existing production systems, including a lot of people whose resumes would make you think otherwise. This has to be covered in the interview.

The question, though, is how. People with systems backgrounds often note that the whiteboard interview process is unnatural and requires practice that is divorced from normal working conditions. It's hard to produce production-quality code for a new problem with the time pressure of a live interview, not to mention the distractions from an interviewer looking over your shoulder and interrupting you with well-meaning suggestions. The result is that the candidate's performance gives no legitimate indication of how well they will write code once in the job.

We suggest that, instead, you take the question offline, offering the candidate a time-boxed take-home coding problem. Then, use the interview to discuss their submission. This allows you to validate that they didn't cheat *and* to go deep on systems questions. This style of interview takes more time and gets pushback from some candidates, but again, we think it's important not to backslide on this point if you really want to build a team with a *platform* culture that will create substantial new software, as opposed to a traditional *infrastructure* or *operational* culture.

Interview for Customer Empathy

In our time managing and working with platform engineering organizations, we've seen some organizations develop abrasive relationships with some of their largest user groups. In certain cases, the engineers treated users' thoughts and opinions with contempt, even as those users struggled with problems caused by the platform itself. It's tempting to dismiss this with "Don't hire jerks." There are two reasons we think this is simplistic.

First, the word *jerk* implies behavior like belittling, agitating, and ignoring. That is certainly some of what you see, but it doesn't cover more defensive behavior, like touchiness around criticism. Here, rather than focusing on helping the user the best they can, the platform engineers sigh, shrug, and point fingers at the past. When the team is under a lot of pressure, this can cause outbursts targeted at users with a clear message of "you users are lucky to have us."

Second, the *user* might be the jerk. There is a reason for the old help-desk meme of "the problem exists between the keyboard and the chair." Some users just cannot accept the facts. Most application engineers are protected by their support or product organizations, which deal with the worst of such people directly. However, as we'll discuss in Chapter 6, when you're working on a platform the line between support cases and new features can be blurred, so user support is part of the job.

Handling difficult users while supporting a system you did not create takes maturity and empathy to hold your temper, build bridges, educate the user, and solve the problem. Not everyone can manage it. Unfortunately, this means there are a lot of passionate platform engineers who aren't cut out to work on platforms. Not only does their behavior affect the reputation of the team, but because they are somewhat "right" in their grievances, they can easily affect the culture of the entire team.

While there are many skills you might try to interview for to avoid this problem (negotiation, communication, influence without authority), we recommend that, at a minimum, you screen for a basic level of empathy and ability to put oneself in the user's shoes. We have used questions like:

- Tell me about a time when you helped one of your users understand the system.
- Tell me about a time when you used customer feedback to change the direction of what you were building.
- How do you understand your users in order to figure out whether a new feature or system is interesting or applicable to them?

These questions are not meant to see if the engineers would make good product managers; they make sure engineers appreciate that they are building things for *other humans* to consume. Camille prefers to frame this as *customer* empathy instead of *user* empathy because, to paraphrase a friend, "*Customer* implies obligations; *users* are just some schmucks."

This doesn't mean that engineers need to spend all their time thinking about their customers. But when engineers have some empathy for other people who might need to read their code and a general commitment not just to the most interesting technical problem but also to the larger health of the system, the engineers themselves and the team as a whole tend to be stronger.

What Makes a Great Platform Engineering Manager?

It's great to have a balanced set of platform software engineers and systems engineers, but at some point you need to add engineering managers into the mix. (After all, who's going to make sure all these interview processes happen?) Furthermore, the manager is often the leader who has the most influence on the culture of a team, impacting who feels heard, who feels enabled, and who feels their ideas are being treated equally to those of others.

While there are skills all good managers share, we've found that some skills, tendencies, and experiences make for the most successful platform engineering managers. In this section, we'll cover the main ones.

Experience Operating Platforms

Platform engineering involves operational complexity that many managers with application software engineering backgrounds do not appreciate. Most at least understand the breadth of the underlying systems, but they may miss that these systems tend to have ill-defined boundaries. A problem in one area can cause the whole thing to fall apart in surprising ways. Thus, it requires a lot of humility and patience to manage a team as they slowly yet diligently address systemic issues. When you bring a software engineering leader without operational skills into a platform management role, they can compound problems by encouraging a mindset that the solution is just one "brilliant" engineering fix away. Yes, there are sometimes quick system fixes that buy time, but these are much more likely to be "simple" than "brilliant." For every "brilliant" engineering fix we've seen, we've seen 10 failed ones that compounded operational problems and slowed the team down.

A different failure mode we have observed involves hiring a good manager from a customer organization. This approach has clear upsides—you get an established manager, a fast path to customer empathy, and organizational relationship building. However, be cautious, because this hire is likely coming from a place of less operational complexity. As you'll see in Chapter 6, they can struggle to see the value in routine operational practices, letting things fall through the gaps. Further, they might think that the underlying system problems are easy to solve and the engineers working on them were mismanaged and doing things wrong. That's a great way to end up not just misdiagnosing problems but also alienating the strongest members of an existing team.

Experience on Big, Long-Running Projects

Managers who are used to the "move fast and break things" pace of application engineering may get frustrated by the slower delivery pace of platform engineering teams. When a lot of people depend on your platform, it is necessarily more critical, and that means you need to make changes slowly and operate with careful thought.

This doesn't mean that platform teams shouldn't aim for frequent delivery. A good platform engineering leader will help their team figure out how to deliver their work quickly and safely in the same way that a good application engineering leader does. But there is a difference between leading a team that ships new code to production every day, and a team that has to think through the multi-month process of safely migrating several customers off of one critical platform and onto another one without downtime, data loss, or disruption.

Great platform leaders are able both to take criticism related to the team's inability to ship improvements faster and to justify why the team's delivery pace is right, as they are managing high levels of business criticality, complexity, and risk. In the face of constant pressure and criticism from stakeholders, even the most confident leaders can start questioning their strategy and churn their team's focus by looking for quick fixes to regain face. Instead, they must set aside any emotional reaction to the one-way nature of this feedback, and be willing to spend time and effort on handling tough discussions with technical stakeholders. We'll discuss techniques for building these relationships in depth in Chapter 10.

Attention to Detail

The most successful managers that we've seen transition from "application engineering" leadership to "platform engineering" leadership were detail-oriented sticklers who found motivation in doing project and process management personally.

Managers who spent their early careers as engineers working in infrastructure and platform teams tend to know which details matter and who can be trusted to make the right trade-offs, so they can lead their teams without using too much management process. But for managers from other backgrounds, until you have built these instincts, you'll need to track a lot of details. This can make teams feel "micromanaged," which can be annoying, particularly if former management used less process. However, if the options are "my leader asks micromanaging questions to understand trade-offs" and "my leader misses crucial details in making decisions that impact me," most engineers will grudgingly admit that they prefer the former.

Good managers should eventually build the instincts for when to trust the team and when to probe more deeply, and so become able to put much of the process aside. This is something *actual* micromanagers struggle with.

Other Roles on a Platform Team

Of course, a good platform team includes more roles than just various kinds of engineers. This section briefly covers some other roles you may encounter.

Product Managers

Good platform teams focus on the product and the customer. As we lay out in Chapter 5, building products that reflect this mindset takes ongoing detailed and focused work, particularly around communicating with customers and building that into a strategy. At scale, adding dedicated product managers to your platform group is the only way to ensure this work will be done.

It's a challenge to hire good product managers anywhere, but it's especially hard for platform teams. Most product management organizations see value in the role as closely tied to revenue and to delivering to external customers, so few PMs are experienced in the challenges of platform teams. This means they can sometimes take the short-term mindset of "business obsession" too far. Jordan West, a staff engineer on a data platform team at one of the FAANG companies, captures his negative experience with PMs who think this way: "Why is it so bad if engineers get interrupted every 10 minutes and can't deliver on anything else, as long as the customer is happy?" That can be a useful mindset for a startup, but it's dysfunctional on a platform team.

To address this challenge, platform teams can turn to product-minded people from other technical backgrounds to fill some of these roles. Our experience is that, for every PM we've worked with who came in with formal product management experience, we've worked with two others who moved into product management from engineering or, occasionally, technical program roles. While hiring people without formal product management experience is a gamble, it's one that often pays off.

However, while it can be tempting to fill your product teams with *only* these folks, you also need some experienced product managers who already understand the role. They can help to train the newbies and calibrate whether they are doing product management or just glorified program management, scrum mastering, or tech leading. You can bootstrap this through external coaching and training, but don't skip this step entirely!

What Happens When You Can't Hire Product Managers?

What do you do if you aren't allowed to hire product managers (for instance, if that role is only for external-facing teams in your organization), or just can't find the right person? Even when there are potential internal transfers from engineering this can be an issue, since at many companies their lack of experience in the new role would mean a pay cut.

Engineering managers and project managers can be helpful here, but you have to be careful. While the engineering manager role requires a lot of communicating with customers, it is usually focused on execution rather than product. Further, it's common for engineering managers to struggle with the workload of their other responsibilities. TPMs have similar challenges: they are often unused to conversations about ambiguous long-term and short-term trade-offs, so they tend to treat product problems as ones of execution, to be scoped, stack ranked, and solved as quickly as possible.

Our best successes have been with staff engineers. Perhaps a quarter of staff engineers are strong two-way communicators invested in doing what is right for the business. When they talk to customers, they listen, internalize the feedback, and look for incremental solutions, even if those take them away from building their ideal "next big thing." We don't mean to imply the other three-quarters are bad staff engineers, just that they lack the strengths to personally take on product management responsibilities, so ideally you would partner them with a PM.

So, if you find yourself unable to hire product managers, your best move is usually to identify, empower, and reward the staff engineers who can wear both hats. To learn more about this role, we recommend Tanya Reilly's book *The Staff Engineer's Path* (O'Reilly).

Product Owners

Thanks to the Scaled Agile Framework, a lot of companies today are hiring a role called *product owner*. There's some ambiguity about how this differs from a product manager role. It's sometimes defined as a complement to a marketing-focused product management role, emphasizing the work of backlog grooming and defining user stories. In platform engineering organizations, where all the "customers" are internal and so marketing needs are small, there is no reason to split the roles. Look for people who can make strategic decisions *and* handle the mechanics of action.

Project Managers/Technical Program Managers

The project or technical program manager (TPM)[2] role is often the most vilified role in engineering organizations. Critics argue that the "technical" part of the title is a misnomer, since every decision involves big meetings of stakeholders, and otherwise the job seems to mainly involve harassing overworked managers and tech leads for updates. We think this is less about the role and more about the conditions they are often asked to deliver in—when executives don't prioritize the right projects ahead of time, it creates a situation where the only way a project will succeed is by a TPM driving brute-force cross-organization execution. To avoid these situations, we recommend hiring product managers first and using engineering managers and technical leads to manage all small- to medium-sized projects.

But no matter how hard your executives and PMs try, no one can predict the future, so broad, execution-focused projects are going to happen. Managing those projects well will require 100% of someone's time, and it's a good idea to make it someone who has built their career on doing that.

Finding good platform TPMs is almost as difficult as finding good PMs. We have seen a lot of candidates who had succeeded at their last company totally fail at their new one. The lesson we've learned is to find TPMs who are comfortable delivering on projects using the organization-wide processes you have *today*, rather than blaming those processes for why they can't. Thus, at a relatively small company, you will want people who are good at making things happen by building bottom-up relationships with engineers and delivering without needing authority. On the other hand, at a big company with tens of thousands of engineers, you likely will want someone who makes things happen by bringing hard decisions to misaligned leadership, collecting the details and communicating them upwards in the style your company's executives prefer.

Developer Advocates, Technical Writers, and Support Engineers

Developer advocates, technical writers, and support engineers are highly specialized roles seen in really big platform engineering organizations (generally, those with more than a thousand engineers). Both product managers and engineers can perform these functions to some degree (though not as well as a specialist), so avoid hiring until your team really *needs* a full-time specialist. This usually means pushing back against "not my job" attitudes from your team. It also means ensuring such work is recognized and rewarded, even when it is not directly mentioned in their job's level matrix.

---

2 Like "product owner" versus "product manager," the difference in these titles in terms of role is subtle, especially as usage varies across the industry. We will use the terms interchangeably.

Creating a Platform Engineering Team Culture

We started this chapter by talking about how some teams get stuck with one type of engineer (systems or software) and struggle to create the balanced culture that platform engineering needs. Now, we want to talk about a case where we brought together two teams with divergent cultures and instilled the culture needed to do platform engineering.

A Platform Split Between a Development and an SRE Team

This was a compute platform whose core was a complex OSS system, with the platform cobbled together by a development team of software engineers who were mostly recent PhDs, although in systems-related fields. All of these had been hired according to a company-wide "software engineer" interviewing standard—which means none were screened for systems operational skills or customer empathy. The platform team had recently added a few systems engineers, but they'd been hired into a separate "SRE" organization, which was the by-the-book approach of the time. Their most common manager, three levels up, knew he had a problem, but he was hearing very different proposals about what needed to be addressed.

Strengths and Weaknesses of the Development Team

The development team's culture held that every problem could be solved by growth—building new functionality in collaboration with customers to allow them to move to the new platform, which would later allow the team to hire more engineers. They didn't worry about broad customer understanding, migration plans (other than "build it and they will come"), improving the operational stability of some of the systems, or solving problems through evolving the existing offerings. Instead, at every opportunity, the team immediately went into "new build" mode, thinking this was going to be the "brilliant" solution that all future customers would use.

This had certain advantages. The team created some very innovative solutions. They weren't afraid to tackle problems with the OSS that no one in the community had solved yet, instead of deciding that the OSS wasn't fit for purpose due to the lack of support for their needs. Their fearlessness in the face of unsolved problems helped them knock down barriers and deliver some really big advances, and they didn't get bogged down in the formalities of process while delivering.

As you can probably guess, however, it had some big drawbacks too. There were many stability problems with these new systems, which the engineers often preferred to solve via a new build instead of taking the time to understand and fix the existing infrastructure. The innovative solutions were great for getting the ball rolling, but the team seemed stuck in "pioneer" mode. Perhaps due to the influence of the researchers in the group, they were less interested in the day-to-day grind of stability, reliability, and iterative improvements. Eventually, project delivery and broad customer communication suffered. The customers weren't clear when they could expect things to get done, so they weren't happy.

The creation of the separate SRE team, which was undersized and mostly staffed with newcomers to the company, just made things worse. The development team started to view reliability as "SRE's problem" and a license to stay on the same path, despite significant technical debt. The finger-pointing was more covert than overt, but the thinking on both sides was "Why is that other team not hiring better people who meet the needs of the business?"

Merging the Teams and Adding Product Management

Our first move was to merge the teams under someone from the SRE side with great managerial traits and strong experience operating platforms, executing on long-running projects, and managing stakeholders. The new team balanced people who wanted to build new things with those who were happy to scale and operate existing things and those who would work more closely with customers. As a result, over a period of about six months, they stabilized operationally and consolidated the prioritization around new features, partly by moving well away from the "one engineer, one feature" model toward a roadmap model.

These changes didn't come for free. We lost some of the more innovative research-focused developers: they had preferred the SRE model, as it let them focus on playing with new technologies and building new things. Mostly, we saw their unhappiness growing and were able to move them to more appropriate roles in other parts of the company. But for a couple, we didn't move fast enough, and we lost some good engineers who just ended up stuck on the wrong team.

The next step was finding a PM to take over product management for the team. This too created some tension; we had to ensure that the technical leads still felt heard and that the engineering managers wouldn't be (or feel) undermined by the product manager making all the big decisions. Bringing such a disparate group together while ensuring everyone feels respected and able to do their best work is not easy.

Instilling a Platform Engineering Culture

As these moves were made, an important aspect of our role as organization leaders was reinforcing the new culture. That was harder than we expected, as cultural challenges also came from outside the team. Part of the reason the development team had been empowered was their strong alignment with the broader company culture, which was largely about collaboratively building innovative things on the cutting edge. This culture was great for data scientists whose work had no human users. But the business had other other application teams with much higher reliability needs, and even the data scientists were unhappy with an unreliable platform.

Thus, we needed a platform team that balanced building new things with thinking about stability, reliability, and usability. We needed to create a new platform engineering culture that respected the overall company values of innovation and collaboration while adding our balanced focus on stability and scale.

In truth, most subteams at larger companies have their own distinct cultures, and the larger the company, the more these cultures tend to diverge. Teams develop cultures that reflect where they focus their attention and how they are punished or rewarded, and platform teams' cultures tend to be a bit more conservative than those of their product engineering counterparts. Platform engineering leaders should pay close attention to any culture drift and ensure that it doesn't lead to an "us versus them" mindset. It's OK for your team to have a slightly distinct culture, but when your pride in running highly reliable systems turns into scorn at the product engineering teams who keep shipping broken code, you risk destroying the customer empathy that is so important in building great platforms in the first place.

To create a healthy organization, spend time recognizing and rewarding different roles and skill sets. Talk about how they contribute to the stronger, better whole. Take the time to appreciate your partner teams and their work. This cultural investment will go a long way toward supporting your team and ensuring their (and your) continued success. The next step forward is creating a product culture, which is the topic of the next chapter.

Wrapping Up

In the first part of this book, we emphasized that platform engineering requires a cultural change in how you staff teams, bringing together engineers with a mix of focus areas to collaborate on customer-focused platforms. Mixed-mode management is not easy, though, so it's tempting for platform leaders early in their leadership careers, or early in their migration to platform engineering, to fall back on what they know—which results in teams with either a software or a systems focus. Unfortunately, that usually means the platforms they produce lack either the complex analysis that systems engineers bring or the code development productivity that software engineers bring. The platform product ends up being defined by what the team can produce, rather than what the customers need.

In this chapter, we not only introduced you to the breadth of roles that a platform engineering team needs to have at scale, but also to how to think about your processes of hiring and recognition so that the people in each role can flourish. We also covered the characteristics leaders need to successfully manage platform teams and gave an example of how to bridge the cultural gaps, not just within the team itself, but also in the expectations customer engineers have in interacting with the team. Because culture is such a major contributing factor to your success, it runs through nearly every topic in this book, and we'll talk about it quite a bit more in Chapter 5.

This change is not easy to implement. But if you want to move past operating over-general OSS and vendor primitives held together with in-house tools and glue, you need to start your platform engineering journey by ensuring your teams are staffed to actually build platforms.

Platform as a Product

What's an internal platform but an external platform being built in a hypoxic, lightless, dungheap of an environment?

—Coda Hale

The idea of taking a product approach when building internal technology has become increasingly popular. Unfortunately, like with so many fads in the technology industry, many people who try to adopt this approach have no idea what it actually means, and end up taking the most literal interpretation to solving the problem—which, in the case of platform engineering, means they add a bunch of product managers to the team. While we agree that product managers are important, there's a lot more to building a product-oriented platform organization than just hiring a few PMs. Because there are also some companies that actively resist having PMs for internal products, we've written this chapter so that it's relevant regardless of whether you have a formal internal product management team.

This chapter is for anyone who wants to get their platform organization to adopt a product mindset and apply product management techniques. We start with a deep dive on culture, focusing on customers (or users—we apply the terms interchangeably to mean the people who actually consume your products to do their jobs), because step 1 is to understand the people you're building these platforms for and how to interact with them as customers rather than stakeholders. Then, we talk about product discovery and evolution. With platforms, you will find that many of the best product ideas come from your engineers and engineers in other parts of the company, so identifying new products is often a process of finding a small prototype that could expand to be broadly useful.

For your existing products, we'll discuss strategies for moving them forward, and knowing when to either evolve the offerings or rethink them entirely. We'll also describe how to validate that there is a ready audience for your proposed new product offerings, and how to measure success.

Next, we'll explain how to put all this theory into practice, turning your collection of related technologies into a product vision, strategy, and roadmap that your customers can reference to understand your goals and planned deliverables. We'll finish the chapter by looking at some of the common failure modes we've seen here—because this is a big shift for many teams, there are a lot of ways to stumble that we hope to help you avoid.

Product management practices could fill an entire book, but we hope that by the end of this chapter you'll have a broad understanding of the foundations and how to use them to define and deliver platforms that meet your customers' needs.

Product Culture Focuses on the Customer

Whether you're in a big, established company trying to adopt product management as part of a platform engineering shift or a small startup hoping to build it in early, the first step to creating a product culture is understanding and appreciating your customers. If you want to build good products, you need to build them *for* someone. But internal customers are tricky to understand. They are people you can talk to every day, but that doesn't mean they can describe what they want you to build. They may be passive consumers who only complain when things are broken, or active competitors who want to build their own platforms. They are your colleagues as well as your customers, and you want to keep them happy, but that doesn't mean doing everything they tell you to do.

No matter who you are building your platform for, it's important to view them as customers (not stakeholders) so you can build a product that meets their needs. After all, a business would never just *make* customers use its product, so why would we expect to take that approach with our internal systems? In this section, we'll explore the various characteristics of internal customers and discuss how to engage and empathize with them in order to foster a collaborative relationship that results in a successful platform.

 Engineering leadership also needs to update incentives and focus areas in order to make this shift; while hiring strong product managers is helpful, the engineering team's behavior will make or break your efforts to build good products.

Characteristics of Internal Customers

Having an internal customer base can cause blind spots in your understanding of whether your products are successful, and catering to customers who may undervalue your work or take it for granted can create added friction. To manage this environment effectively, you need to understand the kind of customer you're working with, their unique expectations, and the challenges you will likely face. Let's take a look at some of the key characteristics of internal customers:

Small customer base

Platform product decision making is something of a unique discipline. When many people think about product managers, the image that springs to mind is a PM for a large consumer-facing product. Metrics, metrics, metrics! A/B tests and user studies and key performance indicators (KPIs) and design sprints and revenue models! Indeed, any time you are building products for a large user base, all of this is a factor, and PMs for AWS probably have a lot of metrics to guide them. But A/B testing for an audience of hundreds might not teach you much. When you're building a platform for internal customers at a small to midsize company, adopting a metrics-driven strategy is harder. This doesn't mean that there are no metrics to apply, but you need to be thoughtful about how and what you measure to ensure you are capturing real signals. We will discuss how to find these signals later in the chapter.

Captive audience

Not only might you have a small group of customers, but you often have a captive audience, meaning the platform product your team offers is the customers' only option (they can't go off and build their own). You can ask internal customers what they want or how they like your platform products, but they may not want to complain to their colleagues. Platform products also suffer from the problem that some engineers always think they could build something better, if only they had the time, so you likely have a customer segment that seems to never be satisfied no matter how hard you work.

There are two main failure modes in working with captive audiences. In one, you ignore adoption metrics entirely and fail to see that you've built a platform product that is useful for only a small subset of your customer base until it's too late. This can lead to the problem of several overlapping half-finished products built as "obvious" offerings that didn't fit the needs of a majority of customers. In the other failure mode, you look at adoption as the only important metric, and use it as a stick to force your customers to adopt a system that doesn't work for them. Having a captive audience doesn't excuse you from the work of building something they need and want.

Conflicting incentives

In extreme cases, your internal customers may also be the ones "paying" for your team to exist. This can lead to customers who think more about what they could do with the budget you are using and less about what they want in a platform product, especially if the product you are providing is something they are forced to use and don't appreciate. Your customer teams may expect you to build bespoke features precisely for their demands, or to loan them developers to integrate your platform into their systems.

Customer happiness is a moving target

Because so much of what you build makes hard things easy, or removes a need entirely, internal customers can forget about the improvements you have made soon after you make them. This leads to a cycle where your customers never seem satisfied; the minute you remove one bottleneck, they focus on the next, and sometimes it's not until the entire flow sees a front-to-back improvement that they are able to appreciate the work you're doing. Furthermore, new customers are always coming into the company as new engineers are hired, and they start with a fresh set of expectations. If things aren't as good as these new hires believe they should be, it doesn't matter how much better they are today than they were a year ago. And let's not forget that most people don't appreciate the complexity of making all of this stuff work, and they take it for granted until something breaks—customer satisfaction is often simple indifference.

Customers as competitors

Finally, sometimes internal customers behave like competitors. Yes, you read that right. When your customers are engineers and you aren't able to keep up with what they want, they might build the thing they need rather than trying to coordinate with you to get the work done. Staying ahead of what they need and making it clear to them that it's better to occasionally wait for your team to provide a solution than for them to rush ahead and build their own is part of the difficulty of working with this customer base.

Collaborating with Internal Customers

So, you have a tricky internal customer base made up of your colleagues and friends (or enemies). This raises another challenge that a product approach must overcome: existing internal collaboration habits.

If you have built software for internal users, particularly nontechnical users, you will be familiar with the *relationship model* of interaction. This comes about when a team is under pressure to deliver software quickly to solve a business problem. Management, faced with the challenge of negotiating delivery timelines, doesn't also want to argue about whether the features they're being asked to build are the right ones. The engineers therefore end up focusing on building exactly what the customer asks for as quickly as possible, to strengthen the relationship between the team and the customer base and keep their stakeholders[1] satisfied. If the only thing that matters is pleasing that one customer group, taking risks to build things they did not specifically ask for can seem pointless. And the fewer people you are trying to please, the more likely you are to just do whatever they want so that you can shield yourself from blame should the system you build end up not solving the problem at hand.

As you can probably tell, we're not entirely sold on this model, even when building for nontechnical customers. It's even worse when applied to platform engineering teams. Using a pure relationship model to build for other engineering teams—building exactly what they tell you they want to make them happy—sets both of you up for failure. Many engineering teams don't precisely know what they want. Even if you build exactly what they request, they might not adopt it. When they don't, despite having said they wanted it, guess who gets blamed? You do. They'll say you didn't implement it quickly enough, you didn't prioritize the right things, or they've moved on to other concerns and don't have time to adopt this new thing.

It's almost impossible to take a pure relationship approach to other engineering team customers, because they suffer from the same problems all engineering teams do: they don't know how long things will take, they have a bad idea of what their future selves will care about, and they haven't really thought about the problem that carefully.

Moreover, engineering platforms are not just collections of features that have been built up over time, request by request. They need to serve many similar but not identical customers across your company. These customers will all be very opinionated about things that may not matter for platform success, and to get a broadly useful platform you'll need to learn how to look beyond specific customer needs to the generalizable problem to be solved.

This is why product management for platforms is not just stakeholder management. Relationship-based product decision making assumes that you can get away with following people's expressed preferences and get to a good place for your systems. The reality is that when the usability of the system really matters (which is the case in many, if not all, developer platforms), success requires you to identify the customers' *revealed* preferences, meaning the way people actually use the systems and the tasks they perform, rather than the things they say they need or want. You need to understand what they are actually doing and derive plans based on this understanding, instead of relying solely on the customers to tell you what to build.

When you approach customers to ask about their needs, then, be thoughtful about how you ask the questions. Almost every customer will agree that they want the

---

1 In this case, "stakeholders" refers to the management of the customer teams, often business leaders.

best, fastest, most scalable offering, so if you ask them "Do you want a system that is near real time?" they will probably say yes. Platform engineers sometimes use this line of questioning to justify building a more elaborate initial offering, which leads to long-running projects and even failed delivery. By asking more specific questions (such as "How quickly do you need to be able to do X while using this system?"), you can determine what is absolutely necessary for customer success, and you often find a design that is much easier to deliver while still meeting their needs.

Stakeholder Management Versus Product Management

Why isn't internally facing product management the same thing as stakeholder management? After all, your stakeholders are probably just a subset of your customers—perhaps the most important ones or the leaders of customer teams. So if you make your customers happy, you should be making your stakeholders happy, and vice versa. Right?

In reality, we find that stakeholder management is as much an exercise in horse trading, power structure appreciation, and CYA (covering your...angles), as it is about deciding what to build. You can have excellent stakeholder management and build crappy products and systems, as many internal teams prove. Stakeholders can be left with a vague sense that they don't like what they've been given, but that they somehow signed off on what was delivered, and so they are part of the problem in a way they don't quite understand. Stakeholder management, at its extreme, is a political act that works the company power structure effectively in order to protect the interests of the leader in question.

Product management is not about making the most important person happy. Product management is about figuring out what the company actually needs, based on a deep understanding of current circumstances and future demands, and shaping the product features and offerings to meet those needs effectively, in measurable ways. Product management is risky because you are making bets about what to build to make an impact, which is why identifying and tracking impact metrics is so important. These metrics will also help you explain to stakeholders why you are making these bets; if the investments don't pan out, at least they'll understand the reasoning behind them.

Stakeholder management is a big job, and we will discuss some approaches to this challenge in Chapter 10. However, it is cynical to assume that because there are so many obvious technical elements to manage in the platform, and because the internal customers can't provide large-scale user metrics, you can get away with just managing to stakeholders and driving your platform without user-focused product management. There is room, and need, for both of these practices, and we believe that you must invest in each in order to run a successful team.

Empathizing with Customers

In Chapter 4, we noted that the two major groups of engineers in your team will have different motivators. Your software engineers will want to write a lot of new code, and they'll often want to chase the newest technologies. Your systems engineers, on the other hand, will usually prefer to make small, safe changes to products in their operational comfort zone. Bringing these groups together to build platform products that customers will love means you've got to get the whole team to appreciate that their success relies on more than the latest and greatest technology and/or efficient operation of existing offerings. How do you do this? By centering the team's focus on the people who will use the technology, rather than on the technology itself, and developing a culture of customer empathy.

Customer empathy is something you can coach and develop in your team, starting with your own behavior. What do you talk about, celebrate, hire for, and reward? There are opportunities around every corner to reinforce this mindset:

- Interview for empathy when evaluating candidates for "values fit," as we discussed in Chapter 4.
- Set quarterly or yearly goals that are not just about technical delivery but that include customer-focused metrics such as adoption, satisfaction, and engagement.
- Bring users to your all-hands or team meetings to share how they are using your products, offer honest feedback about the problems they are facing, and give kudos for things that are going well.
- Have your product managers present user research and feedback to the team regularly.
- Have engineers participate in customer support to observe common pain points.

You should reinforce this culture of customer empathy through goal setting. Platform teams without a captive audience may complain about adoption as a goal, rightly pointing out that they can't force users to adopt their products; meanwhile, teams with a captive audience may blame their users for slow growth in adoption, citing lack of engagement or other priorities. Both of these reactions lead to the question: Are you building things that people want? How do you know? How are you making it as easy as possible for people to adopt your offerings? Do you know what the potential customer base looks like, and are you being realistic about who needs and wants this offering? Asking your engineers to measure their success through the eyes of their customers shakes them out of a purely technical mindset and refocuses them on the experience, use cases, and purpose of their systems. Some basic questions to start with include:

- If your system is supposed to make people more productive, how much time do you think this change will save your users? It's surprising how many teams claim to improve productivity but neglect to measure what they are planning to improve!

- How many hours a year do your customers have to spend to keep using this platform (through reacting to upgrades, migrations, etc.)? This can help you spot unattended pain points and friction.

- Are your support requests about common repeated issues or unusual situations? The easier the system is to use, and the better your documentation/self-service/ error messages, the more likely it is that the support questions will fall on the "unusual" side.

Over time, you can use customer satisfaction (CSAT) or net promoter score (NPS) surveys to track customer sentiment; when done well, these provide a high-level trending view of how your customers are experiencing your products, and comments can be mined for specific target areas.

You can also encourage customer-focused empathy through the content you choose to highlight in team meetings, as mentioned previously. So much of leadership is repetition and showing people your values through this repetition; using your team meetings to emphasize the customer experience and feedback helps to set the expectation of customer focus. When people get shout-outs for great customer support, when they hear positive feedback from the users on the products they've built, and when you make a show of bragging about the uptick in adoption of the latest offering, you encourage that focus in your team.

Finally, when your challenge is usability and reliability of the systems, nothing creates empathy for internal customers like putting your team on a customer support rotation. Seeing where customers are struggling to use your products is a valuable reminder that the things that are obvious to you are not obvious to others; it's also a good way to hammer in that people generally do not read documentation, stack traces, or previously-asked questions, and so the easier your system is to use without needing to consult these sources the better your support rotation will be. Many consumer startups have everyone do a round or two of customer support work in order to better understand their customers, and we think having your engineers do at least occasional support for their products is priceless for developing a better understanding of these products and how they are experienced by their users. (For more on this, see Chapter 6.)

Escaping the Feature Shop Trap to Serve Customers More Broadly

All of the challenges of dealing with internal customers come to a head in what we call the Feature Shop Trap. This arises when platform teams end up doing nothing but triaging feature requests across their customers, instead of forcing the compromises necessary to deliver a more strategic product roadmap.

Let's take the example of a cloud enablement platform. Anyone who has built out a cloud platform team knows that a lot of infrastructure engineering work is needed to test out and start using new cloud services, particularly when you have security or regulatory concerns to deal with. A scrappy early version of a cloud platform may have the platform team on the critical path of unblocking every new cloud service, and at first this might be OK due to low demand or a limited customer base. Plus, it feels great to be the team that helps others get to the cloud, so the engineers don't mind.

But what happens when there's a huge spike in demand—perhaps a company-wide push for cloud migration? The platform teams go into triage mode and prioritize their work to enable the most commonly requested cloud products first, in order to satisfy the largest groups of customers. They may think this triage is temporary and they'll soon get back to the strategic roadmap, but they often get stuck in enablement request Tetris with no end in sight.

Why does this happen? The power of the internal customer relationships and stakeholder politics start to dominate the platform product. Ignoring any customer group entirely is seldom wise, and there are always some who punch above their relative team size, for whatever reason. So, you find yourself pulled off to enable a specialty service for some customer group, because their business heads are Very Important and they want that service Now. Do this once and everyone starts to wonder why you aren't prioritizing *their* special requests, so you try to prioritize the work by implementing some sort of fair share algorithm: maybe the leaders of each major customer group pick what they want to prioritize, maybe it's determined by some proportion of each team's contribution to your own team's budget, or maybe some other scheme is dreamed up. Suddenly, your product management time is entirely spent picking and justifying each piece of work, with no time to figure out how to escape from this situation.

This challenge is not unique to cloud enablement platforms, and there are two mistakes that lead into this trap. The first is the pressure to scale product adoption before the platform architecture is ready to meet additional demand. The second is assuming that, because the customers are precise in their requests, the best response is to faithfully comply with those requests.

These mistakes feed on one another. When you have a platform that people need and want, but that isn't yet built to allow customers to self-service and customize for their applications, the customers are going to bring you specific requirements that they need to unblock their applications. Each specific requirement may seem small enough, but over time they add to the platform's complexity and entrench the current architecture. The customers get used to providing requirements and waiting for the platform team to unblock them, and there's enough adoption now that it's hard to justify slowing down these specific requests to make the platform more self-service.

Good platforms provide a stable surface that customers can build on top of; you want your customers to build the pieces that are specific to their applications and the platform team to build the common components. To achieve this, you have to look at feature requests and think about the patterns they represent. How can the platform evolve so that categories of features can be unlocked by the customers themselves, rather than making them wait for your team? Don't be afraid to prioritize this further-reaching strategic work instead of directly responding to every customer feature request.

You don't have to be a product manager to do this; you can simply be a lazy engineer (*https://oreil.ly/4mPH5*). Do you really want to have to implement variants of the same thing over and over again for every customer? If you were an engineer using this platform, would you want to have to wait for the platform team to implement specific features for you before you could move on? Probably not, right? So how can you approach your offering to allow others to plug their code in, so that while your platform is supporting them, it's not doing the implementation entirely for them?

Before you release a new platform product, think about how the customer demands will follow its successful adoption and where these demands will create a lot of one-off work for your platform team. What should the platform support its users building for themselves, and what should it provide for everyone? This could be engineering tasks like upgrading versions of the underlying software, and sometimes it will be product features, like providing notifications, billing, metrics, or user administration. A good platform takes on and gets rid of common tasks for many customers, rather than providing bespoke implementations for a few. If you can't find the common thread in your new feature requests, is the common thread that you haven't made it possible for your customers to solve a class of problems for themselves? Your goal should be that most new feature requests bring about a solution that helps this customer and also future customers, with few one-off bespoke demands that require negotiation.

Product Discovery and Market Analysis

We've talked about why internal customers can be tricky to work with, and how you have to create a culture that puts itself in the customers' shoes and thinks about what they need, not just what they're asking for.

But how do you actually decide what to work on? How do you find platform products to build? Some of your products may be obvious, at least at a high level (build, test, and deployment tools; compute and storage orchestration; fully embedded observability and monitoring tools; evolutions of widely adopted platform products built earlier in the company's history), but you'll need to narrow down exactly what you will work on within these broad areas. With a product focus, your goal is to identify what your users actually need and want, and which opportunities will make the biggest difference to them.

In this section, we'll talk about identifying products, applying best-effort estimates to what you believe the impact of this work will be, and putting metrics in place to show whether you have achieved a measurable impact.

Identifying Potential Platform Products

There are a few tried and true ways to identify new platform product areas to develop. Many of these arise from partnerships with internal teams, instead of incubation within the platform engineering team itself. Platform engineering teams are usually not on the cutting edge of innovation, but rather play the role of settlers and town planners (*https://oreil.ly/Q2qa2*), taking ideas that have been successfully pioneered by smaller groups and expanding them to broad usefulness (we'll discuss these roles further in Chapter 8). The culture that you want to encourage is one where you look for the best product ideas that meet customer needs, without getting too attached to where these ideas came from.

Assimilate and expand

You don't have a huge customer base to test things on, so how do you find a successful platform product? Don't be ashamed to take over a system from a team that built it with themselves in mind, if that system seems to be the right general concept for the wider company. A lot of platform teams don't like doing this, because they worry they'll have to live with other people's decisions and their consequences. They forget that when you take a product from a team that built it, you already have a reasonably satisfied customer base to start with! For better or worse, someone showed that they had a problem, and they solved it; you wouldn't be taking it over if you didn't think this problem was worth solving in a holistic fashion, right?

Camille did this when she built a global service discovery solution long ago. Another team had first identified the problem and created their own version of a solution using ZooKeeper. The solution was fine for their needs, but it didn't solve the general needs of everyone at the company for global scaling. So, she took over the idea of the project and turned it into true platform infrastructure, built for a big company and not just one team therein. There were plenty of product decisions to make as part of that work, but the core identification of the problem as worth solving was done for her. There is a lot of interesting work involved in taking a solution that is locally optimized and turning it into something that can be used by a diverse set of applications.

Partner to prototype

Another way to identify promising new opportunities is to partner with another team, and perhaps even embed someone in that team, to understand a problem better. A benefit of building a culture of empathy and collaboration is that partner teams are likely to come by and ask if you are planning to build something to solve their various problems. When you believe that what they want provides a specific example of something that will become a general pattern, take advantage of this request to learn more! Having platform engineers build an application with a prototype idea for a platform within it and then using the lessons from that project to extract a more general system is a productive way to quickly iterate an idea into something that is usable. After all, the hardest part of applying product management techniques to platform engineering is figuring out usability. Want to know how people will actually write code around this offering? Well, writing code around the offering yourself is a good way to figure that out.

The important thing to avoid in this model is having your platform engineering team turn into a solutions engineering team that builds things for partners and never creates broad-use products from these offerings. Be thoughtful about whether the thing you are partnering on is a potential product opportunity (in general, the shape of this is a new system that has operational characteristics as well as code features), and not simply a template, pattern, or bit of infrastructure automation.

Incremental Delivery and Proofs of Concept

One of the ways that you discover which products make sense is by breaking big things down into smaller experimental pieces that you can deliver and learn from. When you are partnering with a team to prototype something, that is an example of taking an incremental approach to identifying a potential new platform. Instead of committing to the whole platform up front, you build a prototype, which you can then pull out as a proof of concept (POC). Only if that POC shows value do you expand to other things.

Breaking platform projects down into incremental parts, whether through POC builds for product discovery or planning a major rearchitecture so that it delivers incremental business value throughout development (see Chapter 8), is a key way for platform teams to sharpen their product and business mindset.

Look for products with realistic paths to adoption

In platform teams, a lot of the product-related work is figuring out how to make open source products or next-generation technology approaches apply to your company. Take Kubernetes as an example. The product challenges around internal Kubernetes come in the decisions you make about how to integrate it into the existing ecosystem so people adopt it without too much argument. For example, if your company is of a certain age, you may already have an old private cloud solution kicking around. Everyone is used to running on virtual machines (VMs), but after some analysis you decide that Kubernetes will give you some operational improvements and encourage the company to modernize its CI/CD practices. So you start to stand up a Kubernetes platform.

That is all well and good, but the product management work is not just telling everyone that you have Kubernetes now and they have to use it. Instead, the work is identifying different types of customers and figuring out what will make it easy for them to migrate. What are the carrots you can provide to get people to do work they don't care about doing? Perhaps the incentives are efficiencies in getting access to compute or storage. Perhaps you can offer a higher SLO with the new product. Maybe it's faster, or more secure. But these things don't just happen—you have to choose which features you are highlighting to your customers, you have to help them understand the offering and its advantages, and you have to deliver on those promises. If you are struggling to find compelling customer benefits for this offering to encourage adoption, your company may not have real demand for the product.

Despite having captive audiences, platform teams are notorious for creating half-finished product offerings that somehow fail to get adopted. When your platform organization is running three different generations of solutions to the same problem with no clear plan to remove any of them, and your customers are confused by and dissatisfied with the offerings, you have a serious product failure on your hands. When evaluating a new product idea, be realistic about the cost of driving adoption; a migration strategy must be a primary part of the product planning (more on this in Chapter 9).

You aren't Google, so don't build when you don't have to

Remember that you aren't Google (unless you are, in which case, hi!). When you have a platform team of 7, or even 100, you must be extremely thoughtful about what you choose to build. Platform teams of all sizes can get bogged down trying to imitate systems that have been built up over years at big companies. Even when those big companies provide their solutions as open source software, they encode assumptions about the surrounding ecosystem of available platform products and the culture and needs of the engineers using them. It's not good product management to say "Google does it, so we should."

Instead, start with a clear understanding of the problem, and an accounting of your existing ecosystem and culture, before diving into a technical solution. Say you find that your data volume is out of control. You might need to solve this with a better storage solution, or you might need to solve it by identifying the top data producers and asking them whether the data they're storing is actually valuable. You'll often find that the data is garbage, or the developers can change their workflow, or a little bit of query performance tuning will make the application scale just fine in a normal relational database management system (RDBMS). Build only when you have exhausted the alternatives.

Great platform teams can tell a story about what they have built, what they are building, and why these products make the overall engineering team more effective. They have strong partner relationships that drive the evolution of the platform with focused offerings that meet and anticipate the rest of the company's future needs. They are admired as strong engineers who build what is needed, to high standards, and they are able to invest the time to do that because they don't overbuild.

Whether you are a platform engineer, engineering manager, or PM, it pays to remember that you need to be customer-focused and strategic about your platform offerings. Without a clear strategy for showing impact and value, you'll end up overlooked and understaffed, and no amount of cool new technology will solve that problem.

Evolving Existing Offerings: Smoothing the Edges or Rethinking the Problem

If I had asked people what they wanted, they would have said faster horses.
—Henry Ford (maybe)

In order to make good product decisions about your platform, you need to understand the problem space you are in. If your platform charter is around improved developer experience, you may believe that any solution that speeds up developers is the obvious thing to invest in. This can lead to a default of choosing projects that make existing things easier through performance improvements, better UX, or cleaner integrations. However, in focusing on smoothing the edges, you risk missing those opportunities where you need to go beyond smoothing the edges to totally rethink the problem.

The evolution from frameworks and tools to platforms is itself a rethinking that some platform teams have not fully embraced. If your mindset is still heavily weighted toward providing pieces of code that your customers will adopt to make their lives easier, you can get caught in the edge-smoothing trap. Sure, having a web framework with plug-ins that you provide for authentication and metrics gathering is useful, and many platform teams have such an offering. But if you can build this into a framework, could you provide it even better in a sidecar that also does traffic shaping and management?

Smoothing the edges is the right platform approach for certain situations. In particular, when your platform is joining multiple activities that need to be coordinated across teams or people (such as a developer experience platform), some of the product focus will naturally be on smoothing the edges and making it easy and obvious for people to see where their various code activities are in the workflow process. Exposing the status of builds, tests, scans, code reviews, tickets, and deployment activities means that you are potentially integrating many different systems into one smoothed workflow. Your platform probably can't take all of this work off the developers' hands completely, because it requires human inspection, collaboration, and sign-off activities.

Still, we encourage you to start your product approach by rethinking the problem. Instead of making something easier, ask whether the users need to know about this thing, whatever this thing is, at all. Could your solution completely remove their need to think about this task, not just make it easier for them to manage the task?

Removing the users' need to think about a task usually means you need to think about it a lot, operate it on their behalf, and provide a rock-solid abstraction for that offering. Many teams fail to deliver true platforms because they do not want to own the operation and support of a heavily used, critical offering. Packaging up some useful code in the form of a framework or tool can make your users' lives better, and it's easier to do this than to go all the way to operating a platform that handles the entire lifecycle of a particular task—but it doesn't deliver the full leverage of a platform, which comes only by owning the process through operations, and it's hard to justify staffing a large team that supports only part of the solution.

So, how can you figure out whether you're in the problem space of rethinking or the problem space of smoothing the edges? Here are some indicators:

Are you optimizing a human-in-the-loop process that involves multiple humans collaborating? Smooth the edges.
As in our developer experience example, some things always need humans involved. The easier you can make those humans' lives—by reducing their need to context switch, highlighting the work at hand, and generally thinking a lot about their user experience—the better your platform will be.

Are you supporting machine processes and data? Rethink the problem.
On the other hand, when the thing you are supporting is actually the running of a system or the storage, retrieval, or analysis of data, you want to work hard to rethink the problem at hand. Almost any time you are writing a playbook, pattern, or common script, ask yourself whether a better option might be for you to operate a platform that manages these components so every team doesn't have to run the same playbooks themselves.

Does the human have to be in the loop? Can you remove that human's work? Rethink the problem.
Don't just assume a human has to be involved. Upgrades are a great example where too many engineers assume that the right approach is to provide better tools rather than removing the problem entirely. How do you make upgrading underlying dependencies no longer the problem of the user population?

To start, look at the coupling. Can you decouple the user's software from the platform in a way that improves the abstraction? Like in our earlier sidecar example, you can decouple the authentication logic from the user's deployed process into something you can deploy. That means you can manage the upgrades and changes of the authentication system in your own processes, without involving the users directly.

Are you creating an offering that brings together many different types of related activities where each is already platform-like? Smooth the edges.
There is plenty of edge-smoothing to be done in making meta-platforms—that is, platforms that do more than one core thing. A platform like Heroku that can manage both the compute side of running your processes and the database side of storing your data is a good example of a combination platform, where a lot of the success came from wrapping the underlying complexity in a great user experience.

Market Research: Validating New Investments

How often have you seen platform teams working on projects that seem to be based on nothing more than the whims of the engineers? These engineers believe they are building something of strategic importance (perhaps based on what they're hearing from other companies, what vendors are selling, what they've experienced in a different job, or just their personal observations), but to outsiders it seems like they're just building something for the fun of it. These projects occasionally pay off, but more often than not, they fail to find the customer demand that leads to adoption.

We've learned that just because you're building for internal customers doesn't mean you can skip the work of understanding the market, especially when introducing brand-new products. You need to know whether the work makes sense for this company, at this time; you need to decide which customers you want to target (and conversely, which you want to skip); and you need to combine your understanding of context with the target customer base to validate the potential for making this investment, at this time. Analyzing the target market for your investments is key to making strategic prioritization decisions.

Product-market fit is context-dependent

Many of the new ideas that platform teams want to build come from the wider technology zeitgeist. However, it's common for developers and companies to write blog posts and deliver conference talks hyping their solutions to problems without giving the full context of the problem or the truth about internal adoption, or lack thereof. A solution that sounds good on paper or in conference form often skips over a lot of pain that the team went through to get it to work, and sometimes these solutions were actually internal failures. Plenty of ideas sound cool and might even be great in certain circumstances, but are poor general-purpose solutions.

The bigger the company, the more likely it is that their solutions rely on undocumented internal context. For example, Google has amazing internal developer tools and has open sourced some of them, including its build system, Blaze, open sourced as Bazel. But what makes Google's internal developer experience great is more than Blaze; it's the entire infrastructure of tools and processes that have evolved alongside Blaze, filling in the gaps that become apparent when you try to use Bazel without the rest of the ecosystem.

Monorepos are a great example of a heavily context-dependent solution. They are indispensable when you have a lot of code that needs to be compile-time linked together, which is one reason companies like Google invested so heavily in them (they have a lot of C++). But the overhead of making a monorepo scale is extremely non-trivial. The near-universal visibility and ease of changing things across all codebases is great for modifying compile-time libraries, but it can create a level of coupling that is detrimental for services-based development. Once you have all the context, it may turn out that Google's solution doesn't make sense for your internal platform.

Also, we can't ignore that one part of the context is the human/cultural element of your organization. If the problem can't be solved just by a change in technology but rather requires a change in the company culture, processes, or people, you may build something otherwise good that still doesn't gain adoption. A company that doesn't (or can't) share code openly between teams won't find much value from the visibility of a monorepo.

So, the first questions in considering the market for your solution are:

- Does the solution context match your tech stack? If you have a bunch of C++ code that is breaking due to library issues, a monorepo might be really helpful. If, on the other hand, you're a Java-based microservices company, you might get more value in solving the problem of code search across repos rather than trying to shove everything into one single logical repository.

- Will this technology solution need a corresponding culture or process change? Is the company open to that?

Who are you targeting?

Once you've considered whether the proposed solution makes sense in the current context, you need to figure out who will benefit from the work. You expect this new offering to fill a gap or solve a problem, and now you need to validate the demand for this offering by talking to potential customers to see what they think. You need to make sure that this investment will benefit an important customer segment, which means first thinking about who the customers are, and then getting feedback from them on the idea. Here are some key questions to consider:

- Which types of engineers or teams would use this offering? You may want to build out the potential personas (*https://oreil.ly/351dh*) for your new product, to think more clearly about who you want to target.

- How many of these potential customers would want this offering? You may think that a hosted search service would be a good platform offering, but when you ask customers you might discover that the few who need search already have their own bespoke systems and don't need you to provide a hosted option.

- Are there people who will sign up to be alpha testers? When thinking about solutions that you believe might unlock future business opportunities, you should be able to find early adopters who will sponsor the initiative.

While we're focused on new products in this section, you'll also want to think about a market growth strategy when prioritizing new features for existing products. Going back to Chapter 2, your strategy might be to invest in a railway offering to make one group of customers even more productive, or you might decide to make a paved path platform usable by a new customer segment through improvements in security, performance, or usability. The most important thing is to avoid turning into a feature shop by being intentional in how you want to grow your customer base.

What's the appetite for immediate adoption?

This market analysis is about who might benefit, but also when they might benefit. It's one thing to spend six months building something that people want immediately, but if most of your users won't have any appetite for adopting it in the foreseeable future, why are you investing in it now?

Determine how long it will take for users to experience the benefits:

- What's the onboarding cost for customers to use this offering? Is it easy to learn how to use and integrate into their workflows?
- Do they have to migrate their systems to take advantage of it? If so, do they want this offering so much that they are willing to do the migration work to adopt it?
- If the offering is useful only for new applications, how many new applications are planned for this year? How much time do your customers spend on building new things versus evolving existing applications?

All of these factors can contribute to adoption drag, which can come as a surprise to the platform engineers who see only the potential benefits of their offering. Make sure that what you are delivering has enough immediate benefit that your users are willing to do the work to adopt it—this is one of the reasons it's worth investing in easy product onboarding.

Finally, be realistic when presenting potential products and interpreting customer feedback. Plenty of people will say yes to nice-to-have things when they are presented as theoretical, but when those nice things are presented as something they actually have to pay for out of their budget or with their own time, they may be less likely to go through with the purchase. Budgets and time are also cyclical. When other teams have to approve funding for your initiatives from their own budgets, don't be surprised if they lose interest in new speculative work when times are tough. Teams that commit to migrate to your new platform offering may discover that they're busy with more important work when the time comes and so delay their migration. All of this can cause your product adoption to stumble and fail.

Your market analysis should boil down to the following tasks:

- Verify your potential user base.
- Quantify the potential benefit to those users.
- Present the adoption cost to potential users.
- Estimate how quickly users can migrate and see the benefits.
- Evaluate user willingness.
- Take into account the current budget climate.

If you're looking for the next big thing, there should be obvious benefits to having a large set of important users. When in doubt, revisit the product offering to see if there is something that will be more compelling, easier to use, or cheaper to build.

Product Marketing

One of the challenges that you will face, particularly at larger companies, is drumming up awareness of your new platform products and capabilities. Good products at big companies can struggle because the people who could benefit from using them aren't even aware of their existence. This can lead customers to build their own solutions or seek solutions from vendors instead of using the internal offering, undermining the value of your platform team.

To counteract this, you may need to think about your marketing strategy for your new and existing products. Good practices here include:

- Creating an internal landing page that outlines your platform offerings in an easy-to-browse manner
- Using mailing lists and chat rooms to announce new features
- Setting up roadshows to present your new and upcoming launches to customer organizations
- Cultivating communities of customer developers who are given early access to new products and features and can evangelize these offerings to their teams

The bigger the company, the harder this is, and the more you may want to formalize this part of the work. That could include hiring formal developer advocates and dedicating meaningful product management time to creating and running the marketing activities.

Product Metrics

If you zoom out to the biggest picture, you want to understand the cost of using the platform, the benefits of adopting the platform, how well you are matching your product offerings to customer demand, and how people feel overall about what you are offering. These translate into metrics like:

- How much migration overhead time do you impose? (Cost of using the platform)
- How much time or money are you saving platform users? (Benefit of adopting the platform)
- What percentage of the potential user base is voluntarily adopting this platform? (Customer demand)
- What's the CSAT score for the platform? (Customer opinion about the platform)

You'll note that the "benefit" metric listed here is pretty vague. We'd love to be able to say that our platform is generating revenue for the business and measure its benefit that way, but it can be difficult to tie the indirect influence of the platform to direct business outcomes. And while voluntary adoption can tell us whether a new product is filling a pressing customer need, it doesn't tell us much about whether the changes to our existing, well-adopted products are making a difference.

So how do we find more specific metrics that will tell us whether we're driving product outcomes that are creating measurable benefits? We asked Leif Walsh, a senior platform product manager, to explain how he approaches *impact metrics* to show whether the product features achieve their target goal. What follows is from Leif.

PLATFORM PERSPECTIVES

Why Do You Need Metrics?

Whether you're being asked to produce metrics for higher-ups or you're asking your team to produce them for you, the most important question to ask is: Why? Why do you need metrics? What is the particular situation that calls for them?

When looking for a why, you will find a few common answers. It helps to be intentional about which cases apply in your current situation, and who the audience is for these metrics. The metrics themselves might include:

Impact metrics
> These help you explain the effectiveness of your teams and projects upward. They can also provide targets to focus on and motivate engineers, who like building important things.

Guardrail metrics

These allow you to avoid tunnel vision on impact metrics. In the DORA framework (*https://oreil.ly/PabHt*), keeping change failure rate low provides a guardrail when your goal is increasing deployment frequency, and vice versa.

General product health metrics and traditional consumer-style metrics (acquisition, conversion, retention, and so forth)

These help you find the largest opportunities, detect products at risk of collapse, prioritize projects, and allocate resources.

We aren't going to spend much time on the guardrail and health metrics; these are important to keep in mind and measure, but your most valuable and challenging metrics will be from the first category, impact metrics.

Impact Metrics: Guiding Strategy

Impact metrics are usually the highest-profile metrics, and a key part of strategic decision making. A strategy requires an impact theory, which means a hypothesis about cause-and-effect relationships. If you improve storage throughput, the data science team will be able to run more experiments, so you'll make better recommendations, so your customers will be more engaged, so you'll be able to serve more ads, which generate revenue. Therefore, you should work on projects that will improve storage throughput.

Imagine constructing a causal graph, where nodes have different inputs you might measure, like storage or experiment throughput, and outputs that are connected to other nodes. Node outputs may be differently sensitive to inputs: maybe the number of experiments you can run increases with throughput at some rate, until you hit diminishing returns because of some other factor. At the end of your graph should be some KPI that's important to the business, like revenue.

You should collect impact metrics at the interesting nodes in that graph. In the previous example, you would of course measure aggregate throughput at the storage layer, but you'd also measure the number of experiments run, and perhaps their individual throughput and overall runtime. Other kinds of metrics show up too; for example, guardrails will appear where there are gating factors or negative influences on your impact theory.

Metrics let you check whether your impact theory is sound and adjust when it isn't. Suppose you increase storage throughput, but the data scientists aren't running more experiments. Now you have a puzzle: Was throughput not the bottleneck on experiment performance? Or did the data scientists simply exhaust the number of variants they could try? You may need to further dissect that causal link, or measure other things along that path, to update your theory and therefore your strategy.

What to Collect?

The metrics that will be meaningful to your strategy are those that have something to say about your platform's users: their desires, their behaviors, and the outcomes of using your platform. At the highest level, you'll be asking:

- What are your users doing? (And, ideally, what do they think they're trying to do?)
- How is the platform performing when they do that? Is it efficient? Responsive? Correct?
- Do you need to make any of your products faster or cheaper or easier?
- Is there an unmet need for a product or integration that you should provide?

Answering these questions requires, at minimum, knowing what people are doing, who they are, how the system behaves in response, and what the outcome is for them.

Selecting metrics to answer those questions requires an ongoing refinement process, which we'll get to shortly. But a few basic guidelines cut across nearly all situations:

- Measure things your system does, from a perspective that centers your users' workflows and goals. Request rates are fine for operational alerts, but if a single user gesture results in hundreds or thousands of individual requests, measure the gesture as one event, with an overall latency.
- Capture point-in-time demographic data, like team membership or ownership. People change teams over time, and you don't want to poison later cohort analysis by attributing a user's activity last year to the team they're on this year.
- In most cases, a single denormalized table with one row per (user-centric) event works well.
- Be careful not to stop at the boundaries of your system. Make sure you're measuring your users' behavior and outcomes; where they pass into someone else's systems, make sure those systems are capturing this data, that you trust their data, and that you know how to connect it with yours. In the context of an impact theory, the strongest metrics-based arguments you'll make are those that speak to the successes of your platform's users, which usually means crossing through several systems to achieve outcomes.
- Surveys and user interviews help ensure you're measuring what matters. (Surveys will be covered later in this book.)

Getting Metrics from Your Team

When you ask your team for metrics, your platform engineers will first think of throughput, latency, and error rate—and they're probably already measuring them somewhere, to detect and diagnose problems. Of course, you need these for any software system, but metrics for product strategy decisions are generally higher-level. Who are the biggest groups of users? Which workflow is the most time-consuming? You can't make strategy decisions based on throughput and latency alone.

Doing metrics well is fundamentally about asking the right questions, at the right level of abstraction, then determining which metrics can answer those questions.

Generally, you or your team will start by brainstorming a list of quantities they want to know. Almost always, your next move should be to ask, "Why is that important?" or "What question do we really want to answer with that?" This raises the level of abstraction to questions that impact your strategy or the business's KPIs, and informs whether those quantities will answer the important questions, or if you'll need additional information to make decisions. Some examples of initial questions and potentially more useful higher-level counterparts include:

- How long is spent on compilation of code changes versus running tests on them before they are merged? Would investment in improving compilation speed or test performance yield higher developer velocity?
- How often is each storage bucket read from? Are you storing data you never actually read, and could you ask the teams in question to stop in order to cut costs? Do systems exist that could benefit from caching?

Getting a team to start capturing these metrics effectively will take some iteration. Often, a good first step is to try to aggregate operational metrics in some way. As your practice matures, you should progress to collecting product metrics directly—they'll have more accuracy and fidelity.

Teams should start where they're comfortable and collect what is easy to collect, but this is often not what you need to know to make the best product decisions. Follow-up questions like "Why is that the case?" will lead them to more useful metrics. If you can have a dedicated data analyst work with them, they'll often be able to ask good questions to get more useful metrics. Sometimes you will have to be that person.

Misuse of Metrics

When you ask for metrics, some people will not want to provide them, out of fear that they'll be misinterpreted or abused to support the wrong conclusions. This fear is often well intentioned (and well placed), but you still need to collect the data. Some misuse will likely happen, but the useful insights and decisions the metrics contribute to will outweigh that.

To overcome this obstacle, it can help to frame the initial metrics collection as a prototype that you'll refine over time—after all, it's very hard to collect the right metrics without first collecting the wrong metrics, understanding why, and adjusting. Good documentation also helps prevent accidental misinterpretation. You should encourage your teams to document their schemas and data generation processes, and keep that documentation up to date.

Don't Wait for Perfection

There's more to metrics than this; you'll need to store the metrics you collect (use something easy to query with SQL) and document them for future interpretation (especially if someone wants to use them in support of their next promotion!). But the most important thing to do is to start asking questions about what the impact of the product changes looks like, and what you can measure to know that you're going in the right direction. Don't let the perfect be the enemy of the good; even basic metrics can make a big difference in driving good product outcomes!

Successful Product Execution: Creating a Product Roadmap

A strong customer-focused product culture and a good understanding of product discovery is helpful, but you must still manage to execute against all of this. It's time to tie these ideas into a roadmap. But that's easier said than done; when you first start trying to make this product shift, it's common to find yourself in a situation that looks like this:

> You have a compute platform team. There are some people working on the base operating system, container, and VM images, some people working on configuration management, some people working on the legacy virtual machine openstack environment, some people working on compute orchestration (Kubernetes), and some working on Terraform for cloud stuff. Phew. Each of these areas is going OK, and they often work together well enough in pairwise groups. But there is no overarching concept of how these pieces join together to create a complete and well-integrated landscape for developers, and so each team builds mostly within their silo, and the overall experience remains disjointed and confusing.

When you find yourself in this situation, the team needs to take a step back and think about the big picture. Where do you want to go with all of this? What's the long-term vision? How should these product offerings fit together? What should a developer using this platform need to care about, and what should the platform just do for them? Once you have this insight, you can start to create a product roadmap that reflects not only a vision, but a strategy for tying all these pieces together to get there.

In the product roadmapping process, we go from vision to reality. Your customers' needs (both immediate and longer term), in combination with engineering feasibility and cost analysis, will help you figure out which pieces you should tackle and in what approximate order. This gives you a rough plan, which you can break down into important delivery milestones and places to potentially pause and reevaluate the next steps. This is supported by impact metrics that show you whether your work is delivering what you expected it to.

The rest of this section illustrates this process.

Vision: Long Term

The vision attempts to paint a picture of the essential characteristics of a better future platform. This vision may never be fully realized, but it is an aspirational starting point, and it serves to align the work in the plan. In your compute platform, your vision might be to enable a developer to provision the environment that they need in two hours, whether it's on premises, in the cloud, or even in your DMZ.[2]

Strategy: Middle Term

To formulate a strategy, you need to understand what is preventing you from achieving your vision.[3] Fortunately, the minute you present this to your engineering team they will immediately identify some technical challenges that need to be addressed. While engineering works through the options for tackling those challenges, product management can start to identify what will need to happen from the users' perspective. This includes understanding their current pain points, how they want to interact with the platform (UI? API? command line?), and when they interact (how often are they provisioning, anyway?). Product management will also make sure they know who the real users of this system will be—you may think it's a specialized group of people when it's actually every developer, or vice versa. Ultimately, this should lead to the high-level product requirements.

Coming back to the two-hour provisioning vision, after doing all this research you may decide that one part of the strategy is "Fast containerized compute provisioning: reduce the application provisioning time for new containerized environments to minutes." This will incentivize application developers who want to move fast to containerize their applications and give you a more achievable intermediate target, rather than trying to chip away at the provisioning time for all types of applications in all environments. That's the point of not jumping straight from a vision to a plan; documenting a strategy makes such decisions clear.

---

2 A DMZ, or demilitarized zone, is a subnetwork where compute/network resources facing the public internet can be isolated from the internal network.

3 For more on strategy, we recommend Richard P. Rumelt's book *Good Strategy/Bad Strategy* (Profile Books).

Goals and Metrics: This Year

Now that you have both the high-level product requirements and a technical sense of the major roadblocks, you can start to put together the goals for the next year. This may be written in an objectives and key results (OKR)–like format, where the objective is an opinionated goal statement and the key results detail specific areas of focus for the year and the metrics that you are monitoring to know that you are executing successfully on these areas. For your compute team, one OKR might look like this:

Objective:
> Bring fast compute provisioning for containerized environments to the user's development context

Key Results:

- Enable provisioning from the IDE or command line for 50% of our supported compute types *(supports: provisioning within the user's development context)*

- Reduce the time from provisioning request to completion with available compute by 25% *(supports: fast compute provisioning)*

- Drive down usage of legacy VM platform by 20% *(supports: moving to modern environments)*

Milestones: Quarterly

Your roadmap milestones will fill in the year. What are the rough pieces of technical work that will need to be delivered to achieve these goals? When do you think features will be delivered to your customers? Do you need to break down big features into smaller, incremental deliverables? You may know some of this now, and you may have placeholders for others depending on what happens in the first or second quarter. Write it all down and start tracking quarterly. In Chapter 7, we will discuss how to merge these pieces of incremental feature delivery with other important platform work to produce an overall prioritized roadmap that platform engineering management can use to track execution.

The Customer-Facing Roadmap

To get to reasonable estimates for product delivery, you need to plan and track the technical work that enables these features. But when it comes to sharing your plans with the customers, we recommend limiting the timeline to only user-visible feature delivery. If users ask why a particular feature will take so long, you can share the underlying technical roadmap, but exposing too many of the internal technical milestones can leave you open to accusations of building "things that engineering thinks are cool" instead of focusing on business delivery.

Specification of Features

Let's assume that you've done the work of creating a compelling vision, you've created some good metrics to guide your execution of this vision, and product and engineering have partnered throughout to figure out the work that needs to be done to, you all hope, deliver on these metrics in a technically feasible way. Your broad roadmap is complete, and you're ready to get into the day-to-day work of delivering it through a set of features.

When it comes to specifying features, the product manager needs to document the feature outcomes: why is this important to the customers, what do they need from this feature, and how does it fit into the overall vision of where you want the product to go? They then share these feature outcomes with the engineering leads for the areas in question. This should turn into a discussion between engineering and product about *what* should be done to achieve the *why* behind a specific need. Deciding what to build cannot be done by the product manager alone, because there are technical, budgetary, and human constraints that are understood best by engineering leadership. Together, they will turn the *why* into *what*, breaking down any *what* that will take longer than a month or so to implement into a few substeps. Take all of this and write it up as a product requirements document, user stories, or whatever format your organization uses to record feature requirements, and you now have the next level of detail that shows work that you'll track during the quarter.

Practice Makes Perfect

These practices are somewhat simple, but they are not easy. Developing a compelling vision is hard. Breaking it down into measurable items that reflect impact and not just output is hard. Documenting feature outcomes and working with engineering to figure out what to build to achieve these outcomes is hard. But keep doing this exercise, and over time you will get the rhythms, you'll start to get a sense of what "good" feels like, and with luck you'll get to experience the satisfaction of dreaming big and, eventually, making it happen.

Why Can't I Ask My Customers to Tell Me What They Want?

Customer empathy is about more than appreciating that your customers have an opinion and that you are building to help them. It also means understanding their limitations and what you can realistically ask of them. Take the following example:

> I've been tasked to build a new central platform for my company. We have some product managers, but far more customer teams than our product managers can really cover, so we've set up some customer working groups to get input on the platform and what we should build, to see if what we're building will work for the customers.
>
> This seemed to be a fine approach, but one of our biggest customer groups continually fails to show up to these meetings, and when they do the representative claims that they can't really represent their whole division. It's becoming really frustrating because we can't figure out what they actually need or whether we're building the right thing, and it's slowing down my team. What should we do?

Let's start with the basics: you cannot just expect your customers to show up in working groups and tell you exactly what the product needs to look like. This doesn't work because your customers are busy, because your customers are not themselves product managers who can write up detailed requirements documents for you, and because your customers might be able to describe problems they are experiencing at the moment, but they are very unlikely to do a good job of reasoning abstractly about how they might use some future system. Most people are not good at thinking at that level of abstraction, particularly about some brand-new technology they have never worked with before.

Going one level deeper, even if your customers are showing up to these meetings and giving feedback, you can't have just this one way to ensure you are building a usable product. The work of building a usable product does not end until people are happily using the product. If you don't have customer touchpoints throughout the cycle of building and deploying product features, and measures for whether those features are useful that go beyond what some customer group said in the design phase, you do not have a fully realized product plan. Again, you almost certainly do not have the product management bandwidth to run a new platform buildout of the implied complexity that you are discussing. You may need to hire more PMs, and you certainly should put in more work to figure out what your customers actually want and need, instead of putting the onus on them to tell you whether or not your ideas will do what they want.

How can you get yourself out of this mess? Start with the boring parts of the new platform—the parts you don't think require nuanced differences to meet the needs of diverse customers; the parts you feel extremely confident that you understand; the parts you have seen built successfully before, or that maybe a customer team has already built for themselves, or that are just obvious no-brainer components— and get to work building those. While you work on those, build up your product management team enough to do market research, to identify potential use cases in as many of the customer teams as possible, to sign up alpha and beta customers, and to figure out metrics for adoption that show the new features are actually delivering value.

Then turn to the next most obvious features, and start thinking about them. Don't think about the most complex stuff. You're not ready for that yet. Are you worried you're going to design something that will never be able to handle the complex stuff? Well, you're just as likely to design something meant to handle the complex stuff that fails to handle everything as you are to design something meant to handle the simple stuff that needs to be reworked for the complex. So, you might as well get started on some simple stuff that works.

Unfortunately, we can't just ask our customers what to build, but we can use them to validate our ideas by getting their feedback quickly on what we build, and making sure there is demand throughout our incremental delivery.

Product Failure Modes

When you first start to adopt product management in your internal platform teams, it's easy to make mistakes that can lead to a failed product transformation. Here are some of the gotchas to watch out for when applying these ideas.

Underestimating the Migration Cost

We talk a lot about migrations in this book because migrations are such a critical part of platform engineering, but we want to reemphasize the importance of thinking about their cost even here, in the product chapter. Product managers need to consider the cost of migrations when they make product decisions, because this cost can dwarf the value of the new offering if they aren't careful.

One of the clearest examples of this that Camille has seen was in a developer experience team, where the product manager was convinced that a new code search tool would add a bunch of value to the company. He did a good job creating a pitch for why this product was valuable, selling the idea to the engineering team, to some of the customers, and eventually, reluctantly, to Camille. This product was going to replace the existing open source code search offering, but she was assured that this would be a reasonably straightforward task.

Fast-forward a couple of years, and the straightforward migration was finally, after much stress and work, done. As you can probably guess, this was not a simple migration. Links to the old search tool were everywhere, and the engineering team had realized after lengthy deliberation that they would need to write a redirector service to send links from the old tool to the appropriate location in the new one. In addition, the old tool had been set up to ignore certain meta-repositories, branches, and other pieces of code that weren't that important, and there were a bunch of annoying edge cases that engineering had to work around to make the offering acceptable. Setting up the new system for that was harder than anyone expected.

But even worse, no one had thought through the user training element of the migration. Because no one had done a detailed analysis of how the users accessed the old tool, there were patterns that were not quite one-for-one, and some training was required for users to onboard. Changing something that is so deeply ingrained and foundational in the developer workflow is tricky, and it led to a lot of complaints from the users when they got an experience that didn't make sense compared to what they were used to.

Product managers must remember that migration costs—both in terms of engineering and the user experience—can be major factors in a product's success or failure. Sometimes, despite a painful migration, the end result is worth it—but going in without having done the analysis often results in users viewing your work as sloppy and ill-considered.

Overestimating the Change Budget for Users

It would be nice if your users could adopt new offerings the minute those offerings were ready. Unfortunately, most users have a long list of things on their plate, and adopting a new tool, workflow, or system has to fit into the wider picture of all this work. Product managers in platform teams want to make new stuff and are evaluated based on the organization's adoption of their offerings, so they clamor for attention to their shiny new product offerings. But most customers can take on only so much change at once, and if your change is anything less than a must-have, you are likely to experience slow adoption. This is particularly true in times of high pressure, when budgets are tight, deadlines are looming, or other fires are burning in the organization. That's why we use the term change budget—because it needs to be budgeted in with all of the other work that is happening in the team.

In our opinion, leadership needs to be realistic about how much platform and infrastructure change can be pushed into an organization in any given period. Few companies can successfully coordinate all change at this level (Camille has tried and failed). Each team is incentivized to clamor for the attention of the same people, to get their migrations prioritized, and to get their products to be the ones that users are focused on. So, you're probably competing in a noisy world, and the bigger the company, the noisier the solution and change space.

At least within your own product area, think about how much change you are really going to push through the company in a given year. Is there a way to make that change easier to adopt so your users can take on more of it without increased effort? As we saw in our source code search example, for users to use the new offering they need to be able to use it to do the same things they were doing before; but to really make that effort pay off, they need to be able to do *more* than they were doing before. Is it easy for them to see immediate benefits once they've gotten used to the new tool? Will it create time savings for the users that they can reinvest into getting more done, and actually drive productivity? Think about all of these factors when you make your product roadmap, because a customer base can absorb only so much change at once.

Overestimating the Value of New Features When Stability Is Poor

This one is painful but true: both engineers and product managers mistake novelty as the most important offering their platforms can provide, and they forget that stability is often at least as important, if not more so. Stability is a factor in both migration efforts and change budgets. When you are using highly stable systems, you have more cycles to spend on migration and other types of change, because you aren't constantly spending time contending with platform failures that distract both the engineering team and the users. Stability is part of the product currency you have to spend, and when you lack stability, your customers lose their trust in your platform. Who wants to adopt something new from a team that doesn't seem to know how to operate the existing system?

When your platform is having stability issues, it's almost always better to invest engineering time into improving stability instead of adding more features or products onto an unreliable base. This might mean that you miss some of your product goals for the year, but who cares about new stuff when you can't even reliably use the existing offerings?

Having Too Many Product Managers for the Size of the Engineering Team

This one might come as a surprise, because most of us have too few product managers. But there is such a thing as too many PMs, and the ratio of PMs to engineers may be different for your platform team than it is for your application engineering teams. When you wind up with too many PMs, they can end up doing tasks that the engineers should be doing themselves, like managing the actual execution of the work. Be wary of letting engineers shut off their brains when it comes to their jobs, including deciding what to work on, when, and how to prioritize work. When you have too many product managers and treat your engineering teams like external contractors who just take in specs and implement them, you create all sorts of unintended downsides, cut off the creativity and ownership of a big part of the team, and generally end up with poor results.

You may want us to give you a ratio here, but our experience is that this is quite variable due to the maturity of the products and the company and the nature of the other people on the team. Our best rule of thumb is that you should feel stretched for product managers but not be starving for them; a decent estimate is usually somewhere between the number of second-line and first-line engineering managers, with Ian preferring the former and Camille closer to the latter.[4]

Having Product Managers Doing the Work That Engineering Managers Should Be Doing

A related point to the previous one is that when you have product managers doing all the project management for a team, grooming Jira backlogs and spoon-feeding the team work, you end up with bad outcomes. Most commonly, engineers hide behind this micromanagement to justify technical debt in their systems by saying that the product manager did not prioritize that work, so they didn't have the ability to address it. Do not give engineering teams this out. Engineering management must at a minimum co-own the actual work plan for the teams (as you'll see in Chapter 7, we call this the "bottom-up" roadmap). This is a universal truth, but it's one that bugs us whether it's in the context of application engineering or platform engineering.

Similarly, product management is not "product ownership" in the Agile sense (*https:// oreil.ly/OoTO3*). Product managers are not glorified scrum masters just because they are managing internal products. You may have people in the "product owner" role of an Agile organization who are doing well as product managers, but in our experience these roles tend to overfocus on the project management elements of the job (backlog grooming, short-term prioritization, status reporting) and neglect the more ambiguous product management tasks. It is hard to be deep in the day-to-day execution details of a product and thinking ahead to shape the strategy at the same time. While good product managers will step in to support project execution as needed, trying to merge project and product management into one "product owner" role is likely to result in a weak and reactive product approach.

Wrapping Up

When we consider the ways in which platform teams fail at product development, we see three broad categories:

Culture
> The team fails to adopt a product culture and continues to expect users to directly tell them what to build, while internally focusing too much on the technology and operations and not enough on the customers.

---

4 The most important aspect is how many engineers are working on actively evolving product offerings and features versus other types of engineering work; PMs are in lower demand when most of the work is related to operational efficiency or scaling, for example.

Product-market fit

The team fails to evaluate new product ideas against internal market needs and so builds things that customers don't want. They also don't establish impact metrics for these product bets to clarify the opportunity.

Execution

The team doesn't bother to align its work with a larger product strategy and fails to consider the overhead costs to the customers (migrations, change budget) in product planning. They may also misuse product managers to do engineering management work.

While the paths to failure are clear, the path to success is nuanced. Good product culture is built on relationships, conversations, rewards, focus, and a day-in, day-out willingness to stretch and question whether you're meeting your customers where they are, rather than where you want them to be. Finding market fit can require many iterations of trial and error before you get to the root of what teams really need. And execution is as much the constant work of building and refining practices such as roadmapping as it is the work of negotiating and developing the right product management team for the organization today.

Distilling everything useful to say about product management into a single chapter would be impossible, so this chapter has given a whirlwind tour of a number of complex topics. We realize that some of you might be disappointed that we haven't presented a surefire way to build great platform products, but great products are always situational, stemming from deep insight into what people need, combined with an understanding of what is realistic to build. This is why it is so important to spend time understanding your customers, and why so many of your best products will be initiated by other teams building for themselves. Platform engineering doesn't have to be the source of product innovation in your company; you merely need to make sure you don't completely drop the ball of customer focus and product discipline in favor of technical and operational concerns.

We know this is a journey, but we hope this chapter has given you some ideas for the next steps on the road ahead.

CHAPTER 6

Operating Platforms

Rare things become common at scale.
—Jason Cohen[1]

No matter how well you build a platform, the systems it depends on are complex, so it will inevitably have operational issues. As useful as the product mindset is for platforms, product-focused teams can underinvest in operations when times are good —they move fast and deliver lots of great features, but pile up operational debt along the way. A successful application team might be able to get away with this, because their contributions to the business's top line are rewarded with extra headcount, which makes it possible to stay ahead of the debt. But that's not the situation most platform teams are in.

Platforms create their value through leverage, and one aspect of leverage is efficiency—supporting substantially more scale without needing to hire more people into the platform team. However, as this chapter's introductory quote suggests, this is in conflict with the fact that systems often run into new problems just because of scale, particularly operationally. This means constant-sized teams supporting scaling platforms can wind up in "operational hell," where neglected operational problems start having ongoing acute business impact, eroding customer trust. As the system is handling critical load at scale, it can take months to remediate the acute impact and years to address the core issues, and all the while new product features are stalled.

To avoid this, platform teams need to routinely invest in operational practices, even when times are good. In this chapter, we cover three operational practices your platform team should own and embrace:

---

1 See Jason's article on this at *https://oreil.ly/MxNyb*.

On-call

This is the fundamental practice of scheduling engineers to be available to respond to issues the system may have in production.

User support

As we called out in Chapter 2, this is usually a large enough problem for platforms that it requires separate practices than just being handled by the on-call engineer.

Operational feedback

These are the practices you need to invest in to ensure you are proactively addressing operational problems well enough to stop them from becoming acute.

Let's dig into on-call practices first.

Essential Practices, Not Processes

In this chapter, we talk about what platforms need as a list of essential practices rather than an exhaustive list of processes. There is no shortage of writing on operational processes in the SRE and DevOps literature, and all of it could be applied to platforms—but there are far too many potential processes to adopt, requiring far too much work to do them all correctly. Too many leaders force processes that they've just read about (or worse, that they used in their last job) onto their organization, without looking at the costs and benefits for the particular set of problems the team is dealing with.

Processes are situational, and the granular details should be tailored to the unique challenges your team is facing. But practices are broad. They provide a framework and allow you to create whatever process you need to solve the specific problem you have today. As your problems change, your processes will change too. But the practice remains.

On-Call Practices

When the inevitable operational issues happen, you need the most skilled and knowledgeable people available to remediate them as quickly as possible. This is where your on-call practices come in. We strongly recommend having a merged DevOps on-call team that goes on rotation 24x7 to handle non-support operational issues. We realize this is not always a popular opinion, but hear us out. As we will explain, with the right management practices to ensure sustainability, we've seen platform teams come to prefer this approach because it gives them more control over their fate.

Why 24x7 On-Call Coverage Matters

A lot of platforms support 24x7 businesses, so the need for 24x7 on-call coverage is not in question. But there are other types of "noncritical" platforms, particularly around developer tools or other purely internal use cases, where we have seen teams tie themselves in knots trying to avoid 24x7 on-call coverage, even as it ends up making some customers furious.

The problem is that these platforms can be critical at surprising times. For example, many companies have applications that can only be deployed during off-hours (i.e., nights and weekends), and the teams that own the deployment tools need to ensure those tools are operational during these periods. Imagine that a bug is discovered late at night and the deployment platform is malfunctioning. Should the application team just wait until the morning for the developer tools team to come in and support them, and leave the bug outstanding? Of course not!

There are rare exceptions to the 24x7 rule, we will admit, but your team likely is not one of the exceptions. When you ignore this best practice to protect your engineers from working outside business hours, you undermine your ability to operate the platform in the face of unforeseen circumstances and risk losing the trust of the customers who are impacted by them.

Why Merged DevOps?

As we discussed in Chapter 1, the industry is divided over whether operational work (like being on-call) should be done by the development team or split out and handled by a separate team, called variously SRE, DevOps, or operations. We acknowledge that the best option isn't obvious for large teams that build planet-scale, business-critical applications. But that's precisely because these teams *are* large—meaning, they have enough people to maintain a deep focus on both development and operations.

Most platform engineering teams do not have this luxury. Because platforms abstract over various vendor and OSS systems, the products these teams are responsible for are usually much more operationally complex than the products equivalently sized application development teams deal with. Indeed, this is the "leverage" of platform engineering that makes it more efficient than application teams operating the OSS and vendor systems directly. However, it also creates a problem: who are the people who can be on-call to quickly diagnose and remediate a problem that could be caused by in-house code, by one of the OSS or vendor systems, or by some interaction between them? Our answer is that only a merged team can staff an on-call rotation with the required level of expertise in a sustainable manner.

Platform software engineers may push back on this. After all, they didn't develop those external systems—their expertise is in leveraging the systems to develop features, not debugging them in production! They may ask you to hire some SREs to be on-call, since they can specialize in deep knowledge of the full system's complexity, and build automation besides. This would be wonderful, but the reality is that most platform teams can't afford to fully staff and skill up a team of SRE specialists. The SRE literature suggests the same thing that our experience shows, which is that few engineers will stay in a job where they are on-call over 25% of the time. So if you go the split approach, then in addition to your platform development team, you need the on-call rotation to be covered by a team of at least four or five SREs.[2]

Because most platform teams can't afford this much dedicated headcount, to make the split SRE or DevOps approach work, companies sometimes fudge things by assigning that team a bunch of different platforms to be on-call for. However, this prevents them from having deep experience with and knowledge of each of those platforms. So, when a critical but complex operational issue arises, you no longer have someone with deep expertise remediating it, and you've just re-created the Ops versus Dev finger-pointing divide we described in Chapter 1.

Avoiding this means you need your software developers to be on the same team as your DevOps/SRE systems generalists, and on the same on-call rotation. That may mean you have to exclude from the team some great software engineers who don't have the skills, mindset, or desire to be on-call. But our experience is that, unless you are building FAANG-scale platforms that can justify having 10 or more engineers working on them full-time, it's not worth the difficulties of trying to make a split system work.

Getting to a Sustainable On-Call Load

For a platform engineering team to be able to staff a 24x7 on-call rotation itself, the load has to be sustainable. By that, we mean that it should support each individual's ability to meet their job's expectations by allowing them to mostly work within typical professional nine-to-five working hours. How do we square this seeming contradiction?

The first step is to ensure that no one is on-call more than one week out of four, and ideally not more than one out of every six to eight weeks. The next step is looking at pager load—the type of operational event needing a human response before the next business day, and usually within 15 minutes. In our experience, a sustainable 24x7 on-call load should involve fielding fewer than five business-impacting pages a week.

Unfortunately, many of you will compare that number to where you are today and laugh in despair. Or worse, you know that if you cite a goal like five pages a week to your stakeholders (i.e., the leadership of your internal customers), they will think

---

2 To spell this out, if each person is on-call only 25% of the time, you need four or five people to make a one-week-on, three-weeks-off rota, with a buffer for vacations, illness, and other time off.

your platform team is out of touch with the business, since they deal with so many more than that. But we firmly believe that a constant demand of more than five pages a week is not sustainable. It may be supportable in the short term, while the platform is in an "exciting growth" stage and team members are willing to go above and beyond despite the impact on their work-life balance, but that lack of work-life balance will gradually lead to burnout and start having an impact on staff retention.

As an example, when Ian worked at Amazon in 2014, his larger organization was experiencing what we call operational hell—a high operational load after years of rapid growth. The early builders who had tolerated the operational load during the exciting phase had moved on, leaving their systems for a second generation. There were monthly operational issues that, while they didn't have a widespread impact, upset some important customers. Annual attrition was running at about 25%, and not only was this a first-order problem in terms of human impact, but it was also leading to a knowledge loss that itself caused more operational issues.

Ian's organization got a new VP who wanted to improve the engineers' on-call experience, in the hopes of reducing attrition and getting to an operationally sustainable trajectory. He started by looking at Amazon-wide developer survey data on team engagement, wanting to correlate the response data with support load. The strongest signal he found was for pager events. He found that:

- Fewer than two pages a week correlated with happy team members.

- Two to five pages a week correlated with some unhappiness with operational load, but did not correlate with a negative response to the question "Do you see yourself on this team in 12 months?"

- More than five pages a week correlated with consistent unhappiness, and also correlated with a negative response to the question "Do you see yourself on this team in 12 months?"

It's compelling evidence, but it's not surprising. We all know our teams would be thrilled if the on-call experience was less terrible. But how do you get there? You start by keeping your focus on the highest priority: platform stability.

This is a good place to reemphasize a practice versus process approach. The practice is sustainable on-call, but the process to achieve that can change. The goal of five pages per week is important, but if it's clear the team is doing well, you may only need a process to track the average number of pages a week, for example, as part of each quarter's OKRs. Alternatively, if the team is struggling with operational hell, you will need a more rigorous process with weekly metrics reporting and actionable remediation steps. Processes are flexible; implementing some type of practice is not.

Prioritize stability

If your platform is having more than five business-impacting events a week, then it's not providing a stable foundation for the business. We don't mean this to feel like finger-pointing. It's a pretty common situation to be in. For instance, you may intentionally underarchitect your platform as you partner with customers to build the right initial feature set, then become a victim of success with broader demand driving too-rapid growth. Having more than five business-impacting events per week is a signal that you've reached critical adoption levels; now it's on you to raise the white flag, put aside feature work, and restore stability.

If you're communicating stability as your team's main value and purpose, then your stakeholders will understand why it's in their best interest for you to do this—you might even find that they're willing to help. However, as part of that argument, they may want to see data about why your on-call metrics are a valid proxy for real impact. And that is often a problem because of false alarms.

Eliminate false alarms

False alarms are a big obstacle to understanding the sustainability of your on-call load. The presence of false alarms means that five high-severity pages a week rarely means five business-impacting events a week. When you have the noise of false alarms to deal with, each team has to provide context to explain what their on-call load really is. A team getting 10 pages a week may be quite healthy if they're mostly false alarms that come in during their own deployments that happen during business hours. Another team getting five pages a week could be in far worse shape if they happen at 2 a.m. each weekday because some application's daily batch job is causing the system to fail.

To complicate matters, some engineers are resistant to eliminating false alarms precisely because they correlate with workday events such as deployments, so they become a "pulse" to remind them of what's happening. Such engineers tend to care little about the managerial value of consistent measurement to communicate and drive decisions. However, most teams also have engineers who feel drained by false alarms—it's noise, distracting them from what is most important. Often the best way to resolve such a situation is to first invest in other feedback mechanisms for those who like to feel a "pulse" (e.g., dashboards). You can then work to eliminate the false alarms, improving the quality of your metrics and the experience of the other engineers on the team.

Use another platform team for secondary rotation

We find this advice from the SRE book to be our best practice as well: "In teams for which a secondary rotation is not strictly required for duty distribution, it is common for two related teams to serve as secondary on-call for each other, with fall-through handling duties. This setup eliminates the need for an exclusive secondary on-call rotation."

In the context of platform engineering, the secondary rotation will be with another platform team that has no direct responsibility for and little expertise on the platform for which they were just paged. All this other team can really do is follow a runbook, or call people further up the chain to get the primary team to engage if the runbook fails. Not only is this frustrating work, it also presents a business cost in terms of increased mitigation time. Thus, it should be extraordinarily rare for incidents to fall through to the secondary team. This is another reason why the goal of five business-impacting pages a week is so important: it makes pages of the secondary team rare.

Paying for on-call coverage won't make an unsustainable load better

According to the Gergely Orosz's Pragmatic Engineer blog (*https://oreil.ly/JORAk*), few US companies pay US employees for their off-hours time on-call, because there is no legal requirement to do so. Most EU companies do—a few pay the legal minimum, but most pay around 500 euros a week, which is more than the legal minimum but still a fraction of their engineers' in-hours rate. This means even when being on-call is compensated, there is a fairness issue to contend with.

If you aren't on top of ensuring the load is sustainable across all teams, the amount of off-hours work and stress will vary significantly by team, so it's not fair to pay everyone the same amount. Some teams will get a nice bonus and no extra work, while others will receive a pittance relative to the amount of off-hours work they put in and stress they are put under. You could try adjusting the compensation for fairness by factoring in parameters like number of pages or total off-hours time engaged, but in practice, we haven't seen this work—it subsidizes management that neglects making the on-call load more sustainable and encourages gamesmanship around the metrics, which results in more unfairness (and bad team politics to boot).

So, the best approach is to focus your efforts on removing all the false alarms and getting the on-call load down to at most five business-impacting issues a week. At that count, off-hour pages should be manageable, and what is seen as fair compensation in your country (if any) should be pretty close to fair. Save the special policies for special circumstances where teams have significant on-call responsibilities during off-hours (e.g., a team in Eastern Europe supporting application teams in the US).

Support Practices

For many application engineering teams, user support accounts for a small percentage of their load compared to other operational issues, which means it can be comfortably handled by the on-call engineer. This is not always true for platform teams. Their users are all internal, and between their number and the breadth of use cases, the load to support them can be too much for whoever's on-call to handle. This is particularly a problem when the business wants support to be staffed 24x7 and paged to help even when it's not clear the platform is the root cause. Trying to combine support with on-call coverage will usually push you well over a sustainable on-call load.

In this section, we'll discuss the different steps that you can take to handle the support load on your team at increasing levels of load. But first, let's talk about why it's essential that your engineers do *some* user support.

Why Platform Engineers Should Do Support Work

We understand why your instinct, as with being on call, might be to protect your platform engineers from support duties. Support is a per-user engagement and seems low-leverage compared to the code they could be developing to make the platform better for all users. However, it's crucial for engineers to directly experience users' problems to understand their needs and build the right features for the platform.

Good platforms add value by abstracting underlying complexity. But even the best platforms can't shield users entirely, because some of that complexity inevitably leaks through. When platform engineers are removed from hearing from users about their problems, they forget that "user problems" are really platform problems, and so build platforms with unrealistic expectations of users. Namely:

- They expect users to understand what is unavoidably complex about the platform.
- They expect users to know what is reasonable to expect and not expect from the system (or to read copious documentation).
- They expect users to have empathy for them and understand why it is impossible for the platform team to do a better job than it's already doing.

As an example of what this looks like, we have seen teams sending notices to users, chiding them for "misusing the platform" and calling out "badly behaving applications," as though the platform's failure to protect against edge cases is the user's fault.

A platform team nurturing the belief that users are thinking as much about the platform as they do is a platform team that is not engaging with their user's problems in a way that leads to building a better platform—but if your engineers live in a silo protected from your users' problems, this is an easy pattern of belief to fall into. Involve all your engineers in user support. They, and your platform, will be better for it.

Stage 1: Formalize Support Levels

You may have nodded in agreement with everything in the last section. But you also face 30 support tickets a week, with half of those marked "business critical, must respond in 1 hour." So, what are you to do?

The first thing to note is that 30 support tickets a week may or may not be a sustainable level of demand. You need to understand what those 30 support tickets really represent, which requires first categorizing them and then taking a deep dive into the problem categories. Diego Quiroga, a senior platform engineering leader, gives the following example of what those categories might look like:

1. Requests for help troubleshooting production issues

2. Noncritical bugs in the platform's implementation, with some being addressable through redirection to diagnostic tools and others requiring in-depth diagnosis

3. Requests for help using the platform, with some quickly resolved by directing users to documentation and others requiring more thorough engagement

4. Platform feature requests submitted as bugs

5. Pull request reviews for augmenting platform services or components

6. Broader or more complex questions better suited for a technical design review during office hours

Once the weekly count in any given category is more than a few, you need to investigate. There could be a lot of repetition in these requests, which you can seek to eliminate through documentation, user training, or by improving the platform itself. It can be tempting to skip this, particularly for leaders with a development background who wish it was someone else's job—but until you are able to explain what is driving your support load, and why it is beyond your ability to get on top of it, you should expect no help from customers in trying to reduce its impact on your team.

Next, define your support levels, often called your support service level agreement (SLA). This means defining categories of response engagement and specifying under what conditions they can be used. The fundamental questions you are trying to answer for a customer who feels (i.e., may or may not be) blocked or is seeing a production issue are:

- Can I immediately engage a platform engineer to help?

- If not, how long will I have to wait for some help?

The first question requires defining what you consider to be a critical issue. If your condition for a critical issue is "any issue that the customer believes your engagement would help remediate," you are going to struggle to hit the sustainable on-call goal of five pages a week. At a large scale of platform adoption, even an added condition of "and that has a critical business impact" will drive you above five pages a week. To resolve this, you need to specify both the type of business impact and the conditions that make it reasonable to think paging your engineer will help mitigate the issue.

This causes tension, because when a system that is critical to the business goes down, it is actually a best practice for incident managers fielding operational calls to proactively page the on-calls for all dependent systems if there is the slightest suspicion they could be the cause. They are thinking in terms of mean time to recovery (MTTR), which is the right thing for the business. But if your platform is a dependency of every team at the business, and you have not given your on-call engineers and incident managers evidence to rule out your platform, your engineers will get paged constantly, even when their system isn't the cause of the incident.

Resolving this tension requires ongoing investment in three additional areas:

1. A strong culture of follow-through on postmortem remediation items—in particular, those that answer the question "Why did this page happen at all?" These come from operational reviews, described later in the chapter.

2. A willingness to invest in observability not just for platform team members, but also for customers and incident managers. The biggest difference-maker we have seen is synthetic monitoring, described later in the chapter.

3. A willingness from the platform team's leadership to push back against unreasonable expectations of application teams and their leadership, helping them understand that a burnt-out team of platform engineers with high turnover will not actually give them the SaaS company level of support they think they deserve.[3] That can be a difficult conversation, which is why we stress stakeholder relationships so heavily in Chapter 10.

Without this investment, trust will be lost. The team's conditions will be seen as unreasonable, leading customers to ignore them and escalate demands for engagement.

---

3 And as those with direct experience know, this is a bit of a mirage; large SaaS companies go out of their way to protect their experts who could help remediate specific customer issues the fastest.

Stage 2: Separate Noncritical Support from On-Call

Even if stage 1 is executed perfectly, complex platforms with broad use can still face an overwhelming number of support issues. Sometimes it's the critical (off-hours pageable) load that stacks up, but just as often it's the low-severity cases that require so much investigation and customer communication that it takes over 40 hours a week to handle the load. When you see teams in such a state, you see support queues with a lot of items open at the end of every week, which is particularly costly because the incoming on-call engineer needs to catch up on all the context the previous engineer had. Meanwhile, the frustrated users continue to wait.

Before we get into how to improve this state, we want to cover a non-solution: having the product manager or engineering manager take on all noncritical support duties on an ongoing basis, under the assumption that one person who has all the context will be more efficient at handling it. This is a bad idea for two reasons:

1. It gives engineers little visibility into user support.
2. Whatever overloaded the engineers will eventually overload that individual, who has other responsibilities, one of them being to help get the team out of this state.

Instead, you need to break out the noncritical support duties from the on-call rotation, with a separate business-hours support rotation. This can sound like a lot of operational load—on a team of, say, six, between the on-call and support rotations, a third of your engineers are now doing purely operational work. But there are benefits. By separating the two types of operational work from each other and from development responsibilities, you improve the quality of that operational work, allow greater focus for development work, and make it easier to measure the support load.

That being said, if the combined operational load gets much above 50%, you are going to have trouble putting sufficient time into improving the platform. This will lead to challenges in motivating, retaining, and hiring engineers who are driven by building systems. Thus, the next step is to hire a specialist.

Stage 3: Hire a Support Specialist

At stage 3, your team has done all the work they can to stay on top of your support load, but they are still overloaded. The next step is hiring someone to specialize in taking on the support load. However, at this point you likely should resist hiring a full-time support engineer—i.e., the type of engineer hired by large SaaS companies to do this for external customers, and who builds their career around the role.

Why should you resist? To answer that, let's define some industry terminology around support engineering tiers:

Tier 1 (T1) support engineer
> The initial point of contact for customers seeking technical assistance. They handle basic customer inquiries and provide general assistance, typically dealing with common and straightforward issues that can be resolved using predefined procedures or scripts.

Tier 2 (T2) support engineer
> Comes into play when an issue goes beyond the scope of Tier 1. T2 support engineers possess more advanced technical knowledge and expertise than their T1 counterparts. They typically handle complex issues that require in-depth analysis, troubleshooting, and problem solving.

For a platform team just crossing this threshold, the problem with hiring a support engineer is that most strong T1 support engineers want to move up to T2 to grow their careers. But platform teams are rarely big enough to offer two separate roles and a clear path of growth between them. They need a "unicorn" capable of doing T2 work, but satisfied also spending a lot of their day doing T1 work. This role is difficult to hire for, and the type of "fast learner" who excels by quickly acquiring skills will likely seek a new challenge within 12–24 months if there is no clear path for advancement.

How do you deal with this? Before you look for a full-time hire, ask yourself if your need for a support specialist is truly permanent. Could you reduce that need over time by investing in training, documentation, or platform improvements? If the need might only be temporary, then you should find a skilled support engineer contractor to do both T1 and T2 work, while you enact the measures to allow the team to function without them.

However, if this is likely to be a permanent need, you have an opportunity. Don't hire a succession of short-term contractors. Instead, look inside and outside the company for people with nontraditional backgrounds (e.g., in boot camps, IT, and T2 product support engineering) who seem to be "quick learners" and who want to break into platform engineering. Add them to the platform team with an expectation that their workload over the first 12 months will be heavily support-focused, but they'll have opportunities to grow their software and systems skills in the second year.

At the end of this period many will have developed the skills to move into a "normal" platform engineering role, and in the meantime you will have benefited from the contributions of an enthusiastic support engineer. Chances are that there will have been enough change on the team within this time frame that you can keep them on, and then restart the process with a new quick learner to help with your next 24 months.

How to Support Customers in a Far-Flung Time Zone

A classic example that stretches our recommendation for stage 3 is when a platform team is asked to support a new acquisition or office in a far-flung time zone—say, Israel for a US West Coast team, where there's a 10-hour offset, so there are no business hours in common. While a lot of platforms can limit off-hours support to extraordinary issues, it is more difficult for some, like developer tool platforms, particularly at the stage of onboarding code and coders from another ecosystem. Here, there is no substitute for direct support during business hours, either through chat or in person.

Your priority is establishing a clear path to reliable business-hours support for the new location, which requires you to train someone either local or time zone–appropriate to provide that support. You have three choices here:

1. The simplest solution is often to ask one of your team members to move to the new office for the first six months, to train someone there to be part of your team long-term. That is, of course, an extraordinary ask, so you usually have to get lucky that someone wants to do this, as opposed to trying to force someone who's reluctant about it.

2. The next best solution is a "reverse embed," where you ask someone from the new location to join the team at the home office for three to six months, get some training, then go back. The main downside here is that you are asking them to uproot their lives and work some tough hours during that integration period.

3. The last option is to hire a new person in the new office to join the platform team as a "local support person." This is the worst option, because they are going to be new to the company, new to your platform, and new to the people they are working with. That's a tough position to be effective in.

We admit, none of these options are pretty—but they're all much better than attempting off-hours "best effort" support with your existing team, which is just going to frustrate everyone and harm the successful onboarding of the new location or company.

Stage 4: At Scale with an Engineering Support Organization

At scale, it's not just one platform team looking to hire support specialists, but many. At this point it is sustainable to hire support engineers and arrange them in specialized teams. Now you have the problems of T1 versus T2 staffing, and defining an escalation process between them and the platform engineering teams. We asked Jordan West, a staff engineer on a data platform team at one of the FAANG companies, how they handle this problem at their massive and global scale. What follows is from Jordan.

Our company is large enough to have a company-wide T1 support team called the Engineering Support Organization (ESO) that handles all platforms, with each platform team's on-call rotation taking T2 escalations. But even with the help of the ESO, it took us iteration to get our support strategy to a point where we weren't burning out our team members on the T2 load. While there is no magic bullet, there were five main aspects of the strategy that got us there:

Tiering applications with different SLAs

We created different SLAs around on-call service quality and response time, conditioning them on application tier. It's important to note that application tier here doesn't refer to T1 versus T2 support, which is more about the depth of knowledge required to address the problem, but rather the importance of the applications themselves.

Applications that impact the business top line, like the product itself, or are crucial to important business functions, such as financial reporting, are Tier 0 or Tier 1 applications. For these tiers, the goal is to identify and react to incidents before they're noticed by anyone else. For the remaining tiers, it's OK for the on-call rotation to be notified of issues by customers before we catch them. In practice, this means having different alert settings across the tiers. Latency, for example, is set strictly for the observability of Tier 0 and Tier 1 application usage, while the others either have no latency alert enabled or have the thresholds set high enough to catch only prolonged increases.

Requiring customers to be on-call

For Tier 0 and Tier 1 applications, we require the application team to have a 24/7 on-call rotation to match our own. The majority of the time, our production incidents are not caused by underlying infrastructure but rather by the applications themselves—for a common example, a sudden increase in traffic, perhaps due to new logic being rolled out. For this reason, we need to be able to reach the application team as quickly as they can reach us. Little is more frustrating to an on-call platform engineer than getting woken up in the middle of the night because of a misbehaving application and not being able to do much, if anything, about it.

Hiring systems engineers

We strongly believe in the merged DevOps model, despite mixed feelings about being on-call. To make the model work, though, there must be a balance of team members with development and systems backgrounds. For a time, after a series of reorganizations, we only hired the former. The result was a languishing body of systems work that the team members didn't enjoy doing, around operational tooling and alert reduction. Changing our approach to hire people with a systems background (we use the SRE title) had an outsized impact, in two ways. The team now had team members who were motivated to do the work that had previously sat on the sidelines, but that didn't mean systems types worked on systems tasks and engineers on development, with no interaction. Rather, folks working on these areas raised the bar across the team, changing its culture. No longer was it acceptable to allow these areas to languish.

Creating an expert network to do T2 support

Even with the last two steps, at our scale and importance to the business, the T2 support load was much too high, as the ESO team was still developing the depth needed to handle anything beyond T1 work. Additionally, going through the new ESO layer was actually a frustration for our advanced customers who already had deep knowledge of our platform systems. Our solution to both of these problems was to develop these advanced customers into a community of T2 expert engineers, so that they would become the first line of support for their peers inside their parts of the organization. These experts are uniquely able to combine an understanding of the platform with a deep knowledge of the applications. Their peers go to them first, then the ESO, and finally us. To establish this network, we used incident reviews and data modeling meetings to identify and build relationships with senior engineers who either had preexisting knowledge of the systems we offered or were quick to learn about them in either context. To incentivize folks to take on this responsibility, the "experts" have a special channel direct to the platform developers. This channel is open to all to view, but only the experts and on-call rotation members can post in it. The result is a more scalable support structure of embedded experts with a fast track to help whenever they need it—a win on both sides.

Constantly reviewing with the ESO

If you're going to move some support functions outside of the platform team, a tight feedback loop is critical. Otherwise, the risk of not understanding your customer's pain increases greatly. To address this, we have a meeting every two weeks between the ESO and the on-call rotations. The ESO brings threads they have questions about, and the rotation brings escalations they think could be handled by the ESO in the future. The ESO also points out areas where our documentation or tooling could be improved and trends they are seeing among customers. From these discussions come action items on how to improve—for example, documenting a process so the ESO can do it themselves, or developing even better tooling that allows them to handle it with a few clicks. This turns a repetitive task into a software problem the team is eager to solve. When this was all done in the same team, the tooling never got built because there was no time budget for it. Having a separate ESO team means there is another leader who's invested and asks our leader for time and budget to fix these things for their team.

Operational Feedback Practices

The third operational area a platform team needs to invest in is obtaining feedback. In this section, we'll identify four essential practices that empower platform teams to balance feature development and operational investment *before* operational problems become acute. These practices cover the lifecycle of production applications: SLOs and SLAs are informed by requirements, change management ensures you know what is being released is of high quality, synthetic monitoring goes beyond basic observability to actively detect failures in our running systems, and operational reviews look at recent history to review what is going well or not and inform upcoming work and areas of focus.

SLOs and SLAs Are Necessary; Error Budgets Are Optional

As you likely know, service level agreements are composed of service level objectives, which are measured and evaluated by service level indicators (SLIs), and SLIs feed into error budgets.[4] These are all good practices for a platform team, but we think error budgets have been oversold and do not always bring enough benefit relative to the cost of using them.

Before we explain, here's where we completely agree with the literature on these topics:

- SLIs are a great way for a platform team's engineers to monitor issues with their platform.
- SLOs are great for triggering monitoring and driving on-call deep dives.
- SLAs comprising a small number of SLOs are a great way for platform leadership and customers to understand what levels of performance, efficiency, and reliability the platform and platform team are committed to providing.
- "Failing minutes" of a small number of SLOs can be a good way to talk about problematic operational issues in a manner that allows leadership to understand why remedial action is needed.

The last point sounds like error budgets, so what's the problem? The problem is that a lot of the literature frames a mature error budget as a contract, allowing the team to take risks until they exceed this contractual budget, at which time they must stop all development work to remediate. This framing was introduced in Chapter 3 of the SRE book, which suggests that error budgets be used as a blocker for feature development: "As long as the uptime measured is above the SLO—in other words, as long as there is error budget remaining—new releases can be pushed."

---

4 For more information, see for example *Implementing Service Level Objectives* by Alex Hidalgo (O'Reilly).

Error budgets can be a useful tool to talk about discrepancies between how a system was planned to be operated versus how it *is* operating. But even setting up the conversation this way is taking you toward "us versus them" finger-pointing between engineers and management over details like thresholds and false positives, as opposed to focusing on the problem at hand. Some people will acknowledge that point but still think error budgets are great, because even if they don't automatically force leaders to acknowledge an immediate change in the team's behavior, they at least prompt a conversation. We agree up to a point, but if you want to get your customers or their leadership to change their behavior in a specific way, then the SLOs behind the error budgets need to be high-confidence signals that those outside your team can relate to.

This requires you to use these three rules when creating customer-facing SLOs:

The fewer customer-facing SLOs, the better—ideally, a handful.
 The point of customer-facing SLOs is helping people outside the platform team understand you have a problem. The more SLOs you have, the harder it is for your stakeholders to understand how those SLOs matter to the business.

They need to minimize false positives.
 This is obvious to anyone who has read "The Boy Who Cried Wolf." If you were failing your SLO last week but the business kept chugging along, then why does it matter this week if you are failing again? This applies even if the underlying signal was real (say, a transient load spike) but there was no discernible impact to the business. People outside the platform team have a hard time knowing how to filter the signal from the noise. This means that, for SLOs that are presented to leaders and customers, eliminating false positives from the metric is crucial.

False negatives are tolerable, but require explanation and improvement.
 Mature leadership and stakeholders should understand that SLOs are imperfect, so they have to choose between occasional false positives or occasional false negatives. Occasional false negatives (i.e., bad customer impacting events not appearing in any SLO) are embarrassing, but if you follow through to address them, they work well as a tool for continuous improvement.

Crucially, all of this is the opposite of how a platform team should use SLOs internally, where they should be most worried about understanding the operating conditions and risks of the system. This means they should instead follow these three rules:

- *More SLOs are better* (much more than a handful), to maximize system coverage.

- *Do not minimize false positives*, as that may mean missing a crucial issue.

- *Both false negatives and false positives require explanation and improvement*, lest false positives drive your operational load too high.

All this is to say that customer-facing SLOs/error budgets are an expensive additional cost on top of internal observability, and they are something we think you should require only when you have teams with issues severe enough to be worth that cost—either chronic availability problems, or customer perceptions of problems that stem from an unrealistic expectation of the platform's capabilities (for example, customers that expect maximum single-millisecond latencies even though your platform stores their data on hard disks with much higher seek times). Further, in both cases, violations of the "error budget" should force a conversation about options and trade-offs, as opposed to forcing a predetermined action.

Change Management

Change management is rigor around the mechanics of *all* changes to production, similar to the best practices for changes to code:

- All changes to production should be documented.
- All changes to production should be reviewed.
- All changes to production should be tested before handling production load directly.[5]

For those who have been in the industry for a while, "change management" will be a dirty term. "Surely," they will say, "for lightweight releases to be done on a continual basis, we all know such practices should be fully automated *à la* continuous integration and deployment, and if this can't be done by relying on a platform, it should be implemented through case-by-case release engineering."

In an ideal world, we would fully agree with such a statement as both an ideal and an eventual goal. Unfortunately, though, platforms usually find full CI/CD very expensive to implement, and change management is a necessary precursor to ensure that investment actually occurs. This is because platforms tend to be stateful and have complex architectures, while supporting some customers with low tolerance for performance and availability interruptions. A classic example is a caching platform—if your CD tools clear the cache as part of a code deployment, you will induce transient latency spikes, which, if large enough, will directly impact customer applications. As a result, when implementing CD best practices like canaries, shadow deployments, and automated rollback, platform systems require more complex logic than most application systems.

---

5 The cautious word "directly" is used here because some types of "testing in production," such as shadow deployments, are good practices for platforms since they are highly unlikely to impact customers. However, overreliance on canaries to detect issues, since they impact customers at just a small scale, is more problematic—they are a safety mechanism, not a testing mechanism.

This complexity usually means that the teams worst served by paved path deployment platforms are other platform teams. Instead, these platform teams need to invest in release engineering. However, due to the pressure to release features and the general reluctance among many developers to write automation, we usually see platform teams underinvesting in this area. This often remains completely hidden when the initial developers of the platform are the ones making the production changes, as they usually have deep knowledge of where the points of risk are and how to work around them. But as the team grows and changes, this esoteric knowledge is lost, and all it takes is the wrong person leaving and suddenly there is no one on the team who can safely touch production.

To avoid landing in this situation, you need to invest in change management, as that will create the feedback that tells you that you are relying on risky behavior and need to invest in release engineering automation while the people who understand the system's sharp edges are still around. This can be quite simple as a process—just a short writeup on a wiki or chat that has to be acknowledged by another team member. But you must build a culture of adherence, using operational reviews to ensure both that the process is being followed and that automation for risky or toilsome steps is being invested in.

This is because until the new automation is written, the additional work of change management adds toil to each change, making engineers less happy and diverting time from development activities, including building the automation. Despite this, we've witnessed too many widespread business outages caused by sharp-edged change tools to believe there's a simpler solution. If anyone on your team doubts this, refer them back to the Amazon S3 outage of 2017. The service, which was nine years old at the time and had hundreds of engineers working on it, suffered a two-hour outage because of a single wrong parameter entered in a command-line tool.[6]

 Be careful of letting the platform team go too far with release engineering, turning what should be platform automation into a full-featured shadow deployment platform. Beyond the costs of duplicated work, this will create political problems. It doesn't matter if there are good technical reasons for the duplication; it gives the impression that the platform engineering teams don't trust their own stuff, and that they have so many spare engineers that they can build their own shadow platforms. If a platform team is spending more than 12 developer months per calendar year on release engineering, they may be overbuilding it.

---

6 Per Amazon (*https://oreil.ly/_xViX*), "At 9:37 AM PST, an authorized S3 team member using an established playbook executed a command which was intended to remove a small number of servers for one of the S3 subsystems that is used by the S3 billing process. Unfortunately, one of the inputs to the command was entered incorrectly and a larger set of servers was removed than intended."

Synthetic Monitoring

Enough has been written about the "three pillars" of observability—metrics, logs, and tracing—that we don't need to reiterate their value here. We agree that deep investment in passive monitoring of all of these is crucial for the operability of your platforms. However, there is one aspect of observability that we think requires far more investment for platforms than for most other types of systems: *synthetic monitoring*. Synthetic monitoring, also called active monitoring, simulates a user interacting with the production platform; it measures not just latency and availability but correctness of function, and it raises alerts when objectives are not met.

As we discussed in Chapter 2, platform teams take operational responsibility for primitives that they did not develop, be they OSS or vendor systems or other internal platforms and systems. Each of these brings its own complexity that makes it difficult to understand where issues will arise and even more difficult to debug them when they occur. By actively exercising the full system, synthetic monitoring is your main way of understanding what is happening within and across those primitives. It leads to four benefits:

End-to-end monitoring
> Synthetic monitoring covers gaps in passive monitoring and alerts you to real issues before your customers report them. This is especially useful for SLOs, where synthetic monitors not only can observe the direct behavior of calling APIs (latency, throughput, error codes) from a client but, more importantly, can compose end-to-end scenarios calling multiple APIs together, similar to what your customers do. Thus, synthetic monitors are usually the best way of monitoring the availability and performance characteristics that your customers will be seeing.

Customer understanding
> Both the development and the operation of synthetic tests force platform engineers to get firsthand experience developing an application that runs on their platform. This means that even though the work the monitoring application does is synthetic, it gives a lot of the same feedback benefits as dogfooding.[7] For example, if flakiness in an API call is causing a false alarm in your synthetic monitors, it's likely bothering your customers too (or it bothered them and they've hid it in a retry loop, which will cause even worse problems eventually).

Operational system understanding
> Even if debugging a flaky synthetic test doesn't preemptively identify a customer-impacting issue, your engineers will get real experience troubleshooting issues in

---

7 Having your own team use the systems you are building for your customers, especially acting as early adopters and testers.

the production platform. This practice should drive down the MTTR when they eventually need to handle real issues.

Triangulation

When a customer is having issues, the well-understood nature of the synthetic test load often helps with triangulation, letting you easily determine whether the problem is in the platform for all users, or just in how the customer is using it. If the synthetic load is seeing it, you will often have a lot more historical data available to understand which system component is the cause.

When Ian was building industry-foundational platforms at AWS, synthetic monitoring was used in place of almost all functional integration testing under the argument that if you wanted to test for something before every release, wouldn't you want to ensure that the same issue was not happening in production? Based on this experience, he estimates the cost of doing this well at 25% of ongoing development time and 10% of the platform's resource cost. Your platform may not have the same scale and complexity as AWS, but it would be unwise to think your investment should be drastically less.

Operational Reviews

All the practices covered to this point create data about your operational health. Operational reviews close the loop to drive action. They are a practice from seasoned operations organizations in which engineers and management come together on a regular cadence (usually weekly) to review broad measures like SLO metrics as well as specifics like incident postmortems. They leverage human attention to analyze data as a group, enabling the identification of early outliers, bad trends, and broader lessons. With management and engineering actively engaged, operational reviews create a shared understanding of nascent problems that drives action well ahead of them becoming chronic. Here are a few of our observations regarding this practice.

Operational reviews are essential for platform teams

For those coming from an application development background, operational reviews likely appear nonessential at best and burdensome at worst. They can feel like grunt work to prove you need to spend more time building a system that doesn't require such reviews. Before Ian joined AWS, he spent three years working on application systems that rendered parts of the live Amazon.com website, and he held exactly this view. While the algorithms driving his application code were complex, the systems were not, because the underlying platforms abstracted most of the complexity away. His team easily managed fewer than two on-call pages a week and could avoid doing formal operational reviews, all while patting themselves on the backs for being "operationally excellent."

Ian got a rude shock when he moved into AWS in 2008, to work on a platform product called EMR. Even with a lower volume of use and a considerably simpler codebase, the operational load was much higher. Some of this was user support, but just as much came from direct operational issues, caused by the fact that the system was composed of many underlying systems (including both other AWS services and substantial OSS). In this relatively small team of five, the practice of operational reviews was the only thing that kept small problems from mushrooming to dominate the time of everyone on the team.

Keep team reviews simple and rigorous

At the team level, the basics of operational reviews are that the team does a 30- or 60-minute weekly review of:

- Pages and lower-severity on-call issues
- Customer support issues
- Incident/outage postmortems
- Production changes
- Highly relevant SLIs and SLOs (often done in what is called a "dashboard review," looking at trends)

Each meeting requires some amount of curation and preparation, which generally should be done by the person who just came off being on-call.

Org-level reviews are essential, but put practice over process

Getting team-level meetings to the point where they drive the right action is a bit of an art specific to your company's culture. With newly formed teams or newly hired managers, it's easy for them to devolve into pointless theatrics that don't have any value. This is why it's important to do at least one higher-level organization review, at least monthly, to develop a broader cultural understanding of how good meetings work. There are two essential things to cover:

- Postmortems for the highest-impact incidents/outages
- Some metric-level review with discussion of outliers (for example, looking at SLOs, support metrics, or pager metrics)

An important aspect at this level is that the meeting is well-curated; information presented and discussed should be relevant to the broader audience. We have found success asking our SREs to drive these reviews; they have the technical skill to ensure that time is not wasted on inessential detail, and (as we covered in Chapter 4) they are usually highly motivated by these types of social problems.

As much as we recommend an operational review *practice*, we have seen some leaders overfocus on a systematic and rigorous metric-driven *process*, missing the point that each platform team's particular issues are situational. If you ask your platform team leaders to spend time on things that don't have any bearing on their situation, you are making them spend less time on things that would have an actual impact on the platform operations.

Leadership engagement drives the right outcomes

The point of operational reviews is to close the feedback loop by shifting engineering time in response to the operational data that the team is receiving. If the leaders who need to make those calls are not actively part of the meeting, then you cannot close this loop. Engineering managers need to be engaged, in a blameless fashion, to effectively drive forward understanding of issues and prioritize actions. This makes it clear to platform engineers and their customers that the platform leaders are accountable for maintaining a well-informed balance between operations and feature investments, putting the platform on a path to a sustainable future.

Wrapping Up

If you come from a systems background, there may have been little new to you here—as discussed in Chapter 4, a large part of the reason why the "software versus systems" divide has persisted is that the systems side almost always took operational discipline seriously. We wrote this chapter for those of you with a development background, for whom it's important to understand that succeeding in operating platforms relies heavily on discipline in on-call, user support, and operational practices. If you find yourself in a team where subpar behavior has become the norm, it's your responsibility to create better practices that address areas of clear pain and do the work to raise the bar.

CHAPTER 7

Planning and Delivery

The best laid schemes o' mice an' men / Gang aft a-gley.
—Robert Burns

We have seen platform engineering initiatives and leadership fail for many reasons. The most difficult failures happened when the team was building the right things, but not demonstrating it to the organization. Sometimes, these teams had insufficiently planned their projects and were caught in a long slog, building in what seemed like the right direction but taking far too long to deliver real value. In other cases the team had planned for incremental delivery but gotten unlucky with operational events beyond their control. They made things worse by failing to communicate the impact of these events to their customers, either flooding them with too much information or communicating too little.

Whether the team is failing to plan, failing to incrementally execute, or failing to educate their stakeholders on the current state of things, the view of those outside the organization is the same: this team isn't delivering. To help you avoid this outcome, in this chapter we'll introduce our best practices around planning and delivery for a platform organization. In the first section, we focus on planning long projects, documenting the details that can get missed when teams make optimistic assumptions about timelines and value. The second section focuses on planning your team's roadmap from the bottom up: we'll discuss how to balance product and project plans with other essential platform work to ensure the plan's milestones are realistic. We finish the chapter by introducing Wins and Challenges, a communication mechanism to keep partners in sync with how the team is delivering on these plans, including what unexpected things are delaying them.

People sometimes think Agile practices are the only planning a team should ever do, lest they fall into the waterfall trap. But as a platform engineering team, your work is far too complex to leave solely to what can be planned in a sprint (or three!). The guidelines in this chapter are intended to be layered on top of day-to-day Agile practices to get the best of both worlds.

Planning Long-Running Projects

One key distinction between platform engineering and much of application engineering is that platform projects often have significantly longer timelines. Building, testing, and migrating to a new system can take months or even years (*https://oreil.ly/MVXI7*), depending on the size of your company. It's not uncommon for a platform team to work for months on something with no user-visible output, including up-front research time that produces little more than proof of project feasibility. This can be frustrating to leaders who are accustomed to frequent release cadences. If you hate waiting for customer impact, working on platforms can test your patience.

As a platform leader, you must get comfortable with overseeing big, long-running projects and helping teams break them down into incremental milestones. Your teams will need your help to figure out milestones and discussion points to guide their efforts. And the best place to start is by clarifying what the project is.

Clarifying Goals and Requirements in a Proposal Document

If you want your long-running projects to go well, everyone should have an idea of what you're trying to achieve in the first place. The project leads need to write down their ideas in a proposal or requirements document for management and other engineers to review and evaluate. Note that this is not a classical engineering design document. Important elements of the design should be covered, but engineering design is usually just one of the major factors that should be considered. We have also seen consideration of implementation costs, migration costs, and timelines or other requirements coming from customers.

We are both fond of Amazon-style six-pagers (*https://oreil.ly/o6Egl*), but we know that getting your company to adopt this specific style might not be appropriate. Ignoring the specific document format, the most important takeaway from this exercise is to write a proposal that covers these five key elements:[1]

Background, tenets, and guidelines
Describe the current situation, providing any relevant information as to how you got here, and establish any core tenets, requirements, or guidelines; for

---

[1] For more ideas, we recommend Tanya Reilly's *The Staff Engineer's Path* (O'Reilly), particularly Chapter 5, "Leading Big Projects."

instance, "We must support cross-regional failover" or "We should be prepared to support X scaling up in the next Y months." Marc Brooker (*https://oreil.ly/ Rh3Nq*) captures the importance of this section: setting a baseline by documenting the current state allows you to resolve fundamental disagreements early in the process.

Details of the problem

This is where you go into depth about the problem you need to solve. A classic one-pager by Leslie Lamport, "State the Problem Before Describing the Solution" (*https://oreil.ly/tvcZk*), observes that outlining the problem before proposing a solution makes it easier for readers to imagine possible solutions beyond the ones proposed. Often, this step also reveals gaps in the project leads' understanding of the problem, forcing them to gather more details and truly understand what they are proposing.

Overview of possible solutions

This section should outline all reasonable options for a solution and your good-faith evaluation of their major pros and cons. It's important to go through this step *before* detailing the preferred solution, to head off counterproposals of solutions you've already rejected. Otherwise, you're likely to get comments like "Can't this be done much more cheaply, as in X?" and "Aren't you thinking way too small and short term? We need to restart with new technology Y!" Sometimes you might hear both from the same person, as they personally weigh the trade-offs.

Proposed solution and rationale

State the solution you've chosen and explain the rationale for your decision, analyzing any constraints (such as time horizon) and other relevant factors.

How long should this section be? The trite but true answer is "whatever is necessary to convince your audience," which will vary according to company culture and how contentious the decision is. That said, this shouldn't be a 20-page monster document where you attempt to prove your thoroughness by drowning the reader in details. Try to distill the top three to five factors and make an argument for why they take priority over other concerns.

Plan of action

You'll formulate a detailed plan in the next step of the planning process, but for this document, paint a picture of the implementation. What does "done" look like, and on what timelines? Lay out some early to medium-term milestones and metrics for measuring success. If they are pertinent, be sure to address nontechnical concerns like timing, staffing, and organizational impact as well.

Once the document is written, review it with management (including product management) and lead engineers in one or more meetings to debate the merits and get buy-in. If you choose to follow the Amazon style, you'll start those meetings with ~20 minutes of reading followed by "walking the doc," taking the group from section to section in the order they appear in the document. Either way, the goal of these meetings is agreement that the project is worthwhile and that an action plan should be created to estimate the cost of implementation and get final approval to begin work.

Going from Proposal to Action Plan

Once you've gained buy-in for your proposal, there is still some writing to be done before implementation. You'll want to create a thorough design document aimed at ensuring the technical aspects are well considered, which should usually be reviewed by lead engineers.[2] On top of that, we have found a lot of value in an "action plan" document, going into a lot more detail than what was in the project proposal. Important considerations to cover are:

Testing and acceptance criteria
> A major project will need some testing. Has the team written anything down about this? You don't need a full testing plan on day one, but someone should be assigned to write a plan that you'll track as part of the project execution. Testing also implies acceptance criteria: what will you be validating with these tests? We don't expect perfect acceptance criteria to start with, but some baseline requirements are important as you plan for testing.

Analyzing dependencies
> What other teams will need to work on this project? Will the project need to integrate with another system? Do you have buy-in, and possibly participation, from the team that owns that system?

> The more dependencies a project has, the harder it will be to deliver. One major dependency that many platform teams neglect is the work for a migration. If this project requires your customers to migrate in order to complete the delivery, this is a major piece of dependency analysis that you should estimate as part of the project proposal.

---

2 We will note that our experience is that design documents should be started before implementation begins but are usually not finished and reviewed until a few months into implementation, when important trade-offs are better understood.

Estimating headcount

Getting your project approved doesn't guarantee that you'll get everyone you want to work on it. As we cover later in this chapter, "funded" big projects are frequently in contention with other demands on the team's time. You need to guesstimate how many engineers you'll need on the project's central engineering team, and also whether you might need personnel surges for testing, integration, migration, etc.

Driving adoption

If you are building something that other engineers will use directly (rather than an internal system component), you should have a plan for driving adoption. This is typically where product managers contribute their expertise. If you don't have a product manager, make sure you plan to communicate what you're building so that customers understand its purpose and are excited to use it. You may want to answer questions such as:

- What will you call the new product or feature? (Having the right name early makes later discussions much easier to follow.)

- Have you lined up teams to be early adopters?

- Will this offering require extensive documentation?

- Do you need to teach people how to use your new product?

- Should you do other "marketing" activities, like giving talks to the wider team or writing internal blog posts?

- How will you announce the launch?

Too often, project leaders assume that "if you build it, they will come." But even for internal projects, you can seldom guarantee eager adoption if you don't spend time with the target users and understand their needs.

Milestones

The best way to bring these considerations together and manage the project implementation is to state them as a series of milestones. We prefer to be highly concrete for the first 12 months, using monthly milestones that fall back to quarterly only for later stages where there is less clarity. For multiyear projects, we also like to have some projections of how the previous elements (estimated headcount, dependencies, etc.) will evolve in future years, as it gives a strong indication of where we have risks from "unknown unknowns" that we can't yet resolve. These milestones form the basis of your incremental delivery; the more you can create milestones that not only deliver technical capabilities but also support business outcomes, the better.

Beware Bringing In Project Managers Too Early

At the point of creating an action plan, it's tempting for platform leaders to assign the project to a project manager to "own" for its duration. The expectation is that the project manager can create a Gantt chart to map out all the project's dependencies and the estimated work for each task, giving the team confidence in tracking its execution.

In our experience, this doesn't usually work out well. Instead of creating confidence, involving a project manager too early in a project creates a culture of scheduling bureaucracy, and reduces the engagement from the engineering lead and product manager. Without their input in planning, the estimates often become overly conservative and less accurate. For these reasons, we advise you to save your project manager firepower for times where the scheduling details create major risks for the project—for example:

- The project has a firm deadline.

- The project has a large number of task dependencies.

- Your company has a culture of bureaucracy around cooperating (for instance, an attitude that no matter how small the ask, "if it's not scheduled in this quarter's OKRs, you have to wait until next quarter").

Avoiding the Long Slog

Most engineers start long projects with a great degree of hope and optimism—if that wasn't the case, we'd probably start far fewer multiyear projects! It's one thing to go into a project knowing that it will take a long time, but some projects that shouldn't be so lengthy still end up dragging on and on. To help you avoid that fate, this section examines some of the reasons that otherwise reasonable platform projects turn into never-ending slogs.

Overreach

Some projects attempt to do more than is realistic for the time frame or product they are part of.

For example, a team we know was redesigning an internal storage system. This storage system had worked well for the company for years for a particular set of use cases, but it was inefficient and lacked some security and performance features that would make it sustainable in the long run. While planning the redesign, the team kept adding new goals. Not only would the new system correct those security and performance gaps, but it would also modernize how the company thought about storage by getting rid of all network-attached, file-based storage options.

The team implemented diligently and rolled out the new system to a new environment that removed access to the old network-attached storage options. They then tried to migrate users into the new system, and riots ensued (metaphorically, but only just).

It turned out that the users were comfortable with command-line file tools and with scripting against POSIX-based filesystems. They didn't understand how to use the new APIs for things that they had previously done through simple files, and they didn't want to migrate every script. It became clear that the core assumption of removing the network-attached storage option was not going to work, and the team had to take their design back to the drawing board.

This failure is an example of overreach. The system rewrite was always going to be a big project, but because the team knew it would be hard, they started to believe that they should make the *absolute most* of the opportunity and go from "big project" to "revolutionary project." There was also an element of ivory-tower thinking, an assumption that they knew better than their users. The team ended up trying to launch a system that was too heavy to get into orbit. (In Chapter 8, we'll talk about techniques to avoid this, particularly around rearchitectures.)

Starting too big

In Chapter 5, we discussed the challenge of getting customers to tell you what they want you to build. This in turn can lead to the team struggling to write a project proposal, because they are unwilling or unable to commit to a proposed solution that might exclude some customer group. Instead, the proposals start to look like increasingly complex design specifications meant to cover all possible eventualities.

While building good products is hard, and building good platforms is hard, building a complex platform from scratch for a diverse user base might well be impossible. It's good to keep Gall's law in mind when you start new platform projects:

> A complex system that works is invariably found to have evolved from a simple system that worked. The inverse proposition also appears to be true: A complex system designed from scratch never works and cannot be made to work. You have to start over, beginning with a working simple system.[3]

When you say that you are trying to build, from scratch, a new platform that needs detailed customer design input from a diverse set of customers, you reveal a few things:

1. This is a novel complex system, not a system that is the internal delivery of a well-known platform or an evolution of an existing simple platform.

---

3 John Gall, *General Systemantics* (Quadrangle/The New York Times Book Company), 71.

2. You don't really know what needs to happen to build this system, hence the desire to have your customers tell you what they need and give you cover to build things.

3. You don't have product management coverage to even begin to understand the nuances of your customers and their needs.

4. You have no business building this platform in this way.

You may be in an impossible situation. If you have been given a grandiose central mandate to build a brand-new thing, and won this mandate without previously having a clear idea of what needs to happen (perhaps due to internal politics, naivete, or other factors), you are set up for failure. Sorry to be the bearers of bad news, but if you've promised a complete platform for all customers, you are going to have a very hard time delivering on this promise.

Writing a concrete proposal that your customers can understand and critique is one way to make sure that you aren't getting into this situation. If you can't figure out how to write this document, it's a sign that you may have bitten off more than you can chew, and the best bet might be to scope down your efforts. As we suggested in Chapter 5, start by looking at the boring parts of the new platform, the more obvious features, and look for the scope that you can confidently define in a proposal.

Unclear problem space

With the storage system project we described earlier, at least the team had an underlying problem they knew they needed to solve. So many platform projects fail because no one is quite sure exactly what problem they are solving. This is why it is so valuable to spend some time up front thinking about—and writing down—your project goals and interrogating your assumptions, before you invest a lot of time and money.

It's tempting for platform teams to believe their job is to make everyone happy by building a generic system that will meet all needs. Rather than choosing one of the kinds of solutions outlined in Chapter 2, they choose both a paved path *and* a railway approach. By failing to commit to one approach, they end up unable to meet the needs of the moment. For example, a team might try to build a generic solution to a broad problem (paved path) but also try to use a railway approach by, say, building a cool drag-and-drop UI to make it easy for other teams to configure and tweak the underlying system. When these solutions don't work out, too often teams double down on them rather than declaring these types of investments as failures. They insist that they just need to find the right use case for their cool UI, or the right users who need exactly what the generic offering can provide. A former colleague of ours in the product engineering world used to call this behavior "sh*terating."

Flailing about looking for product fit is one thing when you're building a product at a startup with a "move fast and break things" mandate. It's quite another thing in the platform world, where this behavior gives platform teams a bad name.

It's critical to define the problem that your initiative is trying to solve, hypothesize a solution, provide evidence that the proposed solution can solve the problem, and (ideally) provide metrics to gauge if the solution is working. You'll get the best proposal by teaming up a staff engineer who can provide technical insight with a product manager to support the customer perspective. Without this up-front work, you're likely to end up in the perpetual situation where it seems just one more feature is needed for your silver bullet solution to get adopted. That's why we advocate thorough documentation, beginning with a concrete proposal before the project is even started.

Project team turnover

Projects also drag on when the team is unstable. Losing people who know about the project slows everyone down. Not only do you lose people who could have done the work, but you also then have to find new people to add to the project, train them on its details, and get them effectively gelled with the rest of the team. All of this hinders productivity. Unfortunately, team turnover is often caused by projects that are already dragging on, which leads to a vicious cycle of project delays and demoralized team members who quit or move to other projects, in turn delaying the current project even more.

This is one of the reasons that documenting the proposal and plans is so important. As Cian Synnott, senior staff engineer at Datadog, told us: "I've often seen a new senior engineer added to a team who questions everything. That's good, and part of team formation in a way, but being able to say 'yeah, we're doing this project this way and <here's why>' is a great way to channel their energy and keep it positive."

Even as a senior leader, you may not have perfect control over working conditions that contribute to turnover; for example, if the company isn't paying enough to retain people in a hot market, that may be beyond your ability to fix. But there are other factors within your control. If the platforms you own are always on fire, your team might be turning over because they're burned out on operational work. Avoiding this situation, or removing your team from it, requires a different type of planning, as we'll show you in the next section.

Bottom-Up Roadmap Planning

The product roadmaps described in Chapter 5 represent the plan for adding new features to a platform. For teams not facing delivery or operational pressures, they can be sufficient to function as the only plan used to ensure the team is on the right track to deliver customer value. However, once a team is under delivery or operational pressure, you need to invest in a second, higher-fidelity roadmap, called a *bottom-up roadmap.*

What causes this change? There's an old Borscht Belt joke about a pair of customers complaining, "The food at this place is really terrible…and such small portions!" Similarly, a platform's stakeholders often complain, "The stability of this platform is so terrible…and they never ship our features on time!" Because scaled platforms are so complex and often support business-critical applications, platform teams need to invest in operations proactively. This means not only maintaining systems, but also changing them to handle increased scale. Without proper planning in place to manage expectations of the feature delivery schedule, platform teams find themselves neglecting operational work, and they eventually get stuck in operational hell. This could mean:

- Mitigating issues with "Band-Aid" patches that add to the system's complexity and create technical debt
- Missing committed deadlines for new features, experiencing recurring operational events, and disappointing customers
- Burning engineers out with heavy operational workloads and stress

Avoiding this outcome requires augmenting feature delivery plans with the work needed to operate and operationally improve the platform. The next subsections describe three pools of work you'll need to estimate. First, there's the *keep the lights on* (KTLO) work: the essential operational tasks that keep systems and services running smoothly. Second, you have *executive mandates,* (almost) nonnegotiable projects handed down from executive leadership. Third, you have *system improvements,* which are exactly what they sound like: the work to improve the platform's operations, efficiency, security, reliability, and compliance. In the final subsection, we talk about how to merge this all together, as illustrated in Figure 7-1.

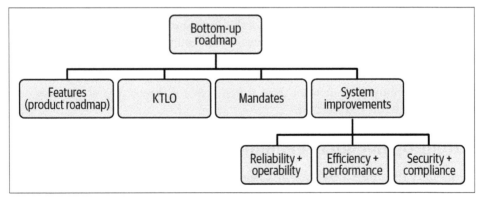

Figure 7-1. The elements of a bottom-up roadmap

"Keep the Lights On" Work

You might call this "operations," but KTLO viscerally captures an engineering team's *truly* nondiscretionary operational work—the absolute essentials required to keep the business running over the next 12 months. This is usually a short list of categories:

- Staffing on-call incident response
- Staffing essential user support (on-call or otherwise)
- Remediating operational and security incidents and critical postmortem action items

If you've followed our advice in Chapter 6 and broken out on-call and support duties into rotations, you should be able to estimate costs for the first two items using your historical data. The third item is the most difficult to estimate, since it involves "unknown unknowns" about future events. Our advice is to look at the volume of this work that the team performed over the last planning period, but strike off any events or action items that took up more than about two months of engineering time. The threshold is somewhat arbitrary, but we would argue that it isn't right to plan with an *expectation* of having future large operational or security events.

Mandates

Mandates are top-down edicts, things that the executive leadership team says *must* be done, often with hard timelines. They might include projects like:

- Migrations driven by other platform and infrastructure teams
- Infrastructure initiatives, like moving to a new cloud provider, integrating after an acquisition, or building out a new geographic region
- Initiatives to improve company compliance, security or operational posture (for instance, deprecating old open source dependencies or achieving HIPAA compliance)
- Large "strategic" business initiatives that are intended to override local priorities (for instance, "we need to have a lot more AI features in all our products")

Mandates present a planning contradiction. There are inevitably mandates that are claimed to be essential at the beginning of the planning process that will be killed once the company realizes the total amount of work involved and how that will cut into other higher-value priorities. This means while no single team can just say "no" to these mandates, if you plan with the assumption that you have to do *all* of them, then the rest of your plan will get derailed.

Thus, estimating the net impact of mandates means taking your best guess at which are both likely to move forward and of high impact on your team, and estimating the effort they will take. This is an art that requires some political awareness and good communication with the executive in your leadership tree who can have some sway on whether proposed mandates move forward. When mandates threaten to overburden your team, tell that executive as soon as possible, so they can give feedback to the leadership team and hopefully help whittle down the list to the truly essential.

System Improvements

While KTLO is the essential operational work for a system supporting a steadily growing business, it's not the only needed work. KTLO doesn't include work that falls into the category of "if the system is not improved soon, it will hurt the company in the intermediate term, by increasing either the likelihood of a problem or the scope of its negative impact." This work arises from three general directions: ongoing growth in scale pushing the system closer to its limits, the system's natural deterioration in a changing environment (sometimes called "software rot"), and standards rising as the platform and its applications become more important to the business.

A lot of organizations call this SRE work. We call it "system improvements," because we have found that the term SRE leads people to assume that all of the work is about improving reliability, whereas we think there are other important categories. System improvements generally fall into one of three buckets:

- Reliability and operability
- Efficiency and performance
- Security and compliance

We suggest creating three separate stack rank lists, one for each category, since the audience for each category's list will be different. This separation also helps the individual stack ranks, by allowing you to compare costs and impact *within*, rather than across, categories.

Reliability and operability improvements

This work has to do with making system operations less costly, risky, or fault-prone. Some examples are:

Reducing toil
  Automating away the hands-on engineering work that scales linearly with the size of the system not only reduces the amount of KTLO work but, by taking the human element out, also reduces the risk of outages.

Improving testing capabilities

If certain bugs continuously end up in production, you might need to invest in new ways of doing unit tests, introduce load testing or fuzz testing, or improve flaky integration tests.

Release engineering

We introduced release engineering in Chapter 6. Specific investments here may be new capabilities, like blue/green testing or canary and shadow deployments.

Observability

While some work to improve observability is small and easy to fit in, other projects, like creating a new synthetic monitoring platform or adding a new type of observability such as APM, will happen only if they are planned and prioritized.

Reducing variations

Much of a platform's technical debt—far more than for applications—comes from variations in the software it runs in production, usually stemming from decisions to enable new use cases "the fast way" rather than "the right way." These variations can include, for example, clients using deprecated versions of APIs, keeping old versions of the platform to support clients who haven't migrated, customer-specific feature flags that have not been removed, or old versions of external dependencies. These often have the most impact during deployments, when slight differences are easily forgotten by the operator, leading to failures.

System changes

These include changes to the system itself to improve reliability: for example, changing a hashing algorithm, tuning a garbage collector, introducing a cache, or swapping out buggy open source libraries.

To find candidates for these projects, look at the lower-priority action items that come out of postmortems. You should also be looking at your customers' postmortems to identify guardrails that you can build in your platform that will eliminate failures for them.

We have had some success by proactively challenging teams to identify prominent issues in their systems in a "system risk register" as a centralized, SRE-led project. However, without strong leadership, such efforts can become highly bureaucratic and return little value. Seek feedback when undertaking such a task to ensure that the process will drive action, rather than create a long list that is immediately forgotten.

Efficiency and performance improvements

Since they own the first layer of software over the underlying infrastructure, platform teams usually have far more responsibility for cost efficiency than their application team customers. However, too often they put little work into that responsibility, underinvesting until a CFO or CTO hears an anecdote about waste and realizes that no one is paying attention to costs. At this point, the platform teams are pushed to do a big one-off drive that randomizes everyone but fixes the immediate waste, and follow it with a heavyweight program to try to avoid it in the future. Unfortunately, such programs, often called "chargebacks," are usually so bureaucratic and rife with untested assumptions that they cause as many problems as they solve.

Doing better than this requires platform teams to constantly invest in efficiency improvements. We have found this is often done poorly because a lot of people miss that the work is split into two categories: FinOps, which is done (at scale) by a team of dedicated specialists, and performance engineering, which is best done by systems engineers within each platform team, and whose larger projects should be included in planning for each team. In the rest of this section, we describe the roles and division of labor.

FinOps, short for "financial operations," is a relatively new discipline born out of the complexity of dynamic cloud usage and pricing models. The FinOps Foundation (*https://oreil.ly/CLdos*) defines it as "the practice of bringing a financial accountability cultural change to the variable spend model of cloud, enabling distributed engineering and business teams to make trade-offs between speed, cost, and quality in their cloud architecture and investment decisions."

The types of things FinOps teams do well are:

- Tagging cloud and infrastructure resources for ownership
- Creating spend reports for financial and engineering leaders
- Using the right reservation duration for virtual machines (instances)
- "Rightsizing" servers and instances to fit the load, including removing unused ones
- Negotiating discounts with cloud vendors
- Working with platform teams to build better models for predicting future costs and optimization opportunities based on customer demand

Aren't there vendor tools that do this for you? Well, yes, but in our experience, most engineering teams and managers struggle to incorporate the complex decisions and actions they require into their regular workflow. It needs to be someone's primary responsibility. The cloud allows you to burn cash quickly in too many ways, and you need someone guarding against that. This is a large enough problem that you need a FinOps specialist once the engineering organization gets to about 200 engineers.

In smaller organizations, we often assign this responsibility as a part-time role to the systems engineers on our compute platform teams, because they are already close to the cloud vendors, and because compute use cases often carry the most cost complexity. But while FinOps work is complex, most systems engineers don't enjoy it as a full-time role, because it is not "hands-on" enough in terms of production systems. What they *do* love doing is the second category of efficiency improvements: *performance engineering*, a system-wide approach to design, analysis, and tuning systems for performance and efficiency. When performance engineering leads to well-tuned systems, it can create the "quick wins" CTOs and finance teams love, where weeks of work produce hundreds of thousands of dollars in yearly savings. But doing this requires deep knowledge of the production platforms.

Companies often respond to this need by creating a "performance team," hiring one or more performance experts to focus full-time on the company's highest-impact performance engineering problems.[4] Unfortunately, few engineering organizations are large enough to have sufficient hard problems to motivate experts. So, they tend to hire someone more junior, then run into the challenges of "specialist as evangelist" we described back in Chapter 4, where the engineer is more interested in lecturing about the way things should happen rather than fixing the problems on the ground. Exacerbating these problems is that the specialist's "actual" engineering job is changing *other teams'* systems, a trust barrier that's sometimes hard even for experts to cross.

Thus, outside of huge enterprises with thousands of engineers, you're unlikely to find the unicorn candidate for such a full-time job. The more productive path is to give this responsibility to the systems engineers on your platform teams. In our experience, these folks read all the performance-tuning material they can get their hands on and are chomping at the bit to put it into practice. They just need free rein to do it.

So, have the FinOps team lead an ongoing cost-efficiency investigation program that creates time for each team's systems engineers to explore high-potential efficiency improvements. Then, in your bottom-up planning processes, estimate the implementation costs of the highest-value ones, stack rank them by cost/benefits, and prioritize them alongside other systems improvements.

Security and compliance improvements

Last, we have system improvements that increase your security posture or your compliance with regulatory/customer standards. Security engineering is a discipline of its own, and despite the many books that have been written about it, the industry is underinvesting in it. The log4shell zero-day vulnerability in 2021 (*https://oreil.ly/ Uxdf9*) dramatically demonstrated how far a lot of companies are from being able to patch critical exploits in a reasonable amount of time, let alone from keeping up to date generally.

---

4 See Brendan Gregg, *Systems Performance*, 2nd ed. (Addison-Wesley).

Security engineering is easily forgotten by application and platform teams until an incident occurs. But building large security engineering teams doesn't work either. While they provide great analysis of security and compliance issues and implementation trade-offs, it's usually hard for them to make substantial changes to systems owned by other teams, particularly when those changes are design or product-level decisions. This work is best done by platform teams themselves, using the independent security engineering organization to help advocate for, compile, evaluate, and consult on projects.

Some of these projects will be about fundamental changes to platform architecture—we'll discuss how to handle those in Chapter 8. Some will be incremental improvements in the current system, similar to other reliability projects. Furthermore, just like reliability projects, their value will be more about reducing probabilistic risk, as opposed to clearly knowing something has been accomplished. So, just as they do with reliability work, platform teams need to constantly evaluate their highest-value security projects, and invest in them alongside other system improvements.

Bringing It All Together

This section completes our discussion of bottom-up planning with a look at the planning cycle. You should now have the following artifacts:

- A nonnegotiable estimate of KTLO work
- An estimate of all "likely nonnegotiable" mandated projects
- Your product roadmap, which lists the new things customers and stakeholders want out of your platform (this should include ideas from the platform engineering teams themselves, not just work defined by product management)
- Three stacked-rank lists of projects to improve efficiency, reliability, and security

Let's look at the important factors in turning this into a concrete plan.

Cadence

How often should you be creating lists, estimates, and plans? The default approach is to do this whenever your company requires you to. However, since application-centric organizations can get away with doing much less (and less rigorous) planning, they probably won't ask for it as often as you need to do it to keep them satisfied. Our preference for platform teams is to do "deep" from-scratch planning annually, then a lighter refresh in the other three quarters.

Merging lists

How do you merge all those lists of potential projects? It depends, not just on the state of your platform but on how people *perceive* the state of your platform. We can offer a few heuristics to guide you:

KTLO work should account for no more than 40% of your team's workload.
Any more than that and you risk burning out your team.

Individual system improvement projects should not take longer than three developer months.
Unless the problem is acute, when an improvement project is likely to take more than three developer months, you're usually better off thinking of it in terms of creating value as part of a larger project. We'll discuss this in detail in the next chapter.

Use the 70/20/10 model to apportion non-KTLO work.
How much of its non-KTLO time should a platform team spend on incremental work versus big architecture projects or entirely new platforms? We like Google's 70/20/10 model (*https://oreil.ly/zPJsK*):

- 70% on core initiatives (incremental work on current platforms)
- 20% on adjacent innovation (platform rearchitectures)
- 10% on transformational innovation (completely new platforms)

However, at any time, teams will differ in how much leverage they can get from adjacent and transformational innovation. Thus, while it's useful to measure and discuss, resist the urge to communicate the 70/20/10 model as a "budget" that leadership grants and teams get to spend.

Merging roadmaps of platform teams

We've asked you to make the lists we just described because we believe that this effort is always valuable for individual platform teams. This level of detailed analysis gives you more confidence in what you're doing, helps you make the case for growing your team when necessary, and lets you push back against stakeholders who disagree with your proposed investments. So shouldn't you get even more value if you try and "roll up" your roadmap and lists across teams as well?

To start with the easy answer, the most value we have seen in the whole exercise is one level up. At the skip manager level, the collective "planning team" is small enough to have conversations about standards and definitions, and the roadmap can still be represented in a six-page document, which is short enough that everyone can read and understand it. This also allows the skip manager to make better decisions about how to allocate people between teams.

However, we don't recommend further merging at higher levels in an attempt to create a complete overall plan, especially for headcount purposes. After the skip manager level, you begin to lose fidelity in the information. Worse, involving more people, each with their own agenda, can make the process political. This is exactly what Ian experienced as a midlevel manager in AWS's OP1 process (*https://oreil.ly/Q6j32*), where the coupling of management promotions to organization size meant middle managers were incentivized to show that they should own new "think big" projects and otherwise grow their organizations. Team managers in turn started padding their estimates to justify the most hiring for their teams, kicking off a race to the bottom, where even the most principled leaders felt compelled to play the game to protect their teams.

Further, since hiring is a continuous pipeline that takes time, the VPs and directors who "owned" the headcount had often changed their plans for allocating it by the time the new hire offers were made. This was sensible leadership behavior, but it only increased the cynicism around the monolithic planning exercise.

Bottom-up planning is important to protect teams from devolving into operational hell, but don't try to turn it into "one planning system to rule them all." If even AWS can't use it to get headcount allocation right, it's unlikely you will do much better.

Platform Antipattern: Relying on Innersourcing

Once upon a time, Camille was the owner of a large distributed system that provided dynamic service discovery. Services registered themselves in her system, and clients queried it to find the service endpoints. It was built as a wrapper over a distributed coordination system, Apache ZooKeeper, which her team also supported. Because client libraries were an important part of the system and the team didn't have experts in every language, as a way to remove bottlenecks, they allowed other developers to build and contribute their own clients through internal open sourcing, also known as *innersourcing*.

One day, the creator of the Perl client library released a bug in his version that took the entire service down. When they looked into the buggy library, Camille's team realized that this creator had started using ZooKeeper features that were beyond the scope of the discovery service API. This was a powerful two-for-one lesson: not only did she learn the truth of Hyrum's law,[5] but she also learned that it's risky to innersource code that is part of a platform ecosystem.

The idea behind innersourcing is that by allowing anyone to contribute to a codebase, similar to open source software, you create a way for developers to unblock themselves. Executives like this model because it lets them seem open to collaboration by

---

5 Paraphrased, all observable behaviors of your system will be depended on by somebody, no matter what you promise in the contract.

saying, "Anyone who is stuck waiting for a feature is welcome to write the code and contribute it back!" We're big fans of open source, and Camille has been an on-again, off-again open source contributor for most of her career, so we agree with the power of this model in theory.

Unfortunately, the reality tends to be much messier. Most people don't want to read someone else's code, figure out how to fix it, or wait for a code review from some stranger. People are happy to consume open source, but very few want to contribute to it. Of the few who do want to contribute, many are only interested in adding some half-considered feature that tortures the code into doing something it shouldn't to unblock their niche use case. Maintainers know that if they approve these changes, they'll have to support the feature forever, which makes them understandably cautious, picky, and slow to accept unproven contributions.

These challenges persist in innersourcing models. You might trust your colleagues more than you do unknown internet strangers, but ultimately, the team that owns the software will be responsible for supporting it. So, most teams prefer hiring more people over reviewing changes from other teams—and that's for the best, because few internal teams really want to do the work of figuring out how to contribute to your platform code.

Platforms add a second wrinkle to this challenge, as Camille learned. Not only are you taking contributions from others, you are also operating the system to which they contribute. When someone adds a bug to an open source project, nobody is paging its maintainers. But the platform team *will* get paged when something goes wrong with their platform, and it's frustrating to have to fight fires ignited by a third-party contribution.

Don't use innersourcing to avoid hard conversations with your customers about priorities. Giving your customers the impression that they can just build what they want and hand it off is naive; setting up a thoughtful model for contributions that goes beyond the initial code implementation takes a lot of work.

One such approach is the Amazon "away team" model (*https://oreil.ly/417LE*), which is a contract-driven model that lets a stuck application team unblock themselves by developing the platform features they need and giving the code to the "host" platform team to own long term. We offer a caution: in his time at Amazon, Ian's teams used a variant of this model. While the collaboration worked, the formality of the interaction incurred high management overhead, even when the engineers got along well. Instead of an informal agreement within a team that could be flexibly adjusted as necessary, two managers ended up in formal negotiations over small matters like vacations, on-call schedules, and code reviews. This is an unsurprising outcome of a contract-driven interaction model, and one of the reasons we are skeptical about formal innersourcing processes.

The away team approach may be appropriate in an early-stage platform that is still evolving, but as it matures, this model should become rarer. If you find your team using it frequently, treat that as a problem that needs action, not a standard operating model.

Communicating Status with Biweekly Wins and Challenges

So your team is planning well and delivering incrementally? Congratulations! But you aren't out of the woods yet. Even when you plan flawlessly, things break, surprises happen, and schedules change. If your senior stakeholders aren't paying too much attention but don't see their expected improvements, they may assume that nothing is happening. And as the organization grows, it's hard for the leaders to keep track of everything that's happening across the different teams and feel confident that things are going in the right direction.

To solve for this, we use an exercise called Wins and Challenges. It's a way of gathering biweekly updates, tailoring them to be meaningful to stakeholders, and creating value for the team itself by highlighting their accomplishments, alerting their leaders to problems, and recording their progress for posterity. While this section is not specific to platform engineering, Wins and Challenges is a particularly valuable habit for platform engineering teams, whose long-term focus often makes them appear to accomplish very little from day to day. We've used Wins and Challenges at companies big and small to show our bosses, peers, and stakeholders what our teams have been up to and to make sure our managers are paying the right attention to the work and its impact.

The Basics

Every two weeks, we walk up the organizational tree, writing a short number of bullet points that describe major accomplishments ("wins") and issues ("challenges") over the prior two weeks. By "walk up," we mean that the line managers write the updates for their teams, and then each level above in the hierarchy is tasked with selecting the most important, interesting, and/or impactful points from the level below to share, rewriting them as necessary to be consumed by a broader audience.

Before we go into *how* to run this exercise and write these updates, let's start with clarifying *why* it's worth your time.

Why: What's the Value?

For the team and its management, this exercise provides a lightweight, regularly scheduled way for everyone to receive an appropriate amount of information about what other teams are doing. It creates a record, team by team, of what really happened over the quarter, which is useful for writing business and performance reviews. And it forces managers to account for what *really* happened in the last two weeks, which is something sprints and other types of ceremonies often fail to do.

For stakeholders, this exercise provides transparency into the work at regular intervals. Platform engineering teams, because they are often working on long-term, less readily understandable projects, need to spend even more time than most teams on communicating the value and impact of their work. The goal is to help the overall organization see that this isn't just a team of engineers playing around with fun engineering stuff; it's a team tackling hard problems that make a difference to the company. Establishing understanding and trust is crucial, and for both of us, across multiple companies, this exercise has been a keystone of that process.

If you think this sounds like busywork but you don't do any other regular reporting, we encourage you to try it. Platform leaders often mistakenly believe that they don't need to provide transparency regularly, or that their teams' work is so big that it's impossible to summarize. And, kindly, we say: *hogwash.* You owe it to your peers and boss and customers to create transparency into your work, and you owe it to your team to think about how the work can be broken down and delivered more frequently.

If this exercise duplicates things you already do to showcase your team's impact, you might not need it. However, we encourage you to think about whether Wins and Challenges can enhance what you're already doing. Many reporting exercises are largely about output measures, like how many tickets the team closed or how many story points they completed. This is fine, but it doesn't incorporate regular reflection on the *outcomes* of that work. It may be worthwhile to add this as a final step to that output reporting: we got all this stuff done, sure, but what was its impact?

What: Structuring Wins and Challenges Updates

The basic format looks like this:

Wins:

- Point 1
- Point 2
- Point 3
- Point 4

Challenges:

- Challenge 1
- Challenge 2

There are two parts to the "what" of this exercise. The first is getting people to write good updates in the first place. In our experience, the structure is one of the biggest initial sticking points. One of Camille's senior product managers created a useful three-part formula for structuring Wins and Challenges updates[6]—to write an update, start with a short, bolded summary, then break it down into a sentence or two describing the situation, action, and result:

Situation
> What was the situation before the action took place? This gives the audience the necessary context to appreciate why you acted.

Action
> What did you do to address the situation? This explains to your audience the size and shape of the problem, as well as the actual work undertaken.

Result
> How did your actions affect the situation? The best is when you can use numbers to show a measurable change.

The goal is to write something your audience can scan and understand, quickly and easily. Depending on the audience, you may need to expand acronyms, reduce complex system concepts into simpler components, or remove unnecessary details.

Numbers are your friends. Metrics help people understand the size of the problem and the impact of the work. Not everything can or should be quantified, but in business communication it's helpful to quantify outcomes whenever possible.

Some examples of topics to include in your updates are:

- News about major initiatives, such as achieving milestones or running into delays
- News about people, like someone leaving or joining the team, team splits, and reorganizations
- Operations news, such as reporting on incidents, celebrating a good week (in terms of incidents or pages), or acknowledging a bad one
- Changes in product or engineering metrics, such as performance improvements, cost savings, adoption milestones, customer satisfaction survey changes, or notable customer feedback

---

6 Adapted from an interview technique called STAR (*https://oreil.ly/uvw7M*), for *situation, task, action, result*.

Don't Forget the Challenges!

We probably don't need to convince you to share your wins, but it's worth taking a moment to think about the challenges. Why include challenges at all? Which challenges are worth including?

Sharing your challenges serves two important purposes:

Internal health monitoring
> Within the platform organization, challenges give management visibility into where the platform teams are having issues with collaboration, stability, or delivery—even if those issues haven't blown up enough to grab the attention of more senior management. Challenges serve as conversation-starters among the management team and can generate better collaboration within the organization.
>
> Challenges may also highlight problems between platform teams and other external teams: for example, if the platform team is still waiting for a customer team to provide feedback on a new feature, or when the wait for a security review is blocking a release. These can be used to support escalations or to document repeated problems with an external team.

External trust building
> Companies don't often have a place to share what isn't going well, but especially for central teams, transparency is part of building trust. Sharing challenges provides an opportunity for others to step in and help. Sometimes, when a team calls out a challenge, senior managers can see an unresolved priority conflict that they need to look into. At much larger companies, you might not even hear about challenges elsewhere in the company that affect your engineering teams until they show up in an update.
>
> The challenges you choose to share externally should be a meaningful subset chosen because they are useful for building trust, getting help, or highlighting ongoing issues. Things break, and while you may have an excellent incident management and postmortem process, briefly acknowledging bigger incidents can help others trust that your team is on top of things. The Challenges section is also a good place to acknowledge unforeseen shipping delays, vendor negotiation issues, security incidents, or even the loss of key personnel.

It's important to note that you don't want to share collaboration challenges thoughtlessly. If you publish an issue with a partner team that no one has brought to the leadership of that team, they may see it as you calling them out publicly before giving them a chance to respond.

Getting Your Team to Write Wins and Challenges

Having rolled out this process several times now, it is always an iterative exercise. Teaching your team how to write good wins and challenges is the first obstacle, and while this section may help, it's a skill that you will all build over time. Just getting team members to write them in the first place can be a struggle. We've learned that the best way to roll this out is to pull off the bandage: just mandate it. In 6 to 12 months, review the outcomes to decide how it's going, and adjust as necessary.

It's important to be clear about *who* is expected to participate, the *format* you need, and *when* it must be done. If you waffle or express uncertainty as to whether this is a real thing or just an optional exercise, you'll lose your teams' attention and focus.

Set a day and time by which all updates need to come in (for example, every Wednesday by 3 p.m. EST). Set the expectation of who will provide the updates (we'll give some advice momentarily). Put out a template and show them where to save their updates. The more specific you can be about the process, the easier it will be for people to focus on the actual updates.

Some teams may complain about reporting at a time that doesn't match their current sprint cadence. But having to adjust your sprints by a week is not a major hardship, and the value this process creates is worth the inconvenience. Some teams may not run on a biweekly cadence; others might not have major updates for a while (you may see this during holidays). That's all OK! Cadence conflict isn't a good reason not to roll this out.

Who should write the updates?

The person accountable for execution and delivery on the teams should be the one responsible for making sure updates are written and for sharing the most impactful updates more broadly. Most of the time, we think, this should be engineering managers. Line managers should gather updates from the engineers on their teams and share them with directors, who will aggregate them and share them with the VP (by which we mean someone managing an organization of 100+ engineers), who selects highlights to share with their peers and boss. Product management team members and managers may play a role in drafting and editing updates, but engineering managers are responsible for making sure the final product represents their teams' most important work and challenges.

When the team is small, it is tempting for the most senior manager to do all of the aggregation and editing themselves. Reading the list of possible updates is an incredible window into what's going on with the team, and as you ask questions and edit the updates, you teach your team what is valuable to communicate and how to present the information. But like every process that depends on one key person, your process will eventually break if you are the only person who is allowed to do it. So, do it yourself if it makes sense, but when you're on vacation, give the responsibility to someone else. As your team grows, look for more opportunities to involve others in the final product.

Who should receive the updates?

Within the platform team, skip managers should review the Wins and Challenges across their managers. The VP should make sure that the highlights from each skip manager are visible to all skip managers, and may review them in staff meetings as applicable.

More importantly, the VP sends the high-level highlights to their peers, stakeholders, and boss, usually by email. Writing Wins and Challenges for platform team use only goes so far; if you want to get real value, share them outside the organization. Teams should view showing up in the Wins as a mark of honor; this encourages the kind of impact-focused culture that we all want to develop in our organizations. Publishing these Wins and Challenges broadly makes it clear to everyone that the platform team is working on important projects, delivering incrementally against its goals, and providing leverage to the business.

Wrapping Up

If you're feeling a bit daunted after reading this chapter, we don't blame you. There's a lot of detail implicit in what we have suggested here. It's hard to get teams to write good project proposals, design docs, and action plans. Many managers get very stressed when trying to estimate the cost of operating their platform, and they may not have confidence that they have enough delivery to communicate on a biweekly cadence.

We don't suggest that you tackle all of this at once. Pick the options that seem most relevant. It's easier to start a Wins and Challenges communication process when your team is in execution mode, rather than in the middle of planning.

If you manage a single area or team, think about how you might estimate your team's baseline "required" work—your KTLO work. The easiest way is to observe what is happening. In any given week or month, how much of the available engineering time is spent on KTLO and how much on moving the product forward, designing something new, or doing research? You don't have to be perfectly accurate down to the hour; the goal is to quantify the capacity you have for investment so that, at planning time, you have a better sense of the team's ability to take on new things.

Teaching teams to write good documentation takes time. This is an exercise that the staff engineers can and should own, with managers assisting with the work estimations. Those same staff engineers (or perhaps SREs) are the right people to evaluate the state of things in support of incremental changes and advise on what, if anything, might be worth doing to move that forward.

Some pieces of work are easy to break down and important enough to prioritize, no matter what time of year it is. Leave some slack in your schedule for this work. For the big initiatives, get into the habit of going through the design documentation process. This has a way of separating the wheat from the chaff: it helps you distinguish the serious ideas with a high chance of success from the shiny but low-value ideas that aren't worth the effort of writing up a plan. In the rare case where you find yourself with more high-quality proposals than your current capacity can handle, you can use this to justify a request for growth—or, better yet, look for synergies between proposals and see how you might address common needs.

Finally, don't forget to provide transparency to your important stakeholders about what your team is delivering. Combining these planning practices with agile delivery and striving to produce incremental value at all times is a mindset shift that separates good platform teams from exceptional ones. This is hard work, but to gain recognition and reward for your efforts your stakeholders need to know about the great work that you're doing, which ultimately helps you earn the trust and respect of the organization.

CHAPTER 8

Rearchitecting Platforms

If you don't end up regretting your early technology decisions, you probably overengineered.
—Randy Schoup

In Chapter 5, we described a process for delivering new platforms: start small, partner with a few select customers, and make sure you're building something that has broad utility for your customer base through incremental delivery. In Chapter 7, we outlined our practices for roadmap planning beyond your product roadmap, helping you balance investments in KTLO work and new features with system improvements to enhance operational efficiency, scalability, security, and more. This all sounds great: you start small, gain momentum, and keep things moving smoothly by regular investment in system maintenance as well as features. What could go wrong?

Even when following this process perfectly, you can still hit a wall. As the system load increases, it begins to experience more operational issues, despite your incremental system investments. The KTLO work grows as the load increases, which in turn lowers the team's capacity to deliver either system improvements or new features. Eventually, the best software developers leave—not because of burnout, but because of frustration over the lack of progress. Crucial infrastructure becomes frozen in time, remaining critical for the business but no longer able to support new capabilities.

Why don't incremental system improvements prevent this situation? The issue is that while these improvements have the highest short-term benefits for scaling the system, their narrow focus means they struggle to address deeper shortcomings in the system's architecture.

The word "architecture" can sometimes evoke negative connotations: endless meetings debating irrelevant details that are impractical to implement and disconnected from the day-to-day of building and operating systems. Even so, we all know that some system architectures handle scale better than others—whether it's scaling for operational load, feature breadth, users, or the number of people working on the system. With continual growth in any of these areas, a system's architecture will eventually become the bottleneck.

This is why we embrace an approach we call *rearchitecture*, which is an iterative process of reimplementing a system's architecture while it remains live and continues to serve load. This differs from a v2 approach, where a new system with a different architecture and feature set is created to replace the original, requiring customers to migrate from v1 to v2.

We'll start this chapter by making the case for why rearchitecture is a better approach than building a v2. Then we'll talk about a growing focus of platform architecture: how to improve the security profile of your applications. Next, we'll explore the first step of succeeding with rearchitectures, looking at the technical aspects of establishing guardrails that allow larger system changes to succeed. We'll finish with the management aspects of rearchitectures—how to plan for something that shows incremental value throughout its multiyear delivery.

Rearchitectures might seem like a sign that you failed to build the right thing, but we prefer to see them as evidence that you have a successful platform supporting a growing business, and now you have the opportunity to evolve in the face of this success. With that, let's dive in.

Why Rearchitecting Is Preferred to Building a v2

You have a platform that's underarchitected for the scale it needs to handle. Are you better off creating a newly architected system from scratch with a "greenfield" approach, or rearchitecting the current system with a "changing the plane's engine as it's flying" approach? It may seem like it should be easier to build the right thing from scratch than to make complex changes to a system that's already handling critical load. However, we believe that rearchitecting is ultimately the right approach, due to the challenges of designing and delivering a v2 within your typical platform engineering team culture.

Let's start with the well-known phenomenon of the *second-system effect*, first observed in 1964.[1] A team that has only ever built one version of a system tends to assume that they can correct for every deficiency the second time around.[2] Their v2 design grows and grows in reaction to all the flaws they perceive in the v1. Management responds

---

1 The phrase was introduced by Fred Brooks in his 1975 book *The Mythical Man-Month* (Addison-Wesley).

2 It's important to note that Brooks recommends hiring people who have at least two of this type of system under their belts in order to avoid this problem; indeed, we find that when you have people on your team who have gone through a big system design a few times you are less likely to end up trying to build a new v2 in the first place!

---

to the expanded scope by adding more people to the team, which just adds to the project's complexity and slows down delivery. Ultimately, these systems often fail to ship and get canceled. For those that do ship, they may find their users have moved on or found workarounds and no longer need or want the new offering.

We believe the second-system effect is real, but there's more to it than the engineering hubris that comes from having only one success under your belt. After all, there are plenty of hubristic engineers working on all stages of systems, not just v2s!

Rather, we believe that by coupling the problem of defining a new product with the problem of building a scaled architecture to support complex business demands, we're asking the engineering team to successfully hold three different mindsets at once:

- The mindset that iterates to create a useful product out of nothing but an ambiguous need, building a scrappy architecture that puts aside longer term needs to deliver quickly (pioneers)
- The mindset that builds an architecture to handle rapid scaling of load and business criticality (settlers)
- The mindset that builds a robust, cost-efficient architecture to handle a diverse and conflicting set of requirements that are all critical to the business (town planners)

In the next sections we describe these mindsets further and show how they are each equipped to handle different architectural needs of a platform at different levels of scale and maturity. We will argue why a rearchitecture approach is the most optimal way to eventually get to platforms that deliver a lot of business value, with an architecture that supports the scale of delivery.

Different Engineering Mindsets

The idea that there are different "right" styles of engineering is not a novel idea. One model was proposed by Simon Wardley, who describes three engineer types working on the same successful technical business as it evolves over its lifetime of growth: pioneers, settlers, and town planners. Each is motivated differently in the face of a problem with ambiguous value and requirements, which means they make different trade-offs in the robustness of what is built. According to Wardley's blog post "On Pioneers, Settlers, Town Planners and Theft" (*https://oreil.ly/M5oBQ*):

> Pioneers are brilliant people. They are able to explore never before discovered concepts, the uncharted land. They show you wonder but they fail a lot. Half the time the thing doesn't work properly. You wouldn't trust what they build. They create "crazy" ideas....

Settlers are brilliant people. They can turn the half baked thing into something useful for a larger audience. They build trust. They build understanding. They make the possible future actually happen. They turn the prototype into a product, make it manufacturable, listen to customers and turn it profitable. Their innovation is what we tend to think of as applied research and differentiation....

Town Planners are brilliant people. They are able to take something and industrialise it taking advantage of economies of scale. This requires immense skill. You trust what they build. They find ways to make things faster, better, smaller, more efficient, more economic and good enough.

Wardley categorizes them as different types of people, but since this falls along a spectrum, and we think people can (somewhat) change, we prefer to call them "mindsets." However, we concur with his view that it's hard for an individual to adopt multiple mindsets at once, and we think this is even more true for teams. That's because the mindsets focus on very different aspects of a problem, resulting in vastly different ideas of what "right" looks like. From the same blog post:

Each group innovates but innovation is not the same for each group i.e. the innovation of an entirely new activity is different to the feature differentiation of a product which is different from converting a product to a utility service. Unfortunately, despite being different forms of innovation that won't stop people pretending there's only one and it's all the same. Try not to do this.

Each group has different attitudes though aptitudes (e.g. broad skill description such as finance, engineering or marketing) might be the same. Engineering in the pioneering group is not the same as engineering in the town planners.

So, teams of different mindsets will waste a lot of time debating things at the technical and process levels that cannot be resolved without first agreeing on which mindset they should collectively be operating under (and accepting there might be some people on the team who are unable to be productive with that mindset).

Wardely's work describes all of this in the context of business products, but we think it directly maps to platforms and how they are architected.

Architectural Needs Drive Mindset Demands

A way of thinking about system architecture is as the fundamental design decisions that will forever constrain the system's capabilities, even as individual components of the system are improved. In the previous chapter, we introduced three categories of a system's operational capabilities: efficiency, reliability, and security. A system's architecture will make some types of improvements in these areas, if not impossible, at least prohibitively expensive. A classic example is using a relational database to store large "blobs" as if it was S3. While you can scale it up vertically as your data volume and throughput increase, it's expensive. Eventually even that scaling can become impossible, and the architecture will have to change.

Beyond efficiency, reliability, and security, there is a fourth category of system capability that can force a rearchitecture: features. Some feature requests are so substantial, the only way to implement them is with a different architecture. A classic example is when you offer a key/value store, but your customers need it to provide transactional SQL write semantics. This feature request challenges the original system architecture assumptions so much that the only way to tackle it is through a different architecture.

In Table 8-1, we show how the requirements in these four categories typically change as a platform scales and matures, meaning it needs to handle more load, more features, and increasing system requirements. To do this, we nominate three points of system maturity that directly relate to the three engineering mindsets we just discussed. In the following section, we will argue why this leads to a rearchitecture approach.

Table 8-1. Model of architectural maturity, mapping changing requirements to different types of engineering mindsets

	Scrappy platform	Scalable platform	Robust platform
Business needs			
Feature delivery	"Agile." Frequent revision as ambiguity in customer needs is resolved and the values of features are better defined.	Balancing big customers becoming timeline- and quality-driven, versus smaller applications wanting agility.	New and small customers want agility, but are told to wait behind large customers who want certainty that things they require will be done on time.
Reliability	Low. Usually applications themselves are young, meaning users have higher tolerance for outages.	Operational rigor. Established applications now have higher requirements. New onboarders have lower requirements, which creates tension as they want the platform to move faster on features.	Metric-driven. Usually a three nines baseline, five nines desired. Measured on a per-customer basis, at least for the big customers.
Security	Low. Usually applications are assumed to "do the right thing."	Paved paths limit impact of mistakes by application engineers.	Secure by design. Assumes there will be compromises, so engineers/systems cannot be trusted with ad hoc access to production data.
Efficiency	Usually an afterthought given the system's lack of scale	Optimizing performance for dominant loads	Optimizing system-wide efficiency with a focus on dollars saved
Leads to			
Focus of platform team	Customer collaboration around feature delivery to enable growth	Investment in scalability to keep up with growth	Forward planning to simultaneously maximize security, reliability, efficiency, and on-time delivery
Optimal mindset	Pioneer	Settler	Town planner

Why It Is Hard to Build v2 Platforms, but Possible to Rearchitect

With this model defined, we can better understand the challenges for delivering a v2. There are two core issues:

- A v2 brings with it many changes beyond the underlying architecture, as the team tries to correct for past sins in the design while also adding significant new functionality. This makes it a fundamentally high-risk operation, no matter how agile and brilliant your engineers and product managers are.

- The platform organization is operating mostly scalable and robust systems, and the culture of their teams is likely to be aligned to the settler or town planner mindset. This is in direct conflict with the mindset needed to build a greenfield product with ambiguous requirements in an agile "move fast and break things" manner.

Rearchitectures, while still extremely challenging, do not have these specific issues:

- A rearchitecture has natural limits to the change it can offer, particularly if the rearchitected system is incrementally delivered within the logical construct of the existing platform. By limiting the amount of customer-visible change we make during a rearchitecture, we constrain ourselves to fixing the system architecture without adding on a bunch of bells and whistles; by doing it within the platform, we force ourselves to think carefully about the change approach itself to minimize the risk and impact to customers.

- There are plenty of customer considerations to successfully delivering a rearchitecture, but they aren't the kinds of concerns that require a strong pioneer mindset. The work lends itself well to settlers especially, as it requires a balance of rigor and agility to pull off in a reasonable time frame.

This is why we recommend a rearchitecture approach, shifting the mindset of the team as the architectural capabilities need to be rebuilt for more scale and robustness, as shown in Figure 8-1.

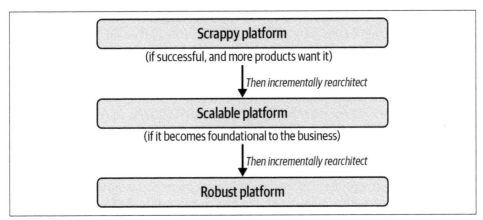

Figure 8-1. How a platform is successfully rearchitected over time

Getting Pioneer Agility on Robust Platforms

You might be wondering, "What about partnering with pioneers on customer teams, like you suggested in Chapter 5?" After all, even if you buy the model of mindsets and architectural maturity, it still doesn't help you with sudden technology shifts that force major platform capability expansion. When you have robust platforms owned by teams of town planners, there will still be times when the business discovers a major new feature need that should be provided by the platform organization. Examples here include moving from data centers to the public cloud, or embracing generative AI capabilities. It could be tied to market opportunities as well; for example, standing up a full application stack on a new cloud provider.

In any case, you need to move quickly, and you not only have complex foundational platforms that make it hard, but also have a team whose mindset is not aligned with fast iteration. Is the only solution to allow the application teams to build shadow platforms? That seems very costly if you are doing it across a suite of existing platforms.

A better approach is allowing the pioneers to start building shadow platform capabilities, but be clear that their best ideas, once established, will get integrated into existing platforms. This sounds like a free lunch, but avoiding the "two platforms" outcome requires a great deal of work by the platform leaders—managers, product managers, and staff engineers. That's because both the pioneers and their early customers will get attached to the early capabilities of their new systems (especially speed of iteration). When you decide to integrate, you can end up making everyone unhappy in the short term—customers, the pioneer engineers, and even the existing platform's engineers, who often get stuck with integrating the "mess" the pioneers built.

We experienced this firsthand when we worked for a platform organization that was years away from fully supporting the public cloud, with application teams starting to demand the elastic compute capabilities that only the public cloud could offer. We staffed a small "Public Cloud Platform" team with pioneers and asked them to embed within the application teams that had specific cloud demands. We tasked them with integrating those application teams into the existing platforms, but stressed that moving fast was more important than doing it right, so some mess was fine.

The pioneers did exactly as asked: they got the application teams onto the cloud quickly, but they also made a mess. This was less about the quality of their code, and more that they didn't put a lot of thought into how they would eventually integrate wider use cases into existing platforms, including overstepping boundaries of existing platform capabilities with "similar but different" functionality. As leaders, we were responsible for easing the tension between this pioneering team and the existing platform teams by communicating a plan to integrate the two eventually, even though the timeline was unclear.

After about 18 months of delivery from the pioneer team, we had to follow through on that plan. The pioneers were now turning their duplicate capabilities into full duplicate platforms. They argued that these new platforms were better, but they had no chance of supporting existing use cases without massive migrations. So, we transitioned the new systems into the existing platforms, emphasizing that it was the platform teams' job to integrate, and then scale up. We offered the pioneers a chance to move with their systems, but were not surprised when most instead found new green fields. Yes, there was some grumbling on both sides, but by showing that we recognized and appreciated the abilities and contributions on both sides, in the end we achieved a smooth transition.

Addressing Security with Architecture

Earlier in this chapter, we listed four major capabilities to think about in a rearchitecture: reliability, features, efficiency, and security. These are all hard, but security is the hardest. It's a deep enough field on its own to have specialists: security engineers. But the collaboration between security engineers and platform teams is challenging, especially when it comes to how their architectures and product choices enable a better overall risk posture. This is a massive loss because, as the world gets more threatened by the oversights that lead to big breaches, platforms that offer "security out of the box" to all application teams could create enormous value for business.

With that in mind, we asked Kelly Shortridge, author of *Security Chaos Engineering* (O'Reilly), to summarize what she would most emphasize in building security resilience into platforms. What follows is from Kelly.

While we cannot prevent cybercriminals from attacking, there are ways we can outsmart them and diminish their harm. We can architect our platforms to prepare our software systems for intrusion, applying the same platform engineering principles we use to sustain reliability, efficiency, and feature delivery to outmaneuver attackers and create better security outcomes.

In my book, I call this a *resilience* approach, meaning security initiatives align with organizational objectives like sustaining growth, satisfying customers, and innovating. Resilience is the ability for a system to adapt its functioning in response to changing conditions, so it can continue operating successfully. Instead of attempting to prevent failure, try to minimize the impact of failure. Rather than imposing awareness training, invest in your ability to change on demand—that is, invest in adaptive capacity—so you can stay nimble like attackers and outmaneuver them (with the added benefit of outmaneuvering your market competition, too).

The best security strategies share the same goal: to ensure the business can succeed and achieve its goals despite the presence of cyberattackers. These strategies do not insist that application engineers must contort and become "security aware." Instead, the best security strategies treat system design as their highest leverage point, trying to infuse security into the platform's features and architecture until it slips into invisibility.

A modern approach to cybersecurity therefore involves designing, building, and operating platforms that enable adaptation, enforce secure configurations, and make the safer way the faster and easier way. This approach should be owned by a team that can develop and deliver software, maintain platforms at scale, and understand system context—all things at which platform engineering teams excel. Adopt the mindset that security is a major facet of platform maturity and invest in building patterns, tools, and frameworks that cultivate resilience capabilities.

Don't try to revolutionize your platforms overnight to be "secure." Instead, iteratively rearchitect them, selecting the security opportunities that best align with your priorities, constraints, and context.

Let's dig into what we mean by rearchitecting a system to sustain resilience.

Platform Architecture to Reduce Security Hazards

As a platform team, resilience helps you sustain security outcomes (and their underlying properties) over time. How can architecture help you gracefully adapt to attacks (or other failures) and conserve your application engineers' cognitive capacity for healthier activities than hypervigilance? Careful platform design can mean that, when an adverse scenario erupts, the system doesn't require human interaction to continue fulfilling its duty. This outcome is what the cybersecurity industry refers to as "security by design."

Like birds sewing strands of spider silk into their nests, you can weave security capabilities into your platform architecture to enrich its flexibility and resilience—allowing you to preserve your customer applications' success against hazards, and stretch to nurture fresh growth. These security capabilities are not the ones that come to mind first, like a firewall or antivirus agent. Rather, you want to imitate the songbirds who select resilient, flexible patterns and materials for nests that can withstand turbulence without active intervention.

To invest in security by design, you can rearchitect your systems to eliminate or reduce hazards—potential sources of harm that include the characteristics of your technology as well as human actions or inactions.

Design-based security solutions feature two key traits:

- They do not depend on human behavior.
- They provide substantial separation of the user from the hazard.

When you eliminate hazards, you excise things or activities that can produce harm—for example, rewriting a component into a memory-safe language. When you reduce hazards, you curtail what can cause harm, even if you don't entirely eliminate all the hazardous things or activities—for example, standardizing an authentication component.

Through the lens of resilience and eliminating hazards, you can reduce the application team's choices to those that:

- Minimize the potential impact of failure
- Minimize the degree of human intervention required to circumnavigate hazards
- Preserve possibilities for growth and innovation

Most of the security solutions within that nexus also offer benefits across the other architecture capabilities: feature delivery, reliability, and efficiency. Let's consider a few examples of patterns created by platform engineering teams that not only help sustain resilience against attack, but nourish other dimensions of success:

- *Automated testing tools* let application development teams focus on their application's behavior—and validating that behavior—so they are not mired in tool selection and customization; if devs don't fiddle with their tools, they can dedicate time to writing tests that improve security outcomes (integration tests, in particular, can catch the interactions between components that attackers love to exploit).

- *Standardized deployment tooling*, especially infrastructure as code, lets application teams focus on building software rather than the challenges of deploying it. A special focus is cleanup; when IaC automatically removes outdated infrastructure, you eliminate the drift, data exposure, and attack paths wrought by stale systems.

- *Configuration management patterns* let application teams focus on building software rather than managing configurations between environments. These patterns also simplify instantiation and destruction of environments, vanquish data sharing between stages of the development workflow, and temper engineers' tendency to pull production data into systems with widespread access.

- *Token and secrets management systems* allow application teams to build systems without worry for how they will safely handle access keys; they also avoid application teams building systems that mishandle the "fissile material" that is secret keys and access tokens.

- *Standardized observability tooling* (especially distributed tracing) allows incident responders to trace operations as they flow between systems, imparting a holistic perspective critical for understanding the behavior of complex systems. More vantage points mean more opportunities to spot unwanted activity before it festers or cascades, and standardization minimizes the toil of data plumbing, the potential for mistakes, and the propensity for silos.

- *Standard service and web frameworks* let engineers focus on delivering business value without the stress of figuring out how to safely package and shuttle data to end users; with appropriate choices, application engineers won't have to think about cross-site request forgery (XSRF), cross-site scripting (CSS), cross-origin resource sharing (CORS), or cookie management.

- *Common authentication/authorization middleware* lets application engineers "plug and play" components and assume that their service will properly validate traffic; the alternative is a DIY approach that foments disaster at scale when teams introduce inconsistencies between how services validate access.

- *Compute platforms with declarative access control* let application teams focus on building services and declaring how they should communicate with specific peers, rather than managing network and computing infrastructure themselves; this prevents departments from creating "infrastructure islands" where all teams share access, avoiding the overly permissive access that attackers could exploit.

- *Tenant-isolated architectures* simplify implementation and performance concerns for engineers, letting them build features without fretting about limiting all operations to the tenant that is accessing the service. Even in the presence of most security failures, this isolation removes attackers' ability to gain access to another tenant's data.

These kinds of patterns help you invest in speedy, safe change—exactly what you need to outmaneuver attackers. But how do you identify which opportunities to pursue first in your organization? And how do you implement these patterns in practice?

Use Paved Paths to Make Applications Secure by Default

We want to make the resilient way the path of least resistance—not just secure by design, but by default. When you implement resilience by default, it means developers must opt *out* of the safe option. You "nudge" them toward your desired outcome but allow room for exceptions. To provide a physical-world example, newer cars lock by default when you walk away with the keys. Your software equivalent might take the form of default service templates using infrastructure as code: you can use automation to demolish unused infrastructure and remove it as an attack path.

A popular name for these "least-resistant" paths is paved paths: well-integrated, supported solutions to common problems that allow humans to focus on their distinct value creation. By blessing certain options by default—and, importantly, making the resilient way the easier way—you endorse standardization and reduce choice overload. You construct a more resilient default for the organization, even when some teams opt out.

How do you prioritize candidates for architecting security into your platforms? Much like you desire in the context of reliability, you want to offload as much security "toil" from your customers as you can. When helping organizations prioritize what patterns, tools, and paved paths to build, I encourage them to ask questions like:

- What security checks or tasks fall on application teams to complete at each stage of software delivery?
- What security mechanisms are standard requirements in software?
- Are there security checklists application engineering teams must complete before deployment?
- What security incidents or near-misses have been blamed on "human error" recently?

As inspiration for your next strategy brainstorm, here are some high-level categories of paved paths I've seen organizations create to successfully solve cybersecurity problems for application teams while improving reliability, efficiency, or feature delivery at the same time:

- API protection—XSRF protection, security header validation, rate limiting, tarpitting and throttling, IP geofencing, distributed denial of service (DDoS) protection, and web application firewall (WAF) integration
- Authentication and authorization
- Caching compliance and static asset caching

- Certificate management and secure network protocols
- Static and dynamic analysis tooling
- Automated testing frameworks—fuzzing, penetration tests, resilience stress tests (i.e., chaos experiments), smoke tests

Application engineering's security fate relies on the platforms underlying their code. Platform engineering teams can achieve substantial leverage by designing platforms with resilience in mind. If you invest in opportunities that minimize the potential impact of attacks (or other failures), minimize the human heroism required to reduce hazards, and enable nimble changes to preserve possibilities, you can shepherd your organization's ongoing success despite the ongoing danger of attackers.

Guardrails for Rearchitectures

For rearchitecting to succeed, you need to minimize the disruption for existing users—ideally so they don't even notice the change. This is a challenge; scrappy platforms are not built with major changes to their underlying architecture in mind, and if you try to make big changes without thinking through the user impact, you can burn a lot of goodwill with those existing customers. Now is the time to think about the guardrails you need to implement in order to lower the cost of change for both your team and its users.

Compatibility

Backward compatibility breaks can kill, and they are exceptionally deadly for multi-tenant platforms. Ideally, you'll never make a backward-breaking change to your API, but when it is unavoidable, treat it as a major version upgrade to a new API. Instead of making a backward-breaking change in one go, introduce the change as a new API, and give your users a long lead time to migrate to the new API before turning off and eventually deleting the old one.

Think about how many versions of the system you want to have live in production at any time. Having many versions supported at once means you can release new versions more quickly, but it also means that the space of compatibility you have to think about with every release grows. If you know that you will never have more than one prior version's compatibility to worry about, you can reason much more clearly about the new code you're writing.

Testing

These days, developers like to brag about testing in production using capabilities like feature flagging or shadow deployments. But when you are releasing foundational infrastructure platforms that people rely on to run core business applications, it is not acceptable to trade delivery speed for even slight perturbations in quality or performance. To support frequent, safe releases, you need to invest in robust testing processes.

For internal platforms, you may have the ability to run full integration test environments with your own users' dependent tests executed as part of the test suite. In companies with large monorepos, this is a common tactic to catch user code breaks early in the development cycle. Even without a monorepo, having a thorough integration testing suite with user-submitted tests is a good strategy for catching some of the integration problems early. Adoption of modern testing methods such as property-based testing (*https://oreil.ly/RcVJ-*) and fuzzing is another powerful approach to identifying failure that doesn't require a fully provisioned simulation environment.

Finally, in Chapter 6, we covered the importance of deep synthetic monitoring. Indeed, when Ian was at AWS, his teams invested so much in synthetic monitoring that it often supplanted functional integration testing—why wouldn't you want the same thing testing your new builds against their complex dependencies in the production environment? But this is not the same thing as YOLO[3] production testing ("we'll just roll it back quickly if we see it break"). If you want to go down this route, you need solid shadow/canary deployments and the ability to ensure that only synthetic monitoring gets scheduled to the new deployment until it passes monitor testing.

Lower Environments

Assuming you have a separate non-production environment for supporting your customers' pre-production testing, you can also use this environment as part of your validation strategy. Once you have vetted changes with your own testing, using this environment for a final pre-release test will give you thorough integration testing as customers run their applications' pre-release vetting on top of your release candidates.

It's important to be careful with this approach; your customers deserve to have high-quality testing, staging, and pre-release support as much as they need high-quality production platforms. If you are regularly releasing broken systems to lower environments because you have not invested in sufficient planning and testing of your changes before this step, go back and invest more into those processes to ensure that your testing is catching fewer issues. But as long as the pre-release environment is kept reasonably stable, it is far better to "test in pre" than "test in prod" by getting real feedback through this early staged launch.

---

3 You only live once.

Tranches, Slow Rollouts, and Staying a Version Behind

Finally, all of those good practices from modern release management of product features apply: canary releases, slow rollouts to tranches of machines, releasing to subsets of customers, beta releases. These all play a role in getting your platform changes safely to production without creating massive failures.

For internal platforms, there is also some wisdom in staying a little bit behind the latest, greatest OSS releases for the underlying infrastructure. This is especially true if you're at a small company, have highly sensitive infrastructure, or have limited money to invest in serious infrastructure testing and validation—let the OSS community test and update on the newest release before you adopt. Just don't be so late adopting that you are essentially "out of window" for community support and miss out on security patches.

Planning for Rearchitectures

A common reason that necessary rearchitectures don't happen is that they get stuck in the planning phase and never get "funded." Your lead engineer analyzes the problems with the current architecture and writes a detailed plan of what new architecture is needed to support the next level of platform maturity. An architectural review confirms that there is alignment from engineering on what needs to be built. It looks like things should be ready to start.

But when you do your annual planning math (as we laid out in Chapter 7), you realize this would cut into your feature budget too much. You need additional headcount if the rearchitecture is to happen, but leadership wants the new headcount to go to new business initiatives, and even when platform leadership gets some budget, it turns out every platform team has its own rearchitectures ready to pitch—so management spreads the budget around, leaving no team with enough headcount to get its rearchitecture off the ground.

The most frustrating outcome is when you get told "let's wait until next year," spend the next 12 months scraping away with incremental system improvements to keep the old architecture operating at a scale it wasn't built for, and then come back in the next round of planning with what you think is an even stronger case for why the rearchitecture is needed—but it backfires because leadership views your demonstrated ability to scrape by as evidence that a rearchitecture is not actually needed!

Is there a path out? Not in all cases. There are many platforms with lots of architectural problems that do not make sense to rearchitect, because the eventual benefits are not high enough when weighed against the costs and risks to get there. But we have also seen many cases where this is what a team assumes, but a deeper analysis of value shows that an incremental rearchitecture investment is worth it. This is the planning framework we use to understand if that is the case:

1. *Think big on final rearchitecture goals.* Use a top-down approach to focus on all the ways a completed rearchitecture adds value to the business.

2. *Factor in migration costs.* Evaluate the migration costs that would be required.

3. *Determine major 12-month wins.* Find high-value needs that are much better when built in the new architecture and can be delivered much faster than full delivery.

4. *Get leadership buy-in, and be prepared to wait.* Finding the right combination of these can take iteration, including sometimes waiting in the hope that some better options come along.

We'll cover these in depth in the sections that follow.

Platform Antipattern: New Hires Leading the Rearchitecture

We want to call out an antipattern that we have seen platform teams fall into: letting newly hired engineers lead the rearchitecture of the platform. This is especially tempting when the new engineer has experience from a prior employer at the next level of platform maturity, and offers great insights in questioning the status quo. The problem is that, while it may be similar, the new architecture your organization needs is going to be different from what they experienced at their last company—but they won't be able to see that clearly, as they will lack a full understanding of the details of your current platform and the culture of your company, as well as established trust relationships with the major users of the platform.

So, in the short term, these new hires can aid your rearchitecture by giving feedback on your longer-tenured engineers' proposals. But to set up both the rearchitecture and the new hire for success, for their first 12 months they should limit themselves to giving such feedback and contributing, rather than leading big new initiatives themselves.

This can be a hard message for high achievers looking to build on their prior learnings and prove themselves, so remember to spend a lot of personal time in 1:1s in those first 12 months to show you are invested in their long-term success, giving them the right projects to quickly build both their understanding and their relationships.

Step 1: Think Big on Final Rearchitecture Goals

At this step, you should be using a planning window of roughly three to five years for full delivery, pushing for the very edge of what's possible. This is the step where lead engineers are often most excited. Finally, they get to sit down like a principal engineer and build (on paper) a better architecture that everyone will work toward. But you need to make sure their sights are set high. Yes, be wary of the "architecture astronauts" who get overly excited by visions of a future so extraordinary there's no way you could ever make it a reality. But not too wary—the later steps of the process are intended to filter those out. If the plan is to improve how your architecture scales for just one system capability like reliability, then you're not thinking big enough.

Look to all categories of system capability

Earlier we talked about the four categories of system capabilities, and a rearchitecture should strive to make *substantial* progress on all four. Questions to ask yourself in each category include:

Features
> What features with substantial business value could a new architecture enable that the existing architecture would struggle to ever support well?

Efficiency
> Can you make the new system substantially more cost effective on aggregate? Can you make the system perform much better for growing workloads, so better performance becomes like a feature, unlocking new application capabilities?

Reliability
> Can you make the system substantially less likely to have operational issues as it handles even more load than it does today?

Security
> Can you make the system substantially less likely to be breached, or substantially less costly to keep compliant?

Look at subsuming adjacent systems

Next, look to existing platforms or customer systems with capabilities adjacent to the platform's. Can you subsume *all* the requirements of any of these within the rearchitected platform, to reduce overall system complexity? In particular, look to similar systems that are significantly smaller, narrower, or growing slower, such as shadow platforms. This may be a chance to finally integrate them into a simpler whole.

Look to big bets around OSS and vendor systems

This complements the last two areas. Look everywhere you use OSS and vendor systems, and everywhere you have an in-house component that duplicates popular OSS and vendor systems. Explicitly ask yourself whether a big bet on a replacement unlocks significant new capabilities, particularly with a view that the new architecture will be with you for the next 5–10 years. The areas to investigate are:

- Replacing an existing OSS/vendor component with another system that will allow you not only to unlock new features but also to ride the wave of innovation around its ecosystem

- Replacing an OSS/vendor component with something developed in-house, so you can customize and optimize for your known use cases

There is a balance here. "Don't compete with open source" sounds like a wise engineering truism. But so too is "don't chase the shiny technology of today." In the following sidebar, we recount a story of when we had to evaluate such a case, and the framework we used for making the decision.

Evaluating a Big Bet on an OSS/Vendor Wave

One of the hardest architecture decisions you will face is when you have a developed platform with a decent amount of success, and then something with massive momentum in the open source or vendor world comes along. On the one hand, people will pressure you to offer the new thing, certain it will have massive upsides in capabilities as a new industry standard with far more investment than you can offer in-house. On the other hand, making the jump means you have to think about how to migrate your current users to the new thing, all with a risk that plenty of apparent next industry standards fail to achieve what everyone believed they were destined for.

We went through this conundrum at a former employer, where we had a Mesos-based compute platform running for about 20% of our total workload. Then Kubernetes came along, and quickly generated momentum and community excitement that was impossible to ignore.

We decided to take a big bet on it, based on three criteria:

1. *Adjacent business need for large investment in rearchitecture.* Containerization coincided with our move from on premises to the public cloud, which came with enough business value (and so headcount) that we knew that over the next five years we would have enough engineers on a rearchitecture project to ensure that the delivery and migration could be done well.

---

2. *Current platform had feature gaps in subsuming adjacent systems.* Mesos was great for the large-scale batch processes it managed, but it was clear that Kubernetes had more "out of the box" support for a broader range of tasks, and we would need this range to successfully containerize 100% of our workloads.

3. *Disparity in ecosystem trajectory.* We could see a lot more momentum in the Kubernetes ecosystem, from conference talks, conference sizes, startup vendors building their business on it, and even Google trends. We also failed to find any companies making new bets on Mesos—everyone in the "start from scratch" case was choosing Kubernetes.

At the time this was not an easy sell to all of our team, who found good reasons to want to invest in improving the platform they had already built—particularly as there were certain ways Mesos was better than Kubernetes. However, we saw the bet as worth the costs, and in hindsight this proved correct; Kubernetes has flourished, while Mesos has not.

We've talked to colleagues who had a different experience at other companies, though: their platform teams faced the same Mesos versus Kubernetes decision, and their bet on Kubernetes was wrong. This was because Mesos was already running almost all of their compute load, and they were already running on the public cloud, so the migration was more or less a costly sideways move.

How do you navigate these trade-offs and make a good bet when faced with a rising OSS core? If you're not meeting all the criteria (feature gaps, ecosystem trajectory, business value), be wary of rearchitecting around an external technology.

Step 2: Factor in Migration Costs

This step is the first counterbalance to thinking big. In Chapter 9, we'll go deep into all the considerations in executing a successful migration. At this point of thinking about a rearchitecture, you need to plan for a plan, and include that in your rearchitecture proposal.

Many great rearchitecture proposals fall apart due to the migration costs they will eventually inflict. Or rather, we should say "should" fall apart, because too often we have seen teams and leaders get caught up in their big dreams of the future and wave their hands at what it means for existing customers to migrate to it. We've seen proposals where only after we asked, "How will existing customers move to it?" did the team consider the migration implications. When they did that analysis, it became clear that the proposed changes would require hundreds of development years to complete—for example, migrating millions of lines of RDBMS-based code to a key/value store, or migrating years' worth of data-processing scripts off of processing from a POSIX filesystem and onto an S3-type object store.

When your engineers are out of touch with business reality, ask a product manager or engineering manager to help you see whether the migration costs of your plan are reasonable. Finding the right balance between costs and benefits can depend on how necessary the long-term rearchitecture wins are, but if you're not factoring the cost of migration into your proposal then you're missing a big part of the picture and risk losing support for your plan.

Step 3: Determine Major 12-Month Wins

So you have a think-big rearchitecture proposal with reasonable migration costs. Time to start, right? Unfortunately, you have more planning to do first. Most rearchitectures take three to five years, and there are going to be many changes in technology and the business over that period. It's too risky if the business will only start to see value toward the end of that timeline. You need to deliver substantial value much sooner than that, partly because of the business risk that if stakeholders have to wait years to see results, politics could kill the project in the meantime, but also because the think-big hypothesis itself has a risk of being wrong, and the best way to validate it sooner is actually shipping something.

We like 12 months as a cycle time for these deliveries, because it's normal for business planning and it gives enough time to deliver a partial implementation that still has substantial value. To find potential projects, a good approach is having the lead engineer partner with the product manager to dig into the product backlog for high-value features that were previously deemed "too hard" given the current architecture. You are looking for three things:

- You can deliver them in 12 months as a partial implementation of the new architecture.
- They show off capabilities of the new architecture.
- You can get a commitment from the stakeholders of at least one application team to partner with you to immediately leverage the new features in their application.

All three of these conditions can be hard to satisfy, but the third is usually the hardest. Often those close to the business can't be sure enough of their roadmaps to be confident they can commit to you. Even when they recognize the potential long-term business value, there is a chance that short-term priorities might crowd it out.

This uncertainty is an inevitable part of trying to build high-value things in a changing business environment. The best way we have found to mitigate it is not to lower the goal of seeking something high in value. Rather, we think about having three goals that are accomplishable with the same initial work:

- Goal 1: Something audacious that moves the needle for the chosen business
- Goal 2: Something smaller that still adds substantial new value to a business (potentially a different one from Goal 1), which the old architecture could not have done
- Goal 3: Getting the new architecture components in production and serving some amount of real customer load

You aim for Goal 1, but you know you have Goal 2 as your first fallback. Thus, you have given yourself two ways (and ideally two partners) to demonstrate the business value of the rearchitecture. Then, should something unforeseen happen (on either your side or the customers'), you can still fall back to Goal 3, getting the new components in production and serving load.

This is all to avoid the "long slog" type of outcome we talked about in the previous chapter. Within a three- to five-year rearchitecture project, this is the step that should be repeated every year—resetting with new goals, new partners, and the next phase of the rearchitecture. If a team cannot deliver any incremental value in a 12-month time frame (i.e., no part of the rearchitecture is in production taking real load), a hard question to address is whether you've learned anything from this delivery failure. Is this rearchitecture really worth it, or are you falling victim to the second-system effect?

Step 4: Get Leadership Buy-in, and Be Prepared to Wait

Platform organizations usually have several rearchitectures to consider at once. Growing businesses will have more than one "legacy" platform[4] built by earlier pioneers, and each one could use rearchitecture work to make it more reliable, efficient, or secure, or give it new features.

Further, when platforms cause operational and support burdens, it is common for teams to want to forgo the incremental systems improvements we recommended in the previous chapter, and instead go all-in on replacing everything as fast as possible. The title of Marianne Bellotti's book on managing aging computer systems and future-proofing modern ones, *Kill It with Fire* (No Starch Press), captures this sentiment as a knee-jerk approach that burns through money and engineering time.

---

4 At startups we've heard the term "legacy" applied to platforms that were less than six months old!

In a well-run organization, the platform organization's leadership must carefully evaluate whether a rearchitecture is the right thing to do, and whether it's the right time to do it. This is particularly the case when:

- The rearchitecture requires additional headcount or internal transfers.
- The rearchitecture demands substantial work from other teams, either in terms of migrations or integrating other platforms.
- The rearchitecture means that shorter-timeline improvements and features will be implemented more slowly or delayed indefinitely.
- The "audacious" business goal of the rearchitecture carries a lot of reputational risk for the platform team if not done well or not done on time.

None of these are reasons not to put forward such a plan. Just realize that you are going to need three to five years of focused investment to succeed, so you'll want leadership buy-in sooner rather than later. They will have to defend this plan to their own senior stakeholders and protect it through unexpected events like layoffs, reorganizations, or high-priority mandates. If a leader does not feel they were brought in to evaluate and commit to a project's value, it's unlikely they are going to risk their own reputation to defend it.

Given all of this, sometimes leaders will say "not at this time." That can be a tough blow. But remember, the costs here are large, and the future is unpredictable; there's no telling what new technologies and new opportunities for the business might appear. When faced with a proposal that promises a good-but-maybe-not-great business impact to justify starting a rearchitecture, the company may well be better off waiting for a great technology with great business impact.

Wrapping Up

No matter how much it improves a platform's security, reliability, efficiency, or feature delivery capabilities, investing in rearchitectures is expensive. Teams go wrong when they invest in too many at once, leading to a platform organization getting a reputation for "building systems for the sake of building systems." The previous section aimed to give you some tools to manage that risk; we will also provide some specific advice for leaders balancing multiple conflicting rearchitecture requests in Chapter 11.

That said, it's also a mistake to push back against the idea of doing rearchitectures at all, believing that technology trends drive massive waves of change every few years and so you should do nothing for now and hope the business allows you to ride the next one that comes along. This mindset is common in leaders with startup backgrounds, where business growth can drive relatively large investment in new platforms built on new technology, and each platform tends to be so much better than the last that existing teams are happy to migrate in order to capture the new benefits.

If you follow this approach, assuming you can always build a better v2 as the business grows, over time the challenge of migrations will start to dominate the discussion. Your new business-driven platform may not be the best replacement for all of your customers, and their enthusiasm for migrating to the newest offering will start to wane as the company grows and they get busy focusing on the demands of their own areas. Those pioneer-heavy teams that love to build new platforms don't think about how they will drive a reluctant customer base through a migration. Eventually you can find yourself in a scenario where you have five platforms in the same area, three of which you have deprecated with the other two not yet ready for robust production usage. We'll bet many of you are currently in this situation, and the next chapter will help you with the migration planning to dig yourselves out of it.

To avoid this outcome, invest in platform rearchitectures. Build guardrails so the business is not disrupted by their execution, and invest in them judiciously, where your confidence in the net benefits of the new technology are highest. Anything less is a poor platform product strategy.

CHAPTER 9

Migrations and Sunsetting of Platforms

A platform is meant to be the stable thing that provides an enduring surface to build on, like a foundation. Platform engineering requires building those stable foundations and not externalizing work onto the things that people build on top of it.

—C. Scott Andreas

The relentless pace of change creates an existential challenge for platform engineering teams. Your underlying systems are evolving all the time: there are regular patches and upgrades to keep up with security issues, vendor changes, hardware updates, and new features. End-of-life timelines for fundamental infrastructure systems, once spanning a decade (*https://oreil.ly/_nJs9*), have compressed to one to two years for cloud products like EKS (*https://oreil.ly/ghq0z*), increasing the frequency of upgrade disruption on application teams. Without a plan to manage the impact of these changes on application developers, platforms become a source of migration pain that outweighs their value.

We've mentioned migrations several times already in this book, and for good reason. In the face of this challenge, great platform teams realize that migrations are in fact an opportunity to prove their value. They see their job as easing the pain of mandatory migrations, limiting and even removing work so their customers can focus on delivering top-line features.

 For the purposes of this chapter, a migration is any mandatory change to your platforms that requires some work by the users in order to adopt. This is a spectrum from the most complex work of migrating physical locations (say, from one data center to another), to migrations due to code or systems upgrades that have backward-breaking API changes, to upgrades that may be in-place or nearly in-place but require acceptance testing from some users to ensure there are no regressions.

In this chapter, we share our advice for doing migrations right. First, we'll look at them from an engineering perspective, considering what you have to build into your platforms to make migrations as easy as possible for your customers. Next, we'll discuss best practices around coordination, and how to make your communication and execution as smooth as possible. Finally, we cover a migration to nothing—"sunsetting" a platform. We'll talk about how to handle the difficult case when your platform has customers, but it doesn't make sense to operate as a platform any more.

But before we get into doing them right, let's review some of the common antipatterns we have experienced during migrations.

Migration Antipatterns

For many engineers there's no dirtier term than "migration," and the bigger the company, the worse these migrations become. Despite executives promising after every painful migration that things will be better next time, we see these same antipatterns play out repeatedly:

Context-free deadlines
> If you've never experienced the random migration deadline handed down from on high, consider yourself lucky. The deadline might come from necessity (say, the end-of-life date for some essential piece of the stack), but it's often thrown out to teams with no discussion or appreciation for what others will have to defer in order to meet this deadline. Worse, somehow these deadlines are always short notice. It might be that the migration turned into a big deal only because everyone ignored it for months, but that doesn't make anyone feel much better about the deadline scramble.

Unclear requirements
> Too often, migration requests come with the expectation that every user understands exactly what they need to do. The team sends out a notice that starts with "If you're using Product X version Y or earlier…" and half of the users don't even know what Product X is, so they either ignore the notice or spend hours figuring out whether it applies to them, wasting everyone's time in the process.

Did anyone test this thing?
> A set of users is already stressed out, and then they try to migrate and the new offering just…doesn't work. Maybe it's just something they have to figure out, like upgrading performance-sensitive C++ code between operating system versions, but often it seems like the team that owns the platform just didn't think about how people were using it before kicking off the migration. There are gaps in the new offering, broken features, or a completely missing set of instructions for how to proceed. The platform team scrambles to get it fixed or work around the gaps, and in the process piles on tech debt just to make the deadline.

Clipboard-carrying scolds

Then there are the people tasked with chasing down users to make sure they did the migration work. This is a thankless job, and we're sure everyone who has found themselves in clipboard-carrying mode knows it. You have to push people to come to meeting after meeting and talk about whether they are on track, why not, and what it will take to get there. You may use "wall of shame" dashboards and reports that attempt to gamify the whole thing, but they just add to the stress, defensiveness, and frustration of those in the red (particularly when they have tried to migrate only to get blocked by missing or broken features!). Once you're at this point, brute-forcing yourself through the exercise, it's unlikely you have time to think about better ways to approach the problem.

Yes, there's a lot of hard up-front work that needs to be done to prepare clear requirements and test your migrations before asking your users to migrate. And yes, sometimes the only way to unblock a project is to create a context-free deadline and put people in place to enforce it. And when you've done as much up-front work as you can and the organizational inertia is still dragging the project down, deadlines and clipboards may be necessary as an option of last resort. Just remember they're the option of *last* resort, not the default approach.

Engineering Easier Migrations

Many human-oriented aspects need to be handled during migrations, but the first approach platform teams should use is an engineering one. Before you start on the communication planning, the inevitable program management, and the other rules and processes you might need to impose, think about the engineering you can do to ease migration pain now and in the future.

Tackle Migrations Early

Migrations start as an annoyance and grow into a strategic opportunity only when your company and software complexity reach a certain scale. At a smaller company, migrations are annoying, but you can often just lean on the goodwill of your colleagues and the hard work of a few scrappy engineers to drive them to completion. However, if you follow our advice and avoid building out a platform engineering team until you're a bit larger, migrations quickly become one of the biggest challenges. The scrappy get 'er done energy that worked when you had a few dozen engineers starts to break down when you have a few hundred. The engineering organization that wants to move as fast as it did when it was small must wrestle with all of the complexity that comes with time, scale, and success, and migrations become a growing source of frustration and anger for them.

Migration support should therefore be one of the first things you tackle with a new platform engineering team, especially if your company is growing quickly and you want to keep moving fast. By this we don't mean starting on the perfect rearchitecture to make future migrations cheap. We mean doing whatever scrappy work you can to make the next pressing migration as cheap as you can.

Use Product Abstractions That Minimize Glue and Limit Variation

In Chapter 1, we introduced our definition of "glue": the code, automation, and configuration built to hold a bunch of disparate systems together. Glue is OK in moderation, but the more glue that exists, the more work is required whenever one of the pieces needs to change. The problem is worst when every application team has created lots of it—platforms should limit the glue that each application team builds for itself over basic infrastructure and common services, because glue is the enemy of change.

If you have built a good platform abstraction, application teams will have minimal glue of their own to change during migration of the underlying components. If you have limited the number of versions of the same system you offer, you'll have less testing to perform when that system needs to change. The more you can standardize and limit variation, the fewer permutations you need to worry about during these changes.

Architect for Transparent Migrations

The easiest migration experience for your customer is one they not only don't have to do any work for, but never even see. As C. Scott Andreas says in this chapter's opening quote, a platform needs to provide an enduring surface for application teams to build on. An ideal platform provides a stable interface to the customer, allowing the platform team to execute the migrations with minimal to no customer impact. Pushing frequent migration work onto your customers undermines that value, and as the platform builder and operator, you can do better.

One way of doing this is with abstract APIs; however, back in Part I of the book, we warned of the folly of overinvesting in a pure "encapsulation" approach. Instead, we think transparent migrations are better achieved with a combination of judicious APIs and newer technologies that make it much easier to run multiple versions of your platform in production during the migration period, slowly and safely moving each customer's requests across as their clients are updated. These technologies include:

- Container-based packaging for fast, lightweight application deployment
- Autoscaling technologies that support changing the size of systems without restarting
- Deployment techniques such as canary and blue/green deployments, combined with advanced health monitoring to detect problems and roll back quickly

These practices make life easier for application teams deploying and scaling their software, but they also support platform teams' ability to manage and update the platform without disrupting the application developers. Yet, to take the most advantage of them, you may need to establish some agreements with your users up front. These agreements include:

Chaos testing and stability guarantees

If you want to do a blue/green upgrade, you need to be able to migrate workloads and eventually kill the old processes. However, if your users expect that the underlying system will never restart unless they tell it to, they won't be able to handle this unplanned change. To address this, we've had teams add an automatic chaos element to their managed Kubernetes offering, which randomly restarted customer nodes. This default offering[1] forced customers to detect and fix certain types of structural bugs, and got them used to operating applications in an environment where they did not have control over the underlying infrastructure and where infrastructure providers could restart their instances.

Acceptance tests

You want to know that your upgrade didn't break anything for your users, but how can you achieve this? One approach is to ask users to maintain a set of acceptance tests that you can run to validate that their applications work after a platform change. And of course, your platform team needs to have a thorough set of its own acceptance tests (ideally, a sample application that you own and operate) as the first pass for validation.

Maintenance windows

True, there's nothing "cloud native" about maintenance windows, but depending on the type of platform you are providing, you may need occasional planned downtime. If this is the case for your system, don't try to negotiate this ad hoc every time you need it. Create an up-front expectation of when maintenance downtime is allowed so that both your team and your users can plan for these disruptions.

---

1 Although the default, it could be turned off as necessary when running certain legacy systems that lacked strong cloud native architectures.

In "Guardrails for Rearchitectures" on page 185, we mentioned some of the practices that big technology companies use for testing and rolling out changes to their wider fleet of systems in order to minimize customer impact, and these practices also support this operator-driven migration model. At a small company you may not have the bandwidth to invest in these advanced guardrails, but understanding what a mature model looks like can provide some ideas for where you might go in the future. Any small investments you can make now, such as establishing maintenance windows and setting up your own sample application for acceptance testing, are valuable gifts to your future platform team (*https://oreil.ly/H6RCn*).

Do Monorepos Help with Migrations?

At some bigger tech companies, monorepos are a popular solution to managing changes to common code—and since everything is code in the end, this raises the question of how much they help with migrations. The nice part of having a monorepo is that you can see into code-level dependencies and can potentially make changes across the entire repository; platform teams can even change the customer code themselves when needed. In practice, this value is much higher for pure in-house library changes than it is for platform migrations more generally, for two reasons:

- Platforms usually have a service component, which means that any change that impacts the clients and APIs is not complete until all clients have redeployed. Because customer systems will not redeploy on your schedule, you will need to support multiple versions of your client and APIs in production.

- Platforms often have thick clients that depend on external code supplied by OSS and vendor systems. Changes to those libraries can have a broad impact on customer applications, which may use them directly for other purposes. This means changes become much more coupled, and thus more impactful and riskier. In the non-monorepo world, this can be managed by versioning internal clients. This can be done with monorepos as well, but that defeats the whole value of a monorepo for this purpose.

The value of monorepos for any company depends on both its culture and its other technology choices (see Chapter 5), but they are not a path to making most platform migrations significantly cheaper.

Track Usage Metadata

One of the trickiest parts of migrating systems is understanding dependencies. As you build more interconnected platforms, you need to know how applications use the different pieces across your platforms—for product metrics, as mentioned in Chapter 5, but also for operations, upgrades, and migrations. Building automatic asset tracking for technologies, deployments, and dependencies and creating graphs of the existing running infrastructure across your company can be extremely valuable in supporting more complex upgrades. This sort of automatic tracking is much easier to build as a smaller company than to backfill into an older, legacy environment.

Things to track include:

- Who is using the platform
- Which applications are using the platform, and which parts of it they are using
- Who owns those applications

Because it is platform-specific, we can't tell you every detail you might need to track for future upgrades. Our goal is to inspire you to think about this as part of the platform organization's work. Make sure you gather metadata about the state of the world, know what is deployed where, and understand how to tie code for deployments to people and teams—this is all powerful knowledge to collect early in your platform engineering journey.

Centrally Track Ownership Metadata

Tracking ownership metadata—which teams or individuals own specific systems and processes—will help you run smooth migrations, target your communication, and operate the platform well. While each platform could track this separately, we have found it valuable to centralize this information to avoid suffering from organizational drift or changes in the organization that haven't been reconciled with the technology.

Anyone who has worked for a company in its growth stages has probably observed the following scenario: a lot of people have come and gone over the years, and now there are a number of technology assets that are still used but that no one seems to own. This might not happen for the most critical systems, but there are often things like cron jobs that no one has looked at for ages, or forgotten data pipelines that just keep on running until they break and everyone scrambles to figure out who's responsible for fixing them.

This is one of the hidden challenges of platform engineering: organizational drift can hamper your ability to evolve the platform itself. When a massive data pipeline is hogging platform resources and no one owns the pipeline to fix the resource issues, the platform team is stuck in a bad place. It's usually not realistic to expect platform engineers to take on the burden of fixing business systems; they can help application developers do this, but they can't own those applications or processes in the long term. If these systems are important to running business processes, then they need clear ownership.

Depending on the state of your company, you may have to tackle this organizational drift in order to create a platform that you can maintain over time. This doesn't mean it is your job to solve organizational drift, but if no one else is thinking about how all the systems get notified of and react to organizational changes, it falls to you to prompt these conversations. Start by partnering with HR to get clarity about offboarding processes and what the system of record is for employment/team status. With a documented system for recording employment changes, you can then work with the rest of engineering to agree on how jobs, systems, and other technology processes should track to human ownership so that they can be automatically reassigned when people leave the company or move teams.

This is one of the reasons we call out ownership metadata in Chapter 2. This is a challenging problem even outside the dynamic world of elastic cloud resources. Without a strategy to address ownership tracking, you seriously hinder your ability to maintain and operate your platforms (not to mention all of the security risks from lack of access visibility!).

Develop Automation to Avoid Clipboards

A good platform team makes the experience of migration as painless as possible for their customers through careful planning and automation. A bad platform team, on the other hand, exposes developers to a great deal of churn and pain with updates and migrations that require significant work and planning on the part of the engineering teams themselves. We know it's hard to vet the impact of a big change on customer workloads, especially when your platform supports a diverse set of performance-sensitive workloads. But rather than giving up and running everything through human clipboard carriers, you can use this as an opportunity to think about your system design and how it can evolve to support automation of this work.

Camille once managed a base platform team that owned, among other things, the standard Linux distributions. The company had a lot of performance-sensitive C/C++, so handling an upgrade to these distributions was a painful process. In fact, when Camille joined, the team was still in the process of a delayed upgrade that had dragged on for so long that they were at risk of losing vendor support for even the newer version of the distribution. The challenge was that their customers found the work they needed to do to verify the new version too tedious and time-consuming, and it took constant nagging and follow-up to figure out who was behind and what was going on. They eventually got the migration done, but not without scars, and when it came time to do the next version there was immediate fear from the team about the timeline and resistance from the customers.

The team asked Camille for headcount to hire project managers to manage the upgrade. They felt it was such a complex project that having humans in the loop would be necessary for success. She was not sure, and pushed back with the following instructions: "I will allow hiring of project managers only when you've proven to me that we have done everything we can to automate the work that those project managers might do. Show me that we've tried to do this without project management and hit the wall, and we can hire. Until then, be creative."

The outcome was brilliant. The team took the pushback seriously, and started to think about why these upgrades were so complex. Part of the complexity was that the upgrades were actually a tree of dependencies. One system couldn't be upgraded until they had validated and completed the work on a subsystem. So, the first step was building out a map of those dependencies and tying that into a project migration cadence. The system would detect when a set of dependencies had been completed, and only then release work on the next step. In this way, they built up a series of observability and tracking workflow tools that were built with the customers in mind. What would make the job easy for the users who needed to upgrade? Which parts of the upgrade could they automate entirely? Which parts could they explain in the context of the ticket that a user got when it was time for their system to proceed?

This didn't completely remove the need for some human-driven project management, and toward the end of the project some of the team ended up working with project managers to finish the process. But the migration was a significant step forward as compared to prior updates, because the team took the time up front not only to plan the migration itself, but also to think about tooling, automation, observability, and customer-centric approaches to ease the pain for everyone involved in the process.

This is a great example of a platform team doing the right thing. Even in a world where they could not auto-migrate everyone, the team took on so much of the heavy lifting that there was little debate when it came time for the customers to finish the process. And this spells out one of the basic requirements for any team attempting to become a modern platform team: you must plan for and take on the bulk of the work for customer migrations if you want to claim this role.

Document On-Ramps and Off-Ramps

Sometimes the migration you are driving is not one that you can automate for your customers. Perhaps you've created a new service management platform, and using it requires customers to move their applications from the old platform (or even their old bare-metal servers) to your new offering. When you are driving a migration of this sort, it's important that you consider the on-ramps and off-ramps you build to make it easy for people to get off the old systems and onto yours.

In the case of a service platform, for example, your customers may want to experiment with moving over parts of their systems to test that the new platform works for them, before moving all of the traffic to the new offering. Showing them how to do these partial migrations (either through tooling that you build or detailed documentation of the process using tooling that already exists) is important to support the off-ramp from the old system and the on-ramp to the new one.

We have not written much about usage-level documentation—by which we mean things you see created by tech writers for SaaS vendors like verbose descriptions of APIs, code samples, and deep getting started guides. The reason for this is that few companies have support for creating good documentation of this kind, and leaving it to the engineers as yet another job is likely to lead to poorly written and rapidly out of date documentation that does as much to confuse people as it does to educate them. But migrations are a case where good usage-level documentation can be a major differentiator, and given that they are a one-off exercise, you can often write it once[2] and forgo the concern about it becoming outdated. In this situation, it's worth an investment to create solid documentation that supports the effort, possibly even hiring professional tech writers to produce it.

So how do you figure out what automation and documentation you need to support the migration? The answer to that question is dogfooding and partnership. If you can, have other platform teams go through the migration process as alpha testers. Using your own platforms during development is a useful, if incomplete, test of their suitability and usability. Once you're ready, approach your advanced customers who may want to be early adopters to get access to new features. These first real customers will give you the opportunity to experience the platform and the migration practices through fresh eyes. Having members of your team embed in theirs and support the migration of these early customers will give you important insights not just into bugs and feature gaps, but also into missing tools and automation that will facilitate the process. As you take early teams through the migration, you have a chance to smooth out the process for the rest of the customer base and document the steps necessary to onboard successfully.

Coordinating Smoother Migrations

While you should do everything you can from the last section to make migrations transparent, most migrations will require some amount of coordination with your customers. What does it mean to do that well? Migrations are never easy, but they can be easier, and there are many things you can do to make it so. In this section we'll cover the most important things to do to ensure the easiest transition for your customers, and balance your own team's workload in the process.

---

2 We don't expect that you will literally be able to write the migration documentation only once; you'll almost certainly discover edge cases that need to be added to it throughout the process. But this is still much more one-off than the live documentation to support an evolving platform or service, so the risk of it becoming out of date is minimal.

Scope, Limit, and Prioritize Planned Changes

Similar to limiting the coupling of the systems themselves, you need to limit the accidental overlapping of migrations across your platform. This takes three forms:

Scope backward from hard deadlines in the next 12 months.
> Some migrations will be completely beyond the platform team's control. If an OSS library is being deprecated or a vendor is demanding a change to the way its APIs are called, these "immovable objects" will restrict the choices you can make later, and you'll need to work out as soon as possible how you will migrate ahead of them.
>
> One thing to highlight is the nominal "12 months" here. This is based on our careers' worth of experience that OSS and vendor dates beyond this horizon, no matter how "hard" they claim to be, are far more nominal than they first seem. When a wide swath of the industry is affected, dates will slip, and often industry-wide solutions will come forward so you don't need to build your own (an example of this was AWS shipping its "Classiclink" VPC migration feature in 2015, meaning customers no longer needed to create bespoke solutions). In light of this, attempting to force your users to migrate today on the basis of an event that will take place well beyond their planning period will at best create a lot of friction, and quite often it will be wasted work even if they agree.
>
> For deadlines more than 12 months out, spend the additional time doing everything we mentioned in the previous section that you can to make the migration easier. Leave the heavy coordination planning until you are closer to that 12-month time frame, at which point you should have a good and, notably, easy-to-follow process to ask of your users.

Limit coupling of in-flight customer work.
> Are you saving customers effort by coupling the data center migration with an upgrade to the databases, or are you making it that much harder for them to complete either of these? There are times when it makes sense to do a group of changes together but it's better if the grouped changes happen internally to the platform, leaving the customer to see only one piece of work. This can be subtle:
>
> - When you're doing a migration that is more than a lift-and-shift for customers, such as one that requires them to rearchitect some parts of their system, it might make sense to couple it with other critical work. For example, if customers are moving from on-premises VMs to container-based compute in the public cloud, bundling that with an update to the authentication system might not add much complexity to the overall project. This approach makes the most sense when the migration is somewhat optional and there is a lot of value for the application teams to go through the rearchitecture.

- If you have a hard deadline for the initiative—for example, the end of your data center lease, or the vendor contract end date for a piece of infrastructure—you'll want to limit other changes to help people get through the process. It's reasonable that you don't want to or can't support the oldest legacy systems in the new data center, but resist the temptation to pile on restriction after restriction with the idea that you can get application teams to fix things you don't like or free you from some of your legacy systems just because they have to migrate anyway.

Keep track of your major outstanding requests, and prioritize.
Do you really need to do a major upgrade of the operating system and change the approach you use for authentication across the company in the same quarter? As part of your roadmap planning, platform leadership should see planned migrations and major changes. Don't be afraid to ask questions about whether these migrations should happen at the same time, what the impact of these changes will be to other parts of the platform, and whether the plans have accounted for these overlaps.

This is important not just for helping your customers, but also for the sake of your own teams. How well can you test the impact of multiple simultaneous changes on your own platforms? It's one thing to bring together new components into a new platform offering, as with our public cloud migration example, but if you're trying to do a build and test system migration at the same time you're changing the object storage used for build artifacts, untangling the impact of these simultaneous changes on performance problems for artifact retrieval can get very messy.

Communicate Early and Publicly

Context-free deadlines are one of the great frustrations that customers experience during migrations—but how can you avoid these deadlines, knowing that users tend to procrastinate on migration-related work until it turns into a fire drill? The answer lies in your communication strategy.

The first step is to tell customers about migrations as soon as you know that they are coming (with the caveat that this should be information-only for most deadlines more than 12 months out). When the migrations are driven by updates in underlying systems (say, your OS or database version going end of life), you usually have a good deal of warning, and not as much flexibility on the due date. These deadlines can be built into the roadmaps that you communicate to your customers, and repeated through newsletters, quarterly planning sessions, and other frequent customer engagements. For changes that also require changes at your own platform layer, you may want to hold off on communicating until you are confident that the project is closer to shipping and you know what the work involved will be—perhaps once you've got an alpha customer using the new version and are confident the change is what you want.

The larger your platform gets and the more pieces you have in play, the harder this early communication can become. At large scale, application engineering teams often designate someone to evaluate the incoming platform migration requests, check the specifications, and then communicate these requests out to the application engineers once they have verified that the requests make sense and are actionable. While this may be inevitable beyond a certain scale of company, it often comes as a reaction to disorganization within the platform and infrastructure teams themselves.

When you're at a big enough scale that your customers are creating migration intake roles, it's time for you to formalize migration coordination for your platforms. The customer coordination may be done best by a project manager (or, depending on the size of your company, a whole team of them), but most of the work to support this role needs to happen during the team's annual bottom-up planning process. Some checks to add to that process include:

- Across the core platform areas, where are there known major changes coming that will require customer work?

- Have you thought about where you can bundle related changes to reduce the customers' work, and where you might delay certain migrations due to already planned churn?

- Does your plan give you enough confidence that you can use it to communicate the major changes for the next two to three quarters, so that your customer teams can plan to absorb them?

Beyond all of this, it's helpful to have a dedicated communication and support channel during the course of the migration, separate from your normal support and on-call rotations. If the channel is public and well curated, customers will often help one another through common gotchas. You can use the channel to collect FAQs to document and to identify rough edges to automate. This can be useful even in cases where you don't have or need a full migration coordination center.

Push Through the Final 20%

So, you've decided to take ownership of migrations. You've done a lot of work to ease the impact for your customers through automation, better communication, and even doing the migration for them. But when you look at where you've gotten, you realize that you've covered maybe 80% of the overall workload. Unfortunately, the remaining 20% is still there, and if you want to fully remove the old version or legacy system, that 20% will still need to be migrated.

What now? As with so many projects, the final 20% can seem even harder than the first 80% (and the last 5% might seem downright impossible). Maybe these are the highest-risk applications, or the oldest, the most critical, or the most customized. It's natural that you would focus on the migration work that gets the most customers finished first, but this long tail can't be ignored forever. As you start on this final set, you will inevitably discover new complications that you'll need to resolve if you hope to complete the work.

The first complication is that your migration is going to take longer than you think, and someone will need to run the old system for as long as it takes to finish the migration. You may want to minimize the work you put into the old system. However, if you allow most of the team to focus entirely on the new system, then those who are stuck on the legacy system may feel underappreciated, worry where their careers are going, burn out due to the combined stress of a limited support rota and a creaky legacy platform, and ultimately leave the team. You'll want to figure out the balance of work to put into the old system versus the new one during these final stages of migration ahead of time, so you don't end up relying on a couple of long-serving employees to hold things together for the final months.

You can expect to run into some unexpected issues in the later stages of the project. If you are running this platform in an on-prem environment, you may want to stop buying new hardware for the old platform, but then what happens if that old hardware needs to be retired before the migration is complete? Camille oversaw a migration that was in its final stages when the data center team insisted that the old servers had to be replaced because the fans were dying. Her team had to negotiate to get that team to do extra work to repurpose or replace just the fans, so her team wouldn't have to spend a bunch of money for new servers that wouldn't be needed six months after purchase. At scale, you'll inevitably miss some underlying dependency that will lead to a scramble during this final drawn-out stage of a major migration. Don't panic; instead, draw on the ingenuity of your team to solve the problem, and in the meantime make sure you are communicating this risk to anyone who might care (or could help!).

Finally, it's not always obvious who should be responsible for the last 20% of the work. This depends on the characteristics of the applications that need to be migrated, and sometimes you don't own those applications. Will the platform team be responsible? Will the application teams be responsible? You may discover that the new system just won't work for some of the edge-case users, which means you'll need to go through a sunsetting process, as discussed in the next section. For the rest, there's likely to be an ongoing negotiation between your team and the application teams, so be prepared. How much power you have to mandate the completion of the migration on a certain timeline (or at all) depends on your organization's culture. For a culture that prefers carrots to sticks, you may need to do more work to sell the platform to the laggards. Either way, the better the new platform and the better the experience of those who have already migrated, the easier this debate will become, because more people will trust you and want to use the new offering. But *easier* is not *easy*, and in the case of legacy applications with minimal customer ownership, expect significant pushback on having to do this work.

Use Mandates Sparingly

Finally, let's talk about a people challenge with migrations, particularly at scale. If you worked at a scaled company when it was smaller, you know that in the past you may have been able to get people to give you the benefit of the doubt on a migration. They knew you personally, and they knew your team; you were all still in the "one team, one dream" stage of company development. But as a company grows, or if you're a leader who has recently joined a new organization, you don't have that built-in trust that comes from deep personal connections. Furthermore, it's likely that your customers will have already seen migrations go sideways. Even if you personally have always run effective, well-communicated migrations, they'll have worked at other companies where this wasn't the case. They are going to instinctively fight you on even thinking about the work they might need to do to support a migration.

"Ah," you might be thinking, "well, this stuff is so important that we'll simply get the CTO to issue a mandate to everyone that they must complete this migration! It worked for Amazon in moving to services, it worked for my friend's company when they moved to the cloud, so surely we can get this support!"

You might get lucky and get agreements on top-down mandates once in a while, for truly critical initiatives. But at scale, you are competing with many other initiatives that also must be completed, from cost-cutting measures to compliance and security initiatives to business expansions. There's only so much attention a company can give to mandates, and even if the leadership is willing to set these mandates, at a certain point people will stop paying attention to them.

We advise you to save your mandate requests for the things that are essential and, if possible, align them with satisfying other mandatory efforts (or even better, align them with major product initiatives!). If your platform improves the security posture and saves money, you may be able to go in with the CISO and the CFO to request that this be one of the few mandates of the year. If the business wants to change the pricing model, this might be a great chance to uplift the billing platform. Strategically planning migrations as part of other important work is usually more effective than annoying your customers with random unscheduled mandatory work that doesn't seem to have any alignment with the other random unscheduled mandatory work coming at them.

Mandates may be necessary to drive that final 20% of a migration effort. There may be a lot of pain in the migration, but there's bound to be just as much pain (and even more risk) in keeping the old thing running, and sometimes the company needs a senior leader to say "we all know this is the right thing" to actually get all parties to commit to doing that right thing. However, platform teams should take care to avoid using the mandate approach too often, as this can create a culture in which it seems like the application engineers only exist to make the platform team's projects happen, as opposed to serving the business.

Sunsetting Platforms

In the previous discussion of migrations, we have taken one thing for granted: you might be moving people from one system to another, but these migrations don't remove functionality. In the case where you are not only asking people to move off of a platform but don't have a near-equivalent system for them to move onto, you are not just asking for a migration; you are sunsetting a system. In this situation, you may not have the capacity to support a full migration for the platform's users, but you'll still want to ease their transition as best you can.

Deciding When to Sunset

There are plenty of reasons to sunset legacy systems: lack of people who understand the old system and can support it, security and compliance gaps, a vendor going out of business, and more. In the case of widely used legacy systems that need to be turned off for any of these reasons, don't go directly to sunsetting. Instead, we recommend that you first figure out a path to another offering, building something new or adding features to an existing platform if necessary, so that you can follow the processes established for a migration, rather than a sunset.

True sunsetting—that is, turning something off without offering an equivalent—should be reserved for the cases that follow:

1. *There are not very many users.* You may have prematurely expanded your product to support many different configurations with the expectation that your customers would demand that variety. This often happens with offerings like databases, messaging systems, or observability tooling. Some teams get very opinionated about these types of offerings and insist that they must have certain advanced configurations enabled, or additional plug-ins that no one else needs. Another common driver for this is a new product team that insists on a specific subtype of a common system: for example, they must have *this* graph database because they need one feature that your standard offering doesn't support. This is a product gamble that does not always pay off, and you may end up supporting a whole stack of infrastructure and integrations for a single team.

   And sometimes you just build a new workflow that you think will revolutionize people's experience and it turns out only a tiny group of users ever latches on. This can happen with superuser features, for example. We've made this mistake in developer tooling for teams that wanted a very particular interaction model with version control, code review, and testing. These noisy customers turned out to be a very small subset of our overall customer base, and the interaction model we built was painful to maintain in the face of other changes; eventually, we had to remove the advanced features because they were too expensive to support for the few users who wanted them.

 Sunsetting should be used only at the very tail end of a migration, when you are down to a small set of customers who are deeply coupled to some feature that is not and cannot be supported by the new system. This often happens when you are rearchitecting a scrappy platform to something more scalable, and you need to eliminate features that don't make sense to offer in a system built for the next order of magnitude of scale.

Platform engineering teams can sometimes lack empathy in dealing with such customers, taking an attitude along the lines of "they should have known that would never scale, so they need to deal with it and figure out how to move off anyway." Needless to say, this is not a product-centric approach, and when you try this with a feature that is critical for more than a small number of edge cases, you may generate enough backlash to force you to support both offerings indefinitely. If you're going to remove critical features you should make sure they really impact only the tail 0.1% of use cases, and begin the sunsetting only after early consideration and communication of all options.

2. *The cost of supporting the offering is high.* If the system runs itself, you may not care that it has low adoption, but when the support burden for a particular feature or offering is high but it has few users, that is a sign that you need to do something. If you don't see a path to increasing adoption, you may need to sunset the offering to reduce the burden for your team. The cost may not come directly in system support, but indirectly in expanding the overall offering. When a feature is complex and fragile, it can make other changes to the platform harder as well—this is often the case for supporting unusual workflows and other superuser offerings.

3. *You have other things you want to focus on.* Finally, there are times when you need to get more focus from your team on higher-priority work, and the only way to do that is to get rid of distractions. When you have an offering that requires continual engineering investment that you need to redirect elsewhere, this can be a sign that you need to sunset the offering to free up bandwidth for other things.

If you are sunsetting because of pressure to deliver in other areas, get specific about where you might redeploy people once the sunsetting is complete. This information should be part of the communication plan to your impacted users and stakeholders, particularly if they are interested in the area that you are reinvesting in.

Sometimes It's the Builders Who Resist Sunsetting, Not the Customers

Sunsetting is often required for projects that just didn't quite go as planned, where the team really believes in their vision but hasn't managed to get it to work. One memorable sunsetting we oversaw was the removal of a build and test tool that the team had been trying to make work for years. They had managed to get far enough that a few application teams were using it, but there was no clear path to getting everyone onto the new offering. Furthermore, the problems with the system that had driven the team to try this new offering had mostly been resolved, and trying to support both the old and new systems was becoming too much for them to handle.

One of the hardest parts of this project was getting the team to realize that the new tool was going nowhere, and despite their best efforts, it wasn't worth the continued investment. They wanted so much for the thing they had invested in to succeed that getting them to accept that the project was at a dead end was nearly as hard as getting the tool itself sunsetted and removed. In fact, we think this is one of the more common challenges that leaders have with sunsetting exercises, because while customers can be frustrated that they have to migrate or give up a feature, the teams that built that feature are often even more attached to the sunk cost they've put in so far. It's never fun to tell someone to kill their darling.

In fact, it gets worse. In the case of our build and test system, it took more than leadership pushing to sunset the offering; it took the die-hard believers leaving the team to really finish off the initiative. We share this as a cautionary tale: when you staff up a team through passion about a particular technology, those people are likely to leave if that technology doesn't pan out in the way they'd hoped.

Coordinating the Sunsetting

Once you've decided you should sunset a system, you have a few options to consider as you plan how to execute it, most involving the coordination approach you will take with the remaining users of the system:

Ask yourself whether you can give the system back to the consuming team.
> Occasionally, the burden of support is beyond what your team can justify, but another team is so dependent on the system that they are willing to take it back and operate it themselves. You may need to do some negotiation here, because sometimes the other team's leadership will expect you to give them people to

support it, and it's likely that you are cutting the offering because you don't have people to spare. In this instance, think about how you can train their team to handle support, and create a transition timeline where your engineers and their engineers pair on the system so they understand how to work with it. You may still end up permanently moving a person or two to the other team, but if it frees up many others on your team to focus on more important things, the trade may well be worth it.

Identify possible off-ramps.

When transferring the system's operations to another team isn't possible and sunsetting is unavoidable, it's time to prepare for hard conversations with the remaining users. The best preparation is to identify ways to soften the customer impact of losing the system and having to move to something else. For example:

- Can you document the steps needed to migrate to a different system so they can understand the effort that migration might take, and can you offer additional support through this migration?

- Can you connect them with a customer who has gone through the sunsetting already to share lessons learned?

- Can you explain how they may use your platform to build their own version of this offering, if it is a minor feature?

- Can you show them how to get the same outcomes with a different tool or feature set?

Talk to the users and explain their options, creating a timeline with their input.

If you're sunsetting something, it should already have a limited number of users, and talking to them (instead of just sending an announcement notice) is a good idea to maintain your relationships. Furthermore, while you might have an idea about the timeline for sunsetting, be prepared to negotiate that in order to give your stakeholders the chance to react. Sunsetting timelines can be as short as quarters or as long as years, depending on the size of the user base and the criticality of the system to that group.

This brings up another key point: you owe it to your users to give them as much warning as possible that this is happening. It is true that they are likely to ignore the problem if you tell them too far in advance, but it's better to give them a chance to do the work earlier. The timeline will depend on the complexity of the feature and the mitigation work they'll need to do. Migration from one database type to another can be as "easy" as running migration scripts, doing performance regression testing, running in prod in parallel, and finally flipping a switch, or it could mean having to read a bunch of stored procedures and understand long-forgotten business logic, rewriting it against a new database, and then doing all of those other "easy" steps.

Don't Be Afraid to Sunset When It Makes Sense

It's not fun to tell a stakeholder that you can't support them anymore, but it's worse to degrade everyone else's experience because your team is spread too thin supporting one-off special-case offerings. So, don't be afraid to edit your offerings from time to time when you launch something that goes almost nowhere. Doing the right thing for the overall company sometimes means disappointing a few people in the process.

Wrapping Up

Migrations and sunsetting are two of the least fun things about owning a platform. No one likes to make their customers do work just to stay in place, and migrations often feel like a tax that customers have to pay for using your systems. But this cost is the reason we see migrations as one of the biggest opportunities for platform teams. This levy will come whether the application teams use your platforms or a smattering of cloud, OSS, and vendor systems. All of that underlying software has to be updated occasionally, whether it's bundled into a platform or not. The promise of platform engineering is that we can minimize the cost of change for the whole engineering organization through better automation, communication, and execution. We aspire to be a stable foundation that makes the whole organization more efficient as a result.

The common themes of this book are echoed in this chapter: think about your users and their experience, and do as much as you can up front to make that experience better. Communicate thoughtfully, and often. Challenge yourself to find places where software and automation can replace manual or human-driven processes. Yes, sometimes you will need to have hard conversations and disappoint your customers, such as when you are sunsetting a system that they still rely on. But the more that you have shown you are doing everything you can to make their experience better, the easier these hard conversations will become.

CHAPTER 10

Managing Stakeholder Relationships

Alice thought she saw a way out of the difficulty, this time. "If you tell me what language 'fiddle-de-dee' is, I'll tell you the French for it!" she exclaimed triumphantly.

But the Red Queen drew herself up rather stiffly, and said, "Queens never make bargains."

"I wish Queens never asked questions," Alice thought to herself.

    —Lewis Carroll, *Through the Looking Glass, and What Alice Found There*, Chapter 9

Back in Chapter 5, we talked about how stakeholder management differs from product management. Product management is about building the right things for your customers; stakeholder management is about convincing their leaders you made the right choices. Sometimes it doesn't matter how well you are delivering a rock-solid, customer-focused platform: if key stakeholders don't believe in your investments, you will be unsuccessful. When your stakeholders don't support you, a charismatic peer with a compelling vision can bleed off valuable investment on the basis of a good idea and a little execution, even when you know that the new platform can't come close to providing all of the features of your current offering.

The painful truth of building internal-focused platforms is that slow delivery and an indirect tie to business value means your stakeholders have an outsized influence on your success. If you want to ensure that your team has enough cover to build the platforms they need to build without getting thrashed by other leadership or engineering teams, managing stakeholder relationships is a must.

In this chapter we will discuss:

- A mapping technique to help you determine which stakeholders need your time
- How best to communicate with stakeholders

- Techniques for finding acceptable compromises, including on the perennial but contentious topic of stakeholders building shadow platforms

- Handling one of the most extreme points of stakeholder contention—justifying the size of your platform team

Your relationship with your stakeholders doesn't need to be a zero-sum game where you lose if they win. You want to be smart about how you approach these relationships, but don't forget that you are all playing for the same larger team, and the goal is to win through the best business outcomes.

Is Stakeholder Management Just Unnecessary Politics?

Many think that stakeholder management is just a bunch of politics and dealing with bad actors, and we used to agree. We've been a part of many big decisions where only one side would get what they wanted, and we've seen many peers seemingly advocate not for the needs of the business but rather to grow their own careers and build their own empires. But we've also seen peers that we admire accused of this self-interest, and even been accused of it ourselves! Once we realized that there was more to this conflict than the company hiring "jerks" that created "politics," we got curious about why this happens and how to handle it better.

What we now understand is that the problem is much more about organization size than individuals. Remember Dunbar's number?[1] At somewhere between 50 and 150 people, organizations split into mini-organizations, with diverging practices, beliefs, and priorities. This means that even with a strong company culture, you will inevitably find situations where the right decision "for the business" from your perspective might not be the right decision "for the business" from someone else's. Stakeholder management is how we make sure our peers have an appreciation of our perspective and context so that when conflicts happen, they don't just listen to their own team's complaints and blame us for everything.

While it's frustrating when your customers act a bit like a clannish village, it's perfectly natural. It is also natural that when their "mayor" brings the village's biggest problems to your attention, they expect it to become your biggest problem too. That's just what happens in villages; we'd bet that when you are frustrated with teams or systems that you depend on, you gossip to your peers to see if there's a common pattern, and ask your mayor (sorry, we mean manager) to help if so.

---

1 Dunbar's number (*https://oreil.ly/yNOlx*) is tied to the notion of community stability from back when humans were hunter-gatherers. There is some debate over the number—somewhere between 50 and 150 people—but the idea is that human brains are limited in how many relationships they can handle (e.g., in the sense of remembering the personal details that matter).

Stakeholder Mapping: The Power-Interest Grid

To think about stakeholder management, you first have to understand your stakeholders and how to measure their influence. To frame this conversation, let's introduce an imaginary platform engineering leader, Juan. Juan is the VP of platform engineering, and his team is building all of the common platforms and tools for every other engineering group. This means that all three of the other major engineering teams that are building the company's big products are his stakeholders. He also builds a few offerings that are used by some internal nontechnical teams, including finance and HR, and works with both the CFO and the chief people officer as part of that work. He reports to the CTO, and his team occasionally gets pulled in to directly unblock a major product deliverable by the business product leadership.

The current state of affairs is that Juan's platform is working well enough for the nontechnical internal employees and when they are pulled to unblock major product deliverables they manage to do it, but they are disengaged from the major product engineering teams, who see them as a necessary nuisance.

How should Juan decide where to focus his stakeholder engagement? Let's start the conversation by using a simple and well-established model called the *power-interest grid*. We'll identify the most important stakeholders by mapping them to a four-quadrant grid, as shown in Figure 10-1. Our y-axis is increasing power, and the x-axis is increasing interest.

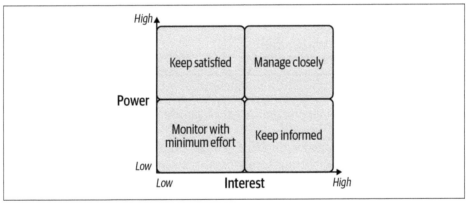

Figure 10-1. Power-interest grid, showing the four quadrants of stakeholders based on their power within the organization and interest in your work

In the top-right quadrant, you have your high-power, highly interested stakeholders. These are the people you want to spend a lot of time understanding. Your powerful stakeholders are critical business leaders or those who have the support of critical business leaders. What draws their interest is the times when they not only rely on the platform in general, but have either a direct product whose delivery depends on you or a team who are unhappy with what you are delivering.

We emphasize the negative here because in our experience, most of these stakeholders are very busy people who do not get deeply engaged with the platform when things are going well and they believe it poses low risk to their own teams' success. If you make this group unhappy, you raise the risk that they will build a shadow platform, or worse, that your team will get broken up and absorbed by those engineering areas, to the detriment not only of your team but also your career and the health of the technology platform.

Let's take a look at what this grid looks like for Juan (Figure 10-2).

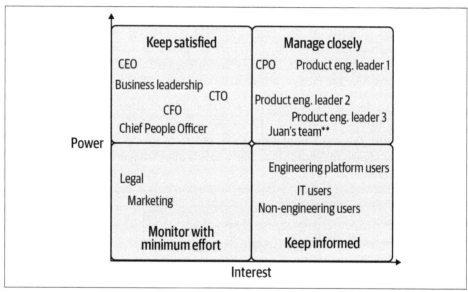

Figure 10-2. The power-interest grid showing Juan's stakeholders

The top-right quadrant contains the chief product officer (CPO) and leaders from the three other major engineering teams (in particular, the ones that rely on his team most for their own product deliverables and the ones that are most ambitious). Because his team is not yet seen as a value-add, the minute the platform starts to struggle, it is likely that someone from this group will make a play. Juan's team is also in this quadrant, but lower on the power axis than his peers.[2] You may be surprised that we categorized them this way, but prioritizing making your own engineering team happy over your most powerful stakeholders is a tempting bargain that we have

---

2 Juan's team is a stakeholder of variable power. Sometimes, Juan may have the power (and mandate) to replace a large part of that team as needed; sometimes, the team's opinion of Juan may mean as much to the company as Juan's opinion of his team!

---

too often seen end in tears. Senior stakeholders can tell when they are being treated with secondary importance to those they see as lower in the ranks and will absolutely use that against you if anything goes wrong.

In the top-left quadrant are the high-power but lower-interest stakeholders. These might include Juan's boss, the CTO, who is content to let things play out without either supporting or undermining him, and business leaders who are busy with other things and don't have time to get into the weeds of Juan's world (people who may move back into the top-right quadrant as new initiatives arise). It also includes the CFO and chief people officer, who are generally happy with Juan's work but spend most of their time thinking about things other than technology. Assuming they are really happy, this quadrant is an opportunity for Juan, because nudging this group into more engagement can improve his odds of surviving a battle with his ambitious peers. However, he shouldn't spend so much time on this group that he is seen as wasting their attention on things that don't directly concern them.

The lower-right quadrant is where Juan finds a lot of overlap with product management, as this is where many of the actual engineering teams who use the platform reside. They have to use this thing day in and day out, and some of them will be very interested in the roadmap and features and how it could be better. The product team does most of the stakeholder management for this group.

Finally, in the lower-left quadrant are people who rarely interact with Juan's team or their software. These folks will only vaguely know what the team does, and they are likely to care only when something is going very wrong.

This mapping shows what we believe to be the political reality on the ground. When you look at the platform team through the lens of building great products, the engineers who use your platforms come out on top. When you look at the platform team through the lens of Juan as an engineering manager and leader, the team itself comes out on top. But when you look at the team through the lens of stakeholder management, the most important stakeholders are unlikely to be either those who use the platforms directly or the team building the platform, but rather the senior people who may judge the delivery harshly, potentially seeing your platforms as at best an impediment to their ambitions and at worst a competitor.

As you build your own stakeholder map, some questions to ask yourself are:

- Who has the ear of the most senior leadership?
- Which teams are considered indispensable, and which are considered nice to have? Where does my team sit on this spectrum?
- If I did everything perfectly but a stakeholder still didn't like me very much, how much would it matter?

- Which stakeholder groups are the loudest? Of these, which are the most respected in the company?
- If my team overdelivered for this stakeholder, would it matter?

By thinking about your power-interest mapping, you can identify critical groups to spend time with. More than this, you can start to understand what they care about, and use that to shape not just your team's plans, but also how you will manage the relationships in terms of communication and compromises, which are the subjects of the following sections.

Communicating with the Right Transparency

Once you've mapped your stakeholders, it's time to think about communication with them. How much do you tell your stakeholders, when do you tell them, and how do you tell it?

Beware of Oversharing Detail

The answer to the question of how much to tell your stakeholders is not as obvious as you might hope. While it's good to keep people informed of your progress (using something like the Wins and Challenges updates described in Chapter 7), too much transparency can cause just as many problems as too little. The problems caused by oversharing include:

External micromanagement
Your team is accountable to your stakeholders, but that doesn't mean stakeholders are responsible for managing and prioritizing your day-to-day. Providing too much transparency encourages some stakeholders to treat you like an execution arm that they control, so this can be a good way to undermine your strategy and create unnecessary second-guessing of the work your team is doing.

Tuning you out
Other stakeholders, when drowned by minutiae in your updates, are instead going to start ignoring you. If everything is going well, that's fine, but when things aren't going well this overload of information contributes to a sense of mistrust from partners who may feel that you are deliberately trying to distract them from the meaningful information by sending them too much to parse.

Focusing on the wrong details
Stakeholders who are given too much information sometimes end up focusing on things that really don't matter to them. You can create problems just by telling them things that they don't understand but that seem like things they should care about. For example, coming back to the challenges with SLOs we talked about in Chapter 6, we have seen stakeholders look at an SLO dashboard with 24 green

graphs and obsess that the platform team needed to get to the root cause on the one that was slightly red, even though the engineering team was comfortable that it was just a noisy measure.

Relationship damage

We have seen highly technical platform leaders try to resolve disagreements by providing the stakeholders with a bunch of engineering details to support their case. Unless the stakeholders are prepared to evaluate these details and motivated to understand this level of nuance, they are likely to be left with the impression that the leader isn't trying to communicate with them or is just a bad communicator in general.

For any broad messaging (including the Wins and Challenges process from Chapter 7), focus hard on what message you want stakeholders to take away. While you don't want to compromise accuracy (this will make them lose trust if they catch it), try to send that message without including extra detail. If some stakeholders ask for specific details, you'll know which ones are important to them, and you'll be able to tune the level of detail to that individual case. For less technical stakeholders, that may mean convincing someone more technical whom they trust, rather than trying to convince them directly.

The Stakeholder Is Always Right

Stakeholders often seem to amplify the worst noise coming out of their own teams. You may have had a small mishap that you handled well internally—maybe an operational issue, maybe a missed release date. It was controlled but still impactful enough that some customers started gossiping among themselves. Now it's "that platform team is a bad owner," or "that platform team builds technology for the sake of building technology." You go to the customer team's leader, your stakeholder, hoping to quiet the noise by having a rational cost/benefits discussion. But rather than understanding, they double down and start questioning not just your strategy but your leadership choices. Then they say they "just want matters solved," leaving all the resolution work to you. And if you don't solve those matters in the way they expect, well, you're the one who has broken trust—they made their expectations clear!

This comes down to an old sales saying: "The customer is always right." Somehow we think that because our stakeholders are also engineering leaders they should have a balanced perspective on our challenges. This would be great, but unfortunately it's rarely the case. Instead, when there are problems between your team and a stakeholder's team, you usually will see some combination of the following:

- *Stakeholders who view you as their "internal vendor"* and don't believe that you can appreciate what *their* jobs entail, especially because they think you are the source of many of their problems. They are therefore resistant to hearing ideas from you about what their own teams could be doing better.

- *Stakeholders who believe they could do your job* and manage your team better than you can, even though the advice they give addresses only the subset of your problems that impact them. (We admit, we have been guilty of this same attitude from time to time.)

- *Stakeholders who have forgotten about what you did for them yesterday*, or how much better the platform is now than it was a year ago. It's human nature to stop noticing the absence of problems, especially when there are more improvements to be made or problems that haven't been addressed yet.

The sooner you accept that your customers will rarely be satisfied, that their leaders will always bring you problems, and that your job as a platform leader is to roll with it and keep moving forward, the happier you will be in your role.

Use Regular 1:1s Judiciously

Incoming platform leaders should begin by conducting several 1:1s with stakeholders to hear about their concerns with your platform, assess their power and interest, and understand their needs and motivations. But beware of relying on this technique indefinitely. While we encourage you to keep a regular cadence of 1:1s with your critical stakeholders, we have three words of warning:

- They are time-consuming, linearly scaling with the number of relationships. This means that as your platform grows, you will find yourself without the time to build new relationships of the same depth; equally, if you attempt to slow down the cadence with some stakeholders to make room for others, they may interpret this as you signaling their unimportance.

- When the relationship is not in a good place and the stakeholder is not of mind to invest in it, they will likely view an unnecessary 1:1 as yet another cost that your team is imposing on them.

- The privacy of 1:1s is as much a weakness as a strength—-for instance, when most stakeholders tell you in 1:1s that they're happy with your trade-offs, your unhappy stakeholders aren't there to hear that. Telling the unhappy stakeholders "I think my other stakeholders agree with my decision" sounds whiny, even when it's accurate.

It's not realistic to rely solely on 1:1s to get feedback, share information, and develop trusting relationships. Plenty of busy managers would rather you just get things done, broadcast information more broadly, and save their calendar for times when it is really important to talk in private. In the steady state, we recommend a quarterly 1:1 with most of your "Keep Satisfied/Keep Informed" stakeholders, and monthly 1:1s with your "Manage Closely" stakeholders.

Track Expectations and Commitments

This is Communication 101 advice, but some new platform leaders get tripped up by it because they are used to roles with fewer stakeholders and fewer day-to-day surprises. A typical day in the life of a platform leader might look like this:

- In a stakeholder 1:1, you commit to looking into something that's bothering the stakeholder's teams.
- Without writing down the specifics, you go straight into another meeting, or more likely, a series of additional meetings.
- You then get paged into an operational event, and the details of what you were supposed to look into get forgotten, never to be acted on.

The stakeholder may not even raise the issue in the next 1:1 (they probably didn't track it either), but it's sure to come to their mind at an inopportune time. And now it will be seen as a missed commitment, contributing to their difficulty in trusting you and your team.

If you are new to a leadership role in a platform team, don't rely on your memory just because it worked in the past—write down commitments in a way that will help you remember to act on them. It's not necessary to take down minutes of all 1:1s in a common document; in fact, doing so can come across as tracking stakeholders' words in an act of political scorekeeping. Instead, take notes privately, and ideally email the stakeholder with the exact expectations, so they can clarify if they wish.

Scale Up with Interlock Meetings and Customer Advisory Boards

Because 1:1s don't scale, you'll need to have broader meetings as well. One of the most popular forms is the *interlock meeting*. In this meeting, representatives of the platform group meet with the stakeholders to discuss work in progress and get feedback. These can be held biweekly, monthly, or quarterly, depending on the stakeholder sensitivity. At the quarterly level, we have also called them customer advisory boards (CABs).

Interlock meetings and CABs are often owned by the product management team, but beware of leaving all of the communication to product (or program/project) management leaders; when stakeholders are struggling due to your team's operational challenges or engineering delivery issues, the best people to own this communication are the engineers who are operating and delivering the platform. Product management should run the roadmap and feature interlock discussion, but engineering needs to be there to speak to other matters.

We can't emphasize enough how important it is to prepare for these meetings. Get clear on:

- What you want to get out of the meeting
- What information and decisions will be presented
- How you're going to let the participants have a voice but also keep the conversation structured (an antipattern here is presenting a slide deck for 55 minutes, leaving 5 minutes for questions at the end)

When these meetings work best, they help your loudest critics understand that they are actually in disagreement not only with you, but with what most of your other stakeholders want. When they go poorly, it's often because you are attempting to solicit opinions from stakeholders on decisions that extend beyond their understanding of the trade-offs, so the meeting turns into a battle over which teams' needs are most important.

Increase Communication During Rough Patches

We'll end the communication section with this final advice: when things are going well, when the platform is stable, when stakeholders are getting what they need, and when there is little budgetary pressure to scrutinize every project, stakeholders are likely to be happy. You will need to communicate what is happening, but in these cases, much of the stakeholder management work can be subsumed by the product management team as part of their general customer engagement. Keep your stakeholder meetings lightweight and only as frequent as needed to maintain the relationships.

When things are *not* going well, whether due to operational instability, features that aren't being delivered, or a budget crunch that has everyone questioning investments, you need to ramp up transparency and communication until the rough patch has passed. In this case, make sure you are bringing the right information, conveyed by the appropriate owners, to your stakeholders, and supplementing any meetings with additional email/chat updates as needed.

Finding Acceptable Compromises

Even when you have done all the planning we laid out in Chapter 7 and are communicating to stakeholders well, you'll still need to deal with disagreements and escalations from your stakeholders. In their view, being closer to business revenue and growth must mean they understand what is "right" for the business better than some internal-serving platform team. You will have to address these issues thoughtfully, ensuring stakeholders feel that their perspective is considered even when you think they're being unreasonable.

As our many stakeholder discussions have shown us, determining the truth of "what platform work will be of highest value to the business" is generally simply not feasible, as it involves different judgments regarding the probable value of what will be built on top of it. Yes, you should attempt to gather as much information as possible, including escalating up the management chain to those with more global responsibility who might have an overriding opinion. But you will often find that they demur, as there are too many uncertainties for them to make a definitive call around a single platform's roadmap. Instead, they want you to compromise.

Maybe your stakeholders need something that you think you just can't support. Maybe they want you to reprioritize essential work in favor of a new feature. Maybe they want you to cut costs so that they can recover some budget. Whatever it is, you can't deliver on it without impacting something else you think is more valuable. What do you do?

Be Clear About the Business Impact

When you are the one saying no to their request, the worst thing you can do is lean on excuses when a stakeholder questions the value of your current investments. If you want to get to a compromise, you have to do it in terms that rise above the specifics of each case, which means you have to make your case in terms of business impact.

Too often, platform leaders let themselves get sloppy about business impact. Someone asked for a feature and the team jumped on it without asking whether it was really important or not, resulting in a lot of work that didn't make much of a difference. The team spent too much of their time on speculative investments that didn't really help with current pain points, and the application teams are tired of waiting for those investments to pay off. Or, worst of all, everything just takes too much time and costs too much to build. Even simple features take months to produce.

There's always an excuse that you can find for these situations. The platform is unstable and it's hard to make changes, so new features take a long time to implement. You're convinced that the current system is unscalable and you have to build a new system to future-proof the platform. You've had some turnover, so the team is slower than they should be. Your stakeholders keep changing their minds, and this further slows the delivery. And on and on and on.

At the point of saying no to a stakeholder request, it is critical that you don't just assume your roadmap is correct because you planned it to be correct. You need to look at the current status and value of the work. How much of it is dedicated to things that customers want now as a high priority, and how much of it is invested in speculative work, future-proofing, or stability/debt remediation? You have to balance immediate value with future-proofing, and this may mean moving some people onto different projects in response to your customers' needs.

Even when you find yourself in the situation where the platform is so unstable that you have to pause most of the customer-demand work in favor of stability and remediation, you still owe it to your stakeholders to show them the timeline, goals, and value of this work. You're measuring something to see whether the system is stable or not, right? Report on how that is improving.

Your stakeholders should not need to accept your word about your business impact. They should be able to see it.

Sometimes Say "Yes, with Compromises"

It's common to work against a roadmap that, by virtue of trying to address the biggest challenges, neglects little things that are important to smaller customer groups. But just because a customer group is small doesn't mean it doesn't have influence. Look at their position in your stakeholder map to see if they have an outsized influence. They might be the darling of an important executive. They might be quick to complain and influential drivers of broader customer opinion. They might be working on a high-profile project that everyone is watching closely. Or maybe you just owe them one because you keep having to deprioritize their requests.

Whatever the reason, it's important to remain somewhat flexible and responsive to these types of requests. Particularly when you're asked to do something that does not imply either a large up-front development investment or a high ongoing support burden, you should try to flex to support your high-profile customers to buy some political capital. You might find it odd that we encourage this, given that we spent so much time talking about sunsetting features that are rarely used in Chapter 9. And it's true, sometimes this ends up causing you to build a one-off that costs more than it should to maintain and operate, and ultimately needs to be sunset.

But sometimes, a team knows what they need, and our job as platform owners is to support them and provide the thing they can't live without. There are two extremes that you want to avoid as a platform owner:

Always saying "yes" and turning into a feature shop
> The first is the reactionary extreme. Every request that comes in causes you to jump and try to patch in some feature or offering as quickly as possible. Your platform spirals into something that is harder and harder to evolve and support, ending up like a Frankenstein's monster of cobbled-together features with no overarching goal. This is a sign that you are not comfortable saying no to your stakeholders (and often, your team). It may also be a sign that you don't have a clear platform strategy, but not necessarily: all it takes is a stronger urge to please in the moment than a dedication to your vision to end up in this scenario.

Always saying "no" like you hold perfect judgment of company value

However, the other extreme, where you are totally inflexible and build only what you think is right and aligned with your platform strategy, is equally impossible. You should be working closely with your customers, ultimately trying to deliver value to the overall company and business. Unlike a third-party vendor, your job is not just to build something people are willing to pay you for, but rather to provide something important that's flexible enough to be customized specifically for the needs of the people in the company.

This is why some of the least effective platform leaders we have managed were often the ones who had the strongest technical and product vision for their platform. They mistakenly believed that this vision gave them the necessary knowledge to make the right choices for the business. This led them to refuse to compromise with stakeholders who saw potential value differently, insisting on only doing things aligned with their vision. They would argue that all the problems with the current system were the result of compromises, and their job was not to let that happen to the new one, or to the teams building it. As a result, when their teams hit any setbacks, long-frustrated stakeholders were quick to point out that not only were they impossible to work with, but they couldn't even execute well.

When an important customer needs a favor that you can offer with little sacrifice, it's worth it to say yes. But it's also good to say yes when someone brings you a feature request that should clearly be provided by your platform, backed by a pressing business deliverable and evidence that this feature is on the critical path for that business deliverable. In this case, don't fight with them over the unexpected request; instead, figure out what compromises might be needed to get it done.

Look for compromises around the scope and timing of this new feature. Is there a stripped-down offering that you can create faster that will unblock their most valuable business needs? Or can they adjust their own timelines to give you extra time to deliver while they concentrate on other parts of the work? Once you've negotiated the minimal realistic "yes," you may need to make sure other stakeholders are aware of the priority changes and any impacts this might have on them. But don't be afraid to support a team just because it wasn't in your original plans.

Saying "No" Without Ruining the Relationship

As with all stakeholder conversations, this one depends on the relationship you have with the stakeholder, the positioning of your team, and the magnitude of the request they are making. For the purposes of this section, we assume that you can ultimately say no to this person, although doing so may cost you some political points. If it's a person you can't say no to at all, you need a different playbook; we recommend asking your manager for help (and if they can't say no either, then you need to reevaluate whether this is really a case for a "yes, with compromises").

For times when you can say no, consider these options:

Not yet, priority call

Are you saying no, or are you saying not yet? Sometimes the request is for something that you think is valuable, that you want to do, but that you can't see a way to prioritize at this time. In this case, you want to leave your stakeholder with clarity on when you might be able to deliver it, as well as options they might have if they need it sooner. This could mean you help guide them through implementing this offering themselves, as something you can take back into your platform team at a future moment. Offering someone from your team to partner on the build can be a good idea, both to help them build it faster and to ensure that you have some insights and input into the design. Another option is to show them other priorities that have come from other teams and outweighed their needs. For all you know, they might be able to convince other stakeholders to wait behind them. It's good to be open to options when you get requests for features that you think you should implement, but you just can't justify implementing right now.

Not yet, technical call

A different version of "not yet" happens when you are not technically ready to provide a feature. In this case, the partner team can't do anything to unblock you. You don't have the underlying technical pieces in place to support the request, so it's not possible to start the initiative. You may still want to partner with them, though, to see if there are other workarounds that they could use until you are prepared to build the piece they need. No matter what, take the time to explain the technical blockers to them and do not back down if your team cannot build what they want yet, because pretending that you can will just damage your reputation and stability in the long term.

No, product strategy call

Not everything makes sense to be inside your platform. Resist the urge to become an empire builder who says yes to every feature that might possibly go into your offering just because someone expressed an interest. You need to understand the core mission of your product, and not everything will fit into that core mission. Allowing mission creep is likely to dilute the value of the product and make it harder to support and evolve over time. This will go over best if your platform is built to allow the people making the requests to either work around this gap or build their own self-managed extensions, or when you can point them to a different system that might align with their feature needs.

No, technical call

Similarly, some things aren't technically feasible, and you have to call that out. This is why we have former engineers in leadership positions on platform teams: because they understand that not every good idea can actually be built. Ian has many scars caused by poorly designed networking and knows that the operational overhead of network-based solutions means things that sound quick and simple to implement can often be overwhelmingly difficult to operate. Camille has similar scars caused by magical thinking about distributed shared memory systems. Dreaming big is one thing, but unless you are running a team that can prove they have a solid solution to an unsolved problem, don't be afraid to say no to things that are not technically feasible—just do your best to explain to the engineers why this is the case.

Going in with a hard no is never a fun conversation. Don't make it about your ego! Your stakeholders are not "stupid" because they don't understand the technical limitations or don't see your product strategy as clearly as you do. When you need to go in with a hard no, it helps to have a plan or recommendation for what else they can do, similar to your "not yet" conversations. Should they talk to another team? Can they think about their problem in a different way? Leaving them feeling like you care about their problem even though you can't help them is important for the future relationship, so try to avoid shutting them down completely.

We asked contributor Jordan West how they handle balancing "no" with "yes." What follows is from Jordan.

PLATFORM PERSPECTIVES

Finding the balance between "yes" and "no" was a challenge on a platform team I joined that had formed after a reorg. Because the perception of the prior team was that they couldn't deliver, we started by greatly limiting what we did—we said yes to delivering three things in the next 12 months, and delivered them above and beyond expectations. Unfortunately, the next year there were still plenty of complaints; but instead of being about lack of delivery, now they were about the platform team saying no too much.

Our initial inclination was to keep saying no and so deliver fewer things on faster timelines. But the feedback was overwhelming, so we ended up taking a different approach: saying "yes, with compromises" to many more things but greatly limiting the scope of each, so we could still deliver.

Two examples of this were:

- We committed to add graph storage as an offering, but to only support small and medium use cases in the first release, excluding anything in the "hot" path that could bring our website down. We also communicated that in the next round of planning we would circle back and see if there was still an appetite for a larger-scale solution.

- We committed to adding a scaled-down "versioned datasets" feature—a fancy name for "taking data from the data warehouse and putting it in OLTP databases." Long term, we wanted to support incremental updates of the data, but for the first year we only committed to the data movement portion for a static dataset.

In both cases, we covered a good portion of the use cases to keep early adopters happy, and also satisfied those who wanted the full feature set because we proposed a plan and timeline for the rest. The result of this incremental delivery that allowed us to say yes to more things was the team was perceived a lot more positively.

Compromising on Shadow Platforms

Some of the worst stakeholder relationships stem from the building of "shadow platforms." As we've described in previous chapters, a shadow platform is a system that duplicates the function of a current platform, often using different underlying OSS and vendor technologies, with a slightly different feature set and/or system (cost, performance, reliability) profile.

In an ideal world, these differences would be identified up front and the current platform would expand its capabilities to handle the new use case. Instead, the stakeholder's team uses its own initiative and builds (or proposes to build) something new—similar, but different. This is often infuriating to the platform team's engineers, who want to prevent this "wrong thing" from happening and quickly escalate it to management.

Before you can figure out an acceptable compromise or "right" action, you first need to identify what's driving these teams to build shadow platforms. Common reasons include:

Can't wait, won't wait
> Sometimes the product team has a burning need, and they cannot get on the schedule of the platform team to get this need met. It's true that this may be a false urgency, and the decision by the product team to build this new solution may be driven by the naive view that throwing together a new platform or supporting a new piece of infrastructure is easy and cheap, but there are also legitimately times when a business has a tight window of opportunity to capture

some value and they need something that doesn't exist yet in the platform and can't be added quickly. We can't always fault the application teams for building their own platforms under this kind of pressure, even though it causes the platform team pain later on.

Novel demand

There will be times when an application team needs something that might fit in with the platform offerings, but is not yet on the radar for anyone else. This could happen because there is an opportunity that requires a significantly different technology capability than the rest of the company; for example, if a team needs a graph database offering to spin up a brand-new business. You don't want to support this because no other teams are asking for it, so they go off and create it for themselves.

Don't want to collaborate

A different situation occurs when the application team has a poor relationship with the platform team and doesn't want to deal with the challenges of collaborating with them. This may come down to impatience; after all, coordination takes time even in small companies, let alone large ones. But often the application teams have had bad experiences with the platform organization in the past, perhaps due to an "us versus them" culture that has popped up on one or both sides of the fence. We have all experienced the conflict avoidance of engineers, and know that sometimes people prefer to just go off and do things on their own rather than have to negotiate with another team—especially when there is some outstanding animosity or even just ambivalence about the experience of working together.

Don't appreciate the operator cost behind your "no"

Sometimes a team hears a no from you on something and decides they want to build it anyway, even though you're sure that the operational cost is going to be far more than they bargained for. Their second-guessing can be frustrating, especially when you know that this is likely to boomerang into something you have to support.

Engineers just want to build

Finally, sometimes it's just a case of engineers wanting to build stuff. Application teams inevitably have some engineers who would rather build new systems than add incremental features to products. Some companies even encourage this behavior by making it hard for engineers to get promoted without building new systems, so there's an incentive to invent big problems to solve instead of collaborating with a platform team to add a few features. This is always going to be a factor in the development of shadow platforms, and engineering leaders must pay attention to the incentives they set up for their teams in order to keep this habit in check.

So, given what we know about the drivers that lead to the creation of shadow platforms, what should you do about them? Here are a few suggestions:

Break down the silos

There is no easy answer to solving the problem of an us versus them culture. We discussed this in Chapter 5, but the more you can do to clean up this thinking in your own team and by engaging with the leadership of other teams, the better. This will help you get earlier insight into what their needs are, incline them to consult you as a trusted advisor before they start building on their own, and make it less likely that you will be surprised by shadow infrastructure that you never knew was being built.

Partner on urgent issues

Remember that technology innovation necessarily means getting away from existing solutions, which means that teams will sometimes go off your platform to support their need for innovation. That innovation may only ever be needed in their small area, or it may end up back in your platform someday, powering more parts of the business. If it seems like a genuine need that isn't covered by your platform, it may be best to let them run with it—you might not have the bandwidth to address an urgent product engineering demand for a new platform offering, and even if the team did the right thing by coming to you first, there may be no way for you to reprioritize your current work (or hire additional headcount) to help them.

In this case, we encourage you to refer to the strategies in Chapter 5 for finding new products, and try to partner with the team to help with the build and understand what is being created. This gives you a chance to keep an eye on things and learn whether this urgent demand is something you might want to assimilate into your offerings later, or whether the thing being built is strategic only for the team in question. If it's the latter, you can set clear boundaries early about whether your team will eventually take over support and operations for the platform in question.

Be patient and accept that sometimes you will play cleanup crew

Sometimes a team is going to build something no matter what, and the best thing you can do is watch and wait. It can be infuriating to see engineering time wasted as it's being built, or dealing with the operational mess it will make in years to come. Nevertheless, it is worth coaching yourself (and your team) to be humble and realistic about what you do and don't know, and mindful that sometimes what you can intuit will be clear to your stakeholders only after they see the results of their build.

Sometimes you will be surprised by what the shadow team can pull off, particularly if they have a more "pioneering" mindset (as we discussed in Chapter 8). An idea that you thought was impossible might turn out to be just barely doable, and bring a lot of value to the users despite the operational challenges. At the very least, there is value in that the application team stakeholders are learning exactly what it means to operate a scrappy platform, and so will better understand your own problems.

Yes, sometimes this means you end up having to take over their barely working system, playing the cleanup crew that turns it into a platform-quality offering. But there are a lot of good ideas that come from people close to a problem. Your team will sometimes be the recipient of good ideas, questionably implemented; embrace the cleanup as an opportunity when it comes.

Money Troubles: Cost and Budget Management

One of the most painful moments for platform teams comes in a downturn (whether for the whole economy, or just the company you are working for), when someone starts asking questions about whether your team should really exist, what you are working on, and whether you are *really* adding enough value. The more your stakeholders trust you and understand your team and their accomplishments, the better you will fare. Unfortunately, it's also likely that even if you have done a good job with your powerful and interested stakeholders, the powerful but disinterested ones will suddenly express interest proportional to how much they think the "platform" budget is not creating commensurate value for their part of the business. In this scenario, you will face two very difficult challenges:

Roadmaps don't matter
> You might think you can avoid this with your bottom-up plan, which we described in Chapter 7, but the truth is that while your KTLO estimation will be valuable, everything beyond that will be viewed as irrelevant plans made when times were good. In tough times every team ends up rejustifying its size and roadmap, and business-aligned application engineering teams are not given a pass on this pain any more than platform teams are.

Metrics don't help
> The next thing you may reach for is metrics. The problem is that platform teams at best have loose metrics that align themselves to outcomes. In Chapter 5, we discussed developing product metrics to measure the impact of your work, and in Chapter 6 we discussed some of the operational metrics you might provide to ensure your health. But even if you do all of this well, you may have only second-order metrics to show the value of your work and its impact, particularly against business initiatives. Few care much about developer productivity when the company is trying to survive. Reliability of course matters, but you will be asked why a smaller team building fewer features cannot do better. Even efficiency projects rarely matter, unless you can save a significant amount of money quickly.

If you find yourself in this situation, you need to do everything you can to tie your work much more directly to the success of protected business outcomes. Whether it is enabling someone's pet project, making the engineering lead of the flagship product team happy, or successfully selling a story about the unacceptable risks that will happen if you don't invest in your platform, now is the time to double down on aligning yourself with business outcomes.

How should you approach this? We recommend a three-step process, outlined in the following sections.

Step 1: Figure Out Who Will Benefit Tomorrow

Start by going through all of the work you're doing that is not in the KTLO category, and for each major project, ask which customers want it and what the value is. For those projects that are closely coupled to delivering some high-profile product or business initiative, you're good. If anything, you want to talk those projects up even more. Is there some small, loosely related work that you think is important that you could bucket with those initiatives without too much scrutiny? You can save a small amount of discretionary budget by aligning it with these important mandates. You'll probably also end up building more valuable things in the process by ensuring that your teams are getting creative about how to tie their work to the highest-value customers.

In the process of doing this, you're going to find some projects that don't easily line up with any big business cases, and this is where things get painful. You may be right that experimenting with a new scheduling algorithm can, over time, improve the performance and cost profile of your machine learning platform, but right now that seems like a distraction from the business of surviving. You have a few choices in these scenarios:

Pause the project
> If the project was early, unclear, and had too many people working on it, you should probably pause the initiative completely. Now is not the time to maintain expensive speculative work.

Shrink the project
> Shrink it and fold it into something that everyone agrees is important. As mentioned previously, you will need to buy yourself some breathing room, and aligning speculative work with necessary work is a good tactic for this.

Do the work to show business value
> This means making a case for how this project could benefit the business, getting stakeholders aligned, and accelerating the roadmap to value creation. You may want to go so far as to get a specific important stakeholder signed up as a senior sponsor for the project. If your team feels strongly about the project's value, you

should give them a chance to sell it—cutting it will likely be very demotivating, and this is a great opportunity to teach them how to sell their ideas to skeptical stakeholders.

Step 2: Group the Work into Teams (Don't Go Person-by-Person)

Unless your team is very small, you do not want to report on which individuals are doing what work. Offering up this detail invites pointless scrutiny, and you are pretending to have accuracy you probably can't deliver.

Instead, group the work into chunks that are no smaller than a single project team (say, 3–5 people at the smallest) can handle, and no bigger than a double-sized team (up to 10–12) can manage. This is a reasonable approach for teams of up to a couple hundred engineers. If you run a bigger organization, make sure someone is grouping all project work into similar-sized chunks across all the teams.

Grouping work by project-sized teams like this prevents you from the mistake of saying you can trim every area evenly and have things continue as normal. Your teams should not be uniformly overstaffed by some percentage, so when you need to do justifications (or worse, cuts), your goal should be to determine whole initiatives to cut so that you can spare other initiatives and retain their focus.

Step 3: Come with Suggestions of What to Cut and Strong Opinions About What to Keep

People respond to strength and weakness. If you try to defend every single thing your team is working on and justify why you can't possibly cut anything, you will signal to your stakeholders that you aren't taking this situation seriously and aren't listening to the message that you need to make changes. It is important, however, that you make the case for why the most important work matters, particularly if it is a speculative investment or deeply technical.

Having coached many teams through budget downcycles, we recommend that you preemptively decide what you think should be reduced or eliminated and come to the table ready to make those suggestions. This should be informed by customer and stakeholder feedback (if no one understands why you're doing something and you can't explain it yourself, that's a red flag), but it shouldn't be entirely decided by their feedback. You are the expert and owner of this area—show that expertise and ownership by defending the things that others don't understand or appreciate but that you strongly believe are essential.

At the end of this exercise, you may have cut your team more than you want, but by strategizing ahead of time you should be able to preserve your most important investments (barring an unavoidable mandate to do a massive 40–50% cut). Strong stakeholder relationships coming into this exercise will minimize the pain; there's no escaping the cuts, but the trust you've established should give you the power to shape them in the way you think is best.

Wrapping Up

In our experience, platform teams live and die on their success at stakeholder relationship management, and we can't overemphasize how valuable it is to develop good practices throughout your team. You need to understand how your stakeholders relate to your team, what they care about, and how to communicate and negotiate effectively with them. This doesn't always come naturally to engineers, in particular, but you can't just delegate it to product management and hope it will take care of itself. Your stakeholders can make your life easier or harder, and it's up to you to manage those relationships for the good of your team, the platform, and the company as a whole.

When developing these relationships, think about the different touchpoints. Yes, you'll have 1:1s, but you'll also have interlocks and advisory meetings where you give your stakeholders a chance to hear from you and one another, to improve overall alignment. Increase communication, especially in tough times, to maintain the right level of trust and transparency.

The day-to-day reality of stakeholder relationships kicks in whenever you need to negotiate and compromise. It's crucial to stay flexible and responsive, even when plans seem to change out of the blue. Say yes when it's easy, and say yes when the request has clear, pressing business value. Sometimes you'll need to say no, or not yet, and accept that the application team might build their own shadow platform. Always aim for the win/win: if you can even just provide advice on their platform, it sets you up to learn from what they build and possibly even take over the platform in the future if it becomes successful.

Finally, there's the issue of budgets. When money is tight, everyone is looking for corners to cut, and without good stakeholder relationships your platform team might end up first on the chopping block. Get ahead of this by figuring out for yourself which areas could be cut, and which areas are must-dos. The more you show that you are invested in taking budget cuts seriously, the more likely you are to end up with an outcome you can live with. If you've done all of the other work in this chapter and come in with strong relationships already established, you'll ward off the worst outcomes and live to fight another day.

PART III

What Does Success Look Like?

"Well, in our country," said Alice, still panting a little, "you'd generally get to somewhere else—if you run very fast for a long time, as we've been doing."

"A slow sort of country!" said the Queen. "Now, here, you see, it takes all the running you can do, to keep in the same place. If you want to get somewhere else, you must run at least twice as fast as that!"

—Lewis Carroll, *Through the Looking-Glass, and What Alice Found There*, Chapter 2

A platform team running as hard as it can can often appear to be making little progress. You get some systems into a steady state, enabling your team to focus on other areas, only to be pulled back a year or two later when the systems are outdated and no longer serve the company. Your paved paths that make the 80% happy still leave the other 20% grumbling that their needs haven't been addressed. You hire the perfect balanced team, only to go through a budget crunch that forces you to lay off some, or a growth cycle that sees great people leave for greener pastures. On top of this, even when you are progressing, delivering value is slow; it takes time to build a high-quality product, time to convince customers to use it, and time to migrate everyone.

This is why we oppose textbook "metrics and measures" approaches as the primary way of talking about platform engineering success. That's not to say they are useless; we will cover adoption and customer satisfaction metrics in this part of the book, and we recommend the CNCF platform engineering maturity model (*https://oreil.ly/VcKqO*) as a way of benchmarking your team and looking for ways to improve. But these metrics and models are most useful as broad signals that measure past actions, too simplistic and lagging to capture the full picture of your situation and point you toward your next successful investments.

Thus, we recommend a holistic approach to evaluating ongoing success by focusing on four areas that will tell you whether you are on the best path:

- Your platforms are aligned.
- Your platforms are trusted.
- Your platforms manage complexity.
- Your platforms are loved.

Success as a platform engineering leader requires you to continually evaluate how you are doing in each of these areas, to which the following four chapters are dedicated. Sometimes changes underfoot mean you will be failing, and often in correcting you will face trade-offs. But if you adjust direction when the balance is not right, and are patient in waiting for your journey on a calibrated path to start showing results, you will get your platform to where the company needs it to be.

CHAPTER 11

Your Platforms Are Aligned

The purpose of a team is not goal attainment but goal alignment. When the team is fulfilling its purpose, team members are more effective because they're more directed.

—Tom DeMarco and Tim Lister, *Peopleware: Productive Projects and Teams*

Alignment is the first criterion for holistically evaluating the success of your platform engineering teams. This requires looking across all the platform teams and asking: are we aligned in what we are doing? Misaligned platform teams create a swamp of a different kind than the "over-general" one we described in Chapter 1. This swamp is filled with overlapping and incompatible products, tricky to use together and often at odds with each other's goals. It's just as hard to navigate and can be even more frustrating, as customers struggle with platform teams who can't see beyond the silos of their own making.

Here are the three areas in which we commonly see misalignments:

Purpose
> Platform teams that do not have a holistic mindset (using a product approach to develop software-based abstractions that are foundations for the business and serve a broad customer base) but rather operate with a narrower focus are misaligned in purpose.

Product strategy
> Platform teams that operate in silos, building platforms that are good for their specific purpose but needlessly duplicate others or make cross-platform use cases hard, are misaligned on product strategy.

Planning
> Platform teams that do not support each other as they execute their most critical projects, but rather get in each other's way and miscommunicate with customers about timelines and changed circumstances, are misaligned on plans.

In this chapter we will dive into each of these types of misalignment and talk about how you can successfully manage them.

A Success Red Herring: Adoption Metrics

When platform teams ask themselves, "What does success look like?" the first answer is often some sort of adoption metric. Strong adoption *should* indicate a platform team that is delivering value for the company by building platforms customers are eager to adopt. However, this line of thinking can be taken too far.

Focusing on adoption, platform teams can start to assume their sole mission is to determine the platforms of the future, drive the usage of those to 100%, and deprecate everything else as fast as possible. But 100% adoption only truly measures success when your customers have a choice of whether or not to use your platforms. The risk of using adoption metrics when you are targeting a captive or nearly captive audience is forgetting to build what people want, and instead building what you think they should want and then forcing them to use it.

Adoption is a better success metric than completion, the ultimate cop-out metric that merely tracks your ability to declare victory, but that's not saying much. When adoption is measured system by system (or even feature by feature), it works against the goal of alignment by creating competition between your teams for user attention. If the platform team also forces mandatory migrations in order to achieve adoption goals, the metric loses all of its value in measuring organic customer demand and turns into a stick to use on the customers. In the worst-case scenario, you have a confusing array of platform offerings and a constant pressure on customers to justify their lack of adoption under the threat of mandatory migration.

This matters because you dilute your leverage every time your platform team generates work for its customers. When the platform team makes the customers responsible for driving their own adoption, whether by expecting customers to write their own requirements or forcing them to migrate to the newest product, they drain the very productivity they're supposed to be safeguarding. When the platform team is out of alignment and competes with itself for customer attention by delivering offerings that don't work well together, it contributes to the complexity and confusion that it's supposed to be solving for.

So, be careful about using adoption as anything other than a secondary metric. Instead, think about how you are delivering leverage by understanding who will benefit most from your platform, and targeting the adoption of those most valuable customers by working with them to identify measurable pain points that your new platform will address.

You don't need to get every single team onboard for every single product you offer. That may be the goal for certain very targeted types of systems—you probably don't want multiple employee identity systems internally, for example—but some platforms are simply more valuable for certain groups than others, and trying to force every

---

team onto the same platform can often cause you to lose sight of where you could be providing the most leverage for the company.

Track adoption, and use it as an input to your product strategy. But don't mistake it for an absolute measure of success.

Alignment to Purpose

One example we've seen of misalignment to purpose was with a continuous integration (CI) platform whose running tasks were regularly disrupted by the underlying operating system platform running OS updates. This would cause the CI task to restart, increasing tail latencies for CI users. It might have seemed that the easy fix would be to delay the OS updates until no tasks were running, but that implementation would have been an additional hack on the already hacky legacy operating system platform. Instead, the OS platform team pushed for the CI platform team to prioritize a migration to a new OS platform with immutable images. While both sides agreed this was the ideal engineering goal, the problem was that this project would take many developer months to implement, and in the meantime the OS team refused to implement a much smaller workaround that would have fixed the user impact immediately.

When we dug into why there was such a strong disagreement here, it became clear that the OS platform team's leadership was not yet aligned on thinking of it as a platform engineering team. Instead, they still held an "infrastructure" mindset. They were in conflict with partners because they viewed their goal as prioritizing the technical quality of the solution above all else. Rather than optimizing for the end customer experience, they used unhappy customers as leverage to get their desired migrations done faster so that their technology would be improved. In short, the OS platform team failed to appreciate the product side of their decisions.

For platform teams to be successful, they must share a common purpose. This comes back to the pillars of platform engineering we described back in Chapter 2:

Product
    Taking a curated product approach

Development
    Developing software-based abstractions

Breadth
    Serving a broad base of application developers

Operations
    Operating as foundations for the business

Each platform team will also define their purpose beyond this, specific to their platform area. However, these four pillars are crucial for all platform teams to adopt, because together they create leverage and make it possible to manage the complexity that comes with building on OSS and cloud primitives and interoperating with other platforms. You need to build a team and team culture aligned to this.

Align Teams to Purpose with the Right Mix of People

Alignment to purpose starts with getting the right people on the team, as we discussed in Chapter 4. As you bring teams together and begin to hire new people, openly discuss the balance of roles and skill sets that you're looking for across the team to help everyone understand what the new group needs to look like. In a smaller company, everyone should be involved in the hiring processes, as this reinforces agreement on the type of engineers that platform engineering needs.

Driving people alignment in a larger organization is trickier: you can use cross-team interviewing to support cultural intermixing, but you'll likely end up reorganizing some of the existing teams to make sure you have the right people, with the right skill sets, covering the right product areas. If you're transforming an infrastructure team, you probably have many functionally aligned subteams (think compute, networking, storage, etc.). In the places where these teams overlap, you may want to mix things up, or even pull out separate teams that are more cross-functional to better support platform initiatives.

Align Culture to Purpose with Common Practices

The next step of aligning to purpose is culture. The first part of this is teams sharing common practices around our four pillars. Through a product management culture of approaching your internal users as customers (not just stakeholders) and looking for partnership opportunities with these customers to identify new products, you break out of the "us versus them" mentality and develop the empathy necessary to build great platform products. Similarly, common operations practices, including operability reviews, blameless postmortems, and other practices learned from the DevOps and SRE movements, help break down the boundaries between teams and platforms.

Align Culture to Purpose by Having Teams Collaborate

The approach to collaboration determines much of your team culture, and the more the organization collaborates, the more gelled its overall culture will become. If you are reading this book as a senior leader overseeing multiple platform areas, it is your job to bring your teams together frequently and foster collaboration. For example, everyone within your organization should use one another's platforms. Not only will this create a common culture, but this "dogfooding" will also generate many of your more creative ideas around product strategy.

If you're an engineering manager, senior individual contributor (IC), or product manager, you can contribute to this collaborative culture by looking for chances to work with your peers on other teams and encouraging your teams to pick their heads up from time to time to get a look at the bigger picture of what's going on around them. One approach to this is holding architecture and product strategy reviews, and inviting members of other platform teams to learn about and provide constructive feedback on these strategies. Sharing work to drive collaboration is the core source of those creative ideas, after all.

Alignment of Product Strategy

The next element of misalignment to address is product strategy. We experienced this coming out of a period of rapid headcount growth with no attempt to align across platform teams. Four teams made four different technology bets for the new platform, each partnering with different customers as early adopters. Roll forward a couple of years to our arrival, and the result was five different compute platforms, where the largest one was "deprecated" for new use cases but the other four were "not GA-ready yet"—a clear failure of product strategy.

However, the failures did not stop there. As each of the four new teams was trying to grow their platform beyond a "scrappy" architecture, they realized they could only do so with more engineers, which they could each justify only by trying to capture the same set of use cases. As we discussed in Chapter 3, duplication of common functionality is not always a problem. But if you get to the point where platforms are not just duplicating but actively fighting for the same customers to justify headcount, then collectively you don't have a product strategy.

To align product strategy across platforms, we recommend four tactics, which we detail next.

Foster Cross-Platform Thinking with Independent Product Management

If your product managers report to the engineering managers who own specific platform areas, then your product managers will struggle to think strategically outside those areas. They become an extension of the engineering managers and lead engineers, and spend the majority of their time communicating and planning within their respective engineering silos. This narrow focus optimizes for growing and expanding within the engineering functional domain, but it misses product improvements that cross areas.

As we discussed in the previous section, culture matters for alignment, and can be used to push siloed product managers to be more open to cooperation. However, there is always going to be conflict between each platform area's preferred strategies, and you make it hard on product managers when the engineering manager doing their performance review is deeply invested in just one.

To counteract this, keep the product management reporting structure separated enough from the engineering management structure that they can operate independently. We like to have all of the platform product managers in a separate team reporting to a product management leader, in turn reporting to a cross-area senior platform engineering leader.[1] That way, the leader of product management for platforms can be held accountable for the platforms working well together as products.

When this works best, the product management leader understands that their role is much less about dictating a singular unifying vision (i.e., the Steve Jobs "visionary" version of product leadership), and more about challenging their product management team to cooperate as they build out their plans (called an "affiliative" or "collaborative" leadership style).

Foster Cross-Platform Architecture with Independent Lead ICs

Sometimes it's actually engineering architecture misalignment that is behind a product strategy misalignment. We lived through a version of this with a deployment platform that was struggling with the storage throughput requirements of large container images and scaling container deployments. True, we had a storage platform that could have supported this with some work, but the team members were fully occupied with their own customer problems and so declined to get involved when first approached. Instead of escalating the issue, the deployment platform team went deep into prototyping a storage system rearchitecture to handle more scale. Since this was seen as a technical decision, the product managers weren't involved, and the engineering managers were happy to have a fun technical project for the team, despite this being a clear misalignment of technical ownership and expertise. It was only after significant investment and delivery challenges that the issue was brought to the attention of senior leadership, and the storage team was brought in to eventually take over the system they should have owned in the first place.

To avoid this kind of situation, you need some person(s) in the engineering team who are not just thinking about cross-platform architectural problems, but are in a position to advocate for resolving them. While we don't like the full bureaucracy of an architecture review board, it is useful to have the most senior

---

1 Why not have the most senior leader be a product leader? We are both engineering leaders at heart, and we were worried about a product person managing everything when engineering and operations were so key to success. But hey, maybe it would work!

"principal/distinguished" engineer in the platform engineering organization report to the same senior leader as the product management leader. While this engineer should endeavor to stay somewhat hands-on to be grounded in their decision making, the other half of their role should be helping with architecture-level misalignment—for example:

- Providing escalation and advocacy when junior engineers are trying to reduce architectural misalignment but running into product/engineering management impediments
- Looking for when teams are wrongfully duplicating architecture because it's easier (or more fun) than cooperating
- For larger organizations, overseeing architecture/engineering design sessions across teams to enable cross-vetting of major decisions and knowledge sharing of best practices

Such a role should include talking more with customers about architecture-impacting product decisions as well. But beware of having every big engineering decision flow through a single person's approval—not only will they be a bottleneck, but it will also limit their ability to do the occasional hands-on work. With this in mind, to scale up the role as the organization grows, "staff-level" engineers should start taking on this role for their own platform areas but be challenged by the principal engineer to think about and advocate for platforms beyond their own.

Seek Feedback from Comments in Platform-wide Customer Surveys

With independent product management, you should now have product managers who can be challenged to think outside their silos when they build their strategies. However, particularly for large platforms, such strategy conversations usually take place with a subset of users—often the more senior ones, who may have become accustomed to the platform's flaws and don't see the alignment issues that frustrate newer users. To correct for this, we like to augment direct product management feedback activities with data from the free-form comments of platform-wide customer surveys.

Customer surveys won't find all problems, but when feature-level product misalignment is keeping them from getting their jobs done, this is often the only outlet customers will use to tell you about it. We've found that it's almost always valuable to spend time investigating reported problems to see how bad the situation really is and how pervasive one person's frustration is across the customer base. One comment is, of course, just a sample, but often where there is smoke (coming out of someone's ears), there is a smoldering fire of other users with similar frustrations.

Judiciously Resolve Misalignment with Restructuring

One alignment challenge comes when different teams have platform offerings that provide overlapping feature sets. This often happens with scrappy platforms created through partnerships with application teams, and the overlap can be substantial enough that there are more shared features than unique ones. This leads to both product and engineering concerns. From the product side, is this duplication confusing to users? What would be the downside of limiting the duplication? From the engineering side, is this duplication wasting engineering effort or driving additional costs?

Both sides can make bad choices here. Product managers, eager to concentrate ownership in their product scope, may argue to create consolidation even when that means losing valuable unique features from one of the overlapping options. Engineering leaders, who also desire to grow their teams, will similarly argue that the cost efficiencies of unification outweigh the marginal benefits of the missing offerings. The temptation to solve this problem by reorganizing the team and putting all products under one leader is very strong.

It's important to remember the lessons of Chapters 8 and 9: rearchitecting, migrating, and sunsetting will take a lot of work, a lot of time, and a decent amount of iteration along the way. A reorganization will not change that (even if it is the right long-term move). Worse, reorgs cause churn in the engineering teams and confuse customers on issues like where to go for documentation and support. Yes, an organization's structure shapes the systems it produces, and leaders should keep an eye out for major structural issues. But alignment-driven reorganizations should be reserved for situations where the costs of misalignment are high and the benefits are clear.

In fact, our reorganizations have been driven more by the capacity of strong leaders to take on more scope (or, conversely, by leaders who could not handle their current scope) than by the goal of mapping our ideal product portfolio onto the structure of our engineering organization.[2] Going back to our earlier example with the five compute platforms, that was something that we resolved incrementally over 18 months, as each integration helped us understand our strategy. In the meantime, we asked each platform team's leader to be aware of when they were competing for customer use cases, and to work with their peers to determine how their product strategies were different and so avoid the competition. Seeing how some of these leaders were able to use influence to resolve these differences with peers, and so go beyond dictating a solution to those under their authority, was in fact a large part of how we learned who the strong leaders were.

---

2 Sometimes called the "inverse Conway maneuver."

Alignment of Plans

For an example of planning misalignment, let's return to the OS platform team we mentioned earlier. While yes, their attempt at a forced migration to immutable images was causing issues for the CI platform, they were also experiencing the challenge of working with a build-tools platform team that hadn't planned to do their work on the immutable images project for another two years. This was because the build-tools platform team had stuffed their roadmap with concurrent v2 projects and argued that any deviation from these plans was impossible because of their commitments to customers.

While we had reservations about this v2 approach (those lessons informed much of Chapter 8), it was clear that the build-tools platform team had customers eagerly awaiting delivery. It wasn't enough to align these teams on purpose and strategy; we had to drill all the way down to aligning on plans.

Align Only on Larger Projects, Not on Every Detail

When we talk about aligning plans, we mean taking only the significant projects (one developer year or bigger) and looking at each one's dependencies on other platform areas and justification for being a priority for those areas. This comes back to Chapter 7: the path to alignment success will not come from building a highly detailed plan spanning all platform teams. That's too much work, too much detail, and will keep teams from having some agility (which the business will demand when urgent needs arise).

We've heard concerns about this recommendation—some worry that leaving out smaller projects in assessments means losing visibility of everything a team is planning and increasing the risk of leaders gaming the process by hiding their pet projects as minor efforts. However, gamesmanship happens even when the smaller projects are included, with overly optimistic/pessimistic estimates of effort and risk to fit whatever narrative gets the plan approved or secures the most headcount. The way to avoid gamesmanship is building a common culture and having leadership from all teams reporting up in parallel to engineering management as a checks and balances mechanism. This allows you to focus only on the big projects and trust that your alignment and culture will keep the small stuff in check.

Be Forthright in Confronting Misalignment

Platform leaders will have to collaboratively make tough calls about roadmap items that benefit Platform A's users at the cost of Platform B's plans (e.g., if team B has to contribute work to unblock team A, or delay their plans to avoid forcing too many migrations on the same users). This presents two challenges:

- These trade-offs become political. While we would like platform engineers to rationally choose work based on the needs of the company, most people also want to see "their" work succeed, especially when delivering impact ties to organizational recognition systems like compensation and promotions.
- It's rarely clear which of the competing initiatives is most important. Each team's plans resolve customer pain points and move the product strategy forward. In an ideal world you'd be able to accommodate both, but the reality is that some hard decisions will have to be made based on what's better for the company overall.

Weak platform leadership often takes the easy route of greenlighting each team's proposals to avoid confrontation, thinking they can be agile and make course corrections later. While agility is great for decisions that impact only a single team, it's a different story when those decisions ripple out to other platform teams and their customers. Eventually, those ripples will need to be smoothed out, and postponing that just means more work will get thrown out and customers will be left scratching their heads over missed deadlines and shifted roadmaps. It's important to bite the bullet and hash things out early to avoid a bigger mess later.

Amazon, where Ian spent a decade of his career, has a leadership principle (*https://oreil.ly/RTnjM*) aimed at avoiding this conflict avoidance trap—they want leaders committed to their cause, but also willing to commit to an outcome otherwise:

> **Have Backbone; Disagree and Commit**
>
> Leaders are obligated to respectfully challenge decisions when they disagree, even when doing so is uncomfortable or exhausting. Leaders have conviction and are tenacious. They do not compromise for the sake of social cohesion. Once a decision is determined, they commit wholly.

People often focus on the "Disagree and Commit" part of this principle, but miss that "Have Backbone" comes first. Your platform team has strong leaders. If you want them to eventually commit to a decision they disagree with, they first need a forum in which to put forth their best case.

Final Alignment Comes from Principled Leadership

But how do the platform leaders get to a final decision they can commit to? Is it up to the platform engineering organization's "biggest boss" to pick winners and losers? We've all experienced situations where a senior leader picked the winners in a seemingly arbitrary fashion, leaving teams with the impression that the leader didn't understand or care about their needs or those of their customers. On the other hand, someone has to make the final decision, or we end up hurting our customers by making plans we can't deliver on.

To resolve this quandary, senior leaders need to apply a deliberate rationale to making decisions, and this must be clearly communicated to everyone involved. The process of getting to the decision needs to be collaborative and transparent. "Disagree and commit" is not in fact a matter of the most senior person arbitrarily deciding; rather, it is about creating a process where the team can get aligned behind the decision because they understand what led to it. Succeeding comes through doing the work of planning and consolidating, as we discussed in Chapters 5 and 7, and applying those plans across the team.

Tying It Together: Getting an Organization to Alignment

Aligning on major initiatives tends to become an acute challenge for platform teams once the combined team is big enough that there are several distinct areas, each with multiple teams working on them. Each of these area teams will inevitably have big things they want to do to move their part of the platform forward, and even if you've developed a pretty high-functioning organization, the question of which of these big projects to work on is a tough one. Camille experienced this when leading a platform organization of around 100 people (out of ~1,000 engineers at the company) with a large surface area and a number of platforms that were struggling to scale. While the team had come together culturally by balancing its skills, focusing on customer needs, and improving support and on-call practices, there was remaining tension around rearchitecture work and major investments. Every area team was sure it needed immediate, deep investment in order to solve underlying technical issues, scale for the future, and deliver the next major customer feature, and these projects were competing for attention and change budget from the users themselves.

In the last section, we talked about such a case of competition between the OS platform team and the build-tools platform team. The OS platform team was sure they needed immutable images to avoid mutating OS updates impacting low-latency and CI customers. The build-tools platform team was sure they needed to decompose their current bespoke platform so that they could support more industry-standard tooling and take advantage of a hot open source build system, Bazel, to improve performance. Each team had done scoping and roadmap planning, which revealed that not only were these large projects with large migrations, but each migration would create significant work for the other team. There was no way they could do both of these migrations simultaneously, so how could they resolve the conflict? Each leader thought their area was the most important, each product management leader also thought their area was the most important, and both had customers advocating for their solutions. The teams were deadlocked.

Resolving this deadlock was not easy. Here's how the process went:

1. First, each team made a bottom-up roadmap with estimates for the upcoming year, where they would invest, and which projects would require additional funding. This was the outcome of the product roadmap process from Chapter 5, feeding into the bottom-up roadmap estimation process described in Chapter 7.

2. Using this input, the leadership team (made up of heads of each area, product management, and the chief architect) identified common themes across the teams that spoke to both technical and product challenges. Five of these became the high-level objectives for the organization, reflecting the areas that everyone agreed were most important and the general approaches they would use to address them. For example, one hypothesis was that they were failing to meet users' needs because they had tried to deliver end-to-end solutions without providing stable building blocks, so the objective was "building blocks, not batteries included." These objectives were used to reprioritize the product investments across the teams. Projects that sounded like good ideas but didn't match the objectives were cut in order to drive measurable progress in the objective areas.

3. Next came a series of meetings where the area heads' roadmaps were reviewed by peer heads, senior ICs, and product managers. These reviews revealed places where the teams had been overly optimistic about the costs of doing something, especially when their plans had impact on other platform areas that had not been considered. Through this exercise, they managed to weed out some overly optimistic projects.

4. Finally, each area head was asked to come to the group with the projects they saw as misaligned to the overall goals and thought should be dropped. This only worked because they had started to trust one another, and they trusted Camille to help them prioritize for the best interest of the overall company, so they didn't play political games to try to kill one another's projects but rather brought their honest opinions. This further highlighted projects that seemed risky or optional, and some (but not all!) of the identified projects were either cut or had their scope reduced for the year. The product objectives were again used to make priority calls based on their potential impact.

5. At the end of this process, the overall project list could accommodate the most important stakeholder work, everyone understood the investments their peers were making, and, while there were still disagreements, the team as a whole could commit to moving forward with the understanding that they would course correct as needed.

This process did not result in perfect alignment across the team, but it laid the groundwork to enable that "disagree and commit" approach. While the OS platform team still thought the company needed to move to immutable OS images, they could see that this was not a top product priority to begin a broad migration in the next 12 months. And while Ian (who the OS platform team reported to) didn't agree with the build-tools platform team's strategy to migrate the build systems to Bazel, he saw that his peer had a reasoned argument for continuing the work, and moreover had sacrificed other projects in the process of planning. This helped him commit to supporting the project, despite lingering doubts. Some of these strategies still failed, including the Bazel migration, but others that were contentious (such as moving the company to Git) prepared the foundations for important platform improvements over the years.

This is what success in driving platform alignment looks like from an execution perspective, and this process applies to major product investment conflicts as much as it applies to rearchitecting and technical investment conflicts. It will be time-consuming, frustrating, and messy, but you can achieve success by proactively gathering the details to justify decisions, putting up with the frustration and possible disappointment, and slowly course correcting. Ultimately, this is much better for the company than leadership avoiding conflict, letting everyone go their own way for far too long, and leaving it for the next generation to make even harder calls after much deeper investments have been made.

Wrapping Up

So, how does alignment contribute to platform success? We're frequently asked the question: how do we know our platform is good, or getting better? Well, the only way to measure success is to agree on a target and aim for it. If you go through the detailed exercise of aligning your teams and their plans, at the end of it you will have a much clearer understanding of what your focus areas should be, and a set of goals and work items to help you achieve those goals. If you have done the product work necessary to identify the market you're targeting, and you regularly get feedback from the users rather than looking only at your internal metrics, you will know whether your platform is getting better at the things you have chosen to focus on. This doesn't mean that you've chosen to do the right things; we can all make strategic mistakes! But without this work, you will never be able to make conscious improvements in the capabilities of your platforms.

Here's a secret about this chapter: nothing about it is particularly unique to platform engineering. If you want to be a successful leader of any type of team, creating a shared purpose and aligning your team culturally around that purpose is critical. You need to have a strategy for what you are going to do, and a way to break that strategy down across the parts of your team to execute against it, so that they all understand what is important overall and can make informed decisions on where to focus.

The particularity with a platform engineering team is that the value you produce is usually several steps removed from clear measures of success such as revenue growth, so it's rare that you have business-driven deliverables dictating your roadmap. The indirect nature of platform value leaves platform leadership with a lot more discretion to choose where to invest. This leads to one of the common causes of platform strategy failure: in the face of many different paths that the team could pursue, and the challenge of having hard conversations to create alignment about which of those options to focus on, leaders just don't make decisions and instead let individual product teams go off and build what they think is right from their narrow point of view. This can create some pockets of siloed success, but the lack of alignment across the team as a whole will always hold it back from greatness.

CHAPTER 12

Your Platforms Are Trusted

Trust is like the air we breathe—when it's present, nobody really notices; when it's absent, everybody notices.

—Warren Buffett

After the internal focus on building alignment within your team and its products, the next area of success is external: earning the trust of everyone else. You may ask, why should we put trust (a feeling or belief) ahead of results? Surely if you deliver platforms that manage complexity and so deliver leverage to the organization's application teams, that is a more important signal than a second-order signal of trust?

When you get your platform team to a point where they are delivering value continuously, trust will follow. However, you have platforms in production today. Features and improvements for these platforms take time to deliver, and their delivery requires customer trust, in the form of patience and partnerships for testing, validating, and adoption. Without trust, a single unfortunate event can render your carefully crafted product roadmaps useless, forcing you to scramble with throwaway work to manage the crisis.

We have seen platforms lose trust in three main ways:

Operations
  Not demonstrating operational ability at the scale customers need

Big investment buy-in
  Not seeking buy-in on large investments before starting, under the assumption that no one outside the platform team should care

Being a bottleneck
  Becoming a bottleneck to business initiatives, and so reducing rather than creating business leverage.

In this chapter, we'll discuss how you can avoid losing trust in each of these areas.

A Success Red Herring: Thinking Trust in a Leader Is Trust in the Platform

One of the worst management mistakes in any type of engineering is when the team leader oversteps their role as facilitator for collaborative decisions and instead acts as a benevolent dictator, personally making all the calls—be they management, engineering, or product decisions. It might seem easier to trust a single person who understands how product, stakeholder, engineering, and management decisions intersect, who can short-circuit conflicts by dictating solutions, and who is most accountable for the team's success. However, this approach undermines trust in the long term by failing to foster trust in any other members of the team.

It's true that the benevolent dictator setup can be efficient, especially when the leader is a strong communicator and decision maker with a small team and few users and stakeholders to wrangle. In these scenarios, the leader can use 1:1 meetings with all of these individuals to understand the nuts and bolts around any conflict, personally commit to the needed action, and provide directions to their team, thereby avoiding lengthy documents detailing trade-offs and contentious deliberation meetings.

The problem with this situation is that what makes it efficient also makes it brittle. It only works because you have one person with deep expertise in the platform who (right now) has the time to have regular conversations with all types of users and stakeholders to maintain their personal trust. Once the number of customers becomes too big for one person to handle, or that person moves on (often burned out from trying to work too many hours a week), you are left with a situation where not only do you no longer have a decision maker, but you also don't have any trust.

Now the platform team will have to start from scratch, building up inherently slower group mechanisms around trust and decision making. It can take months, if not years, for the product teams to figure out how to negotiate decisions and establish trust with one another and their stakeholders. With hindsight, it becomes clear that it would have been far more efficient for the decision maker to delegate and share some of that responsibility earlier, to build trust within the team.

Does this mean you should never allow someone to take on the benevolent dictatorial role? No. In fact, a lot of the agility at the scrappy and scalable stages comes from having someone with a pioneer or settler mindset in this sort of leadership role, making fast decisions with a small team and a small number of customers. However, this approach is not sustainable and does not scale to larger team sizes or customer numbers. If you are such a leader, you need to challenge yourself to start delegating. This will be hard on you and the stakeholders, because it will slow down the decision-making process in the short term. But it's worth it, because you'll be building your stakeholders' trust in the whole team for the long term.

Trust in How You Operate

You're probably thinking this is going to be a rehash of Chapter 6: put in some practices around on-call and support rotations, backed by some SLOs, change management, and operational reviews, and you deserve trust, right? As usual, things are not so simple.

We believe all these practices are essential to ensure rigor and hold platform leadership accountable. However, you can tick all the boxes and still lack the operational trust of many senior engineers in application teams. Before they migrate to your platform, this lack of trust may show up as standoffs, prolonged timelines, and demands for vague "proofs of concept." Even after adoption, it can cause issues—for instance, when some operational hiccup leads customers to pressure leadership into letting them build a "simpler" shadow platform that suits their needs better.

We get it. Earlier in our careers *we were* those senior application engineers who didn't want to adopt shiny new platforms, or who inherited an application on a shaky general-purpose platform that we wanted to change out for something simpler. Beyond the seeming lack of control over our fate, the most frustrating part of being on the application engineering side of things was when the platform team seemed to underestimate how much impact we felt due to their critical failures. It was a double trust problem: "Not only are they bad at operating things, they have no idea they are bad at operating things!"

The root of the challenge is that you only get good at operating foundational systems at scale by operating foundational systems at scale. When Ian was at Amazon, this was such a recurring problem that they developed a saying: "There is no compression algorithm for experience. You can't learn certain lessons without going through the curve." Where does this put you as a leader of a platform team, if you see that your senior users don't really trust your team operationally? You still have two levers:

1. Accelerate the curve by hiring and empowering leaders with operational experience at scale.

2. Optimize the curve by ordering new use cases based on tolerance for operational risk.

Let's look at both, with examples from our backgrounds.

Accelerate Trust by Empowering Experienced Leaders

When Camille started her first head of platform engineering job, much of the team she inherited was struggling with operational stability. The engineering team and the systems had been built in a scrappy fashion, and they'd grown a lot over the prior few years without much investment in system improvements, let alone rearchitectures.

The team had some new managers who had come from operational roles at bigger companies, and they were confident they knew what was needed to stabilize the systems, but they needed help—cover to focus on this work in light of customer demands for features, and help inspiring their teams of mostly software engineers to see the value of doing it.

Looking back, Camille considers herself quite lucky. There was a problem, yes, but all of the ingredients to solve the problem were already there: talented, experienced managers; strong engineers; support from the CTO. With the hiring side taken care of, Camille's contribution was providing empowerment—taking the trust problem seriously, setting a broad cultural mandate about how they would approach operations as an organization, and communicating this in a way that both the team as a whole and the stakeholders/customers would understand.

To do this, she used what is now a key tool in her management toolkit—the operational excellence OKR. OKRs were a well-established practice at the company, but historically they'd always been focused on new capabilities. Camille established an objective of improving operational stability, and got each of her leaders to commit to measurable key results their teams would deliver against this objective. She then shared this broadly to all of engineering as part of their OKR town hall, to her organization in detail in the team all-hands, and even to the executive management team (her peers and so major stakeholders) in quarterly reports.

Creating measurable goals enabled managers to explain to their stakeholders why they were focusing on operational stability work instead of features, and what they could expect to see from the work. Calling this out as an organization-wide focus area made the team take the work more seriously, and as time went on Camille assigned ownership of this objective to key up-and-coming leaders in the organization, which gave them the chance to lead cross-organization initiatives. Tracking this OKR also provided evidence for the impact of operational initiatives. This evidence was useful for explaining the value of the work during promotion conversations as well, which had in the past only looked at new feature delivery as evidence of promotability.

The work delivered meaningful outcomes. Customer satisfaction surveys for these systems showed measurable improvements. The on-call burden for the systems became more manageable, which improved the happiness of the engineering teams. And the conversations at a senior level moved away from blaming the platforms for their constant operational failures and toward more collegial discussions about new opportunities and features.

Optimize Growth in Trust by Ordering Use Cases

Part of gaining trust means waiting to push adoption until you're confident that the systems can support the application's business needs. This reminds us of another lesson from our time working together, when many of the compute and storage platforms were new, and their teams wanted to drive adoption to prove their value. But the teams hadn't done enough performance testing to understand the actual (rather than theoretical) performance SLOs of their platforms. The result was that when an application would try to migrate, the system would struggle to meet its performance needs, causing latency problems and occasional brownouts. Even when this was done as a controlled proof-of-concept trial, the failures fed into a lack of trust, giving the impression that the platforms weren't ready, and the platform engineers could not understand operational demands like application engineers did.

In this case, there was also an opportunity that was being ignored. Many of the potential use cases for the platforms were supporting internal users in their day-to-day workflows. These workflows were important, but could tolerate some amount of latency and downtime. With the new attention to stability, Camille's leaders used the lens of performance sensitivity to think about whether they were moving the right use cases onto their offerings. They started to evaluate based not just on the platform features but also on how confident they were that the platform could meet the customers' operational and performance demands.

This changed the way they thought about their roadmaps and features. Instead of thinking of an offering as done the minute they got one customer successfully onboarded, the teams took a staged approach, starting by onboarding less critical applications. These applications provided data they could use for performance tuning and ironing out other bugs. Once they had these improvements in hand, they used them to gain the trust of the next tranche of more critical use cases, and so on.

There are no shortcuts to scaling up a team's operational ability, but by empowering the right leaders who put trust ahead of adoption, you will move faster up the curve.

Trust in Your Big Investments

Big investments, whether in a new platform or a major rearchitecture, require an enormous amount of faith ahead of demonstrated value. Not only do they take a long time to fully deliver (usually years), but they pull developers away from delivering faster value on the current platforms. As a result, customers waiting on the results of this big investment are prone to criticize the motivation behind the project. They may accuse the platform team of prioritizing "resume-driven development," putting fancy new technologies ahead of more mundane work that they believe would provide more immediate business value. Engineers love to grumble about each other, and you can't avoid all such feedback. Success means that your key stakeholders understand and trust the rationale behind the investment.

If you skip this and initiate the work by saying "Trust me, this is important; it's my team, and I'm responsible," you are headed for trouble. When users come to you with pain points and you respond that you can't address their needs because the platform is undergoing a rearchitecture, you can expect that they will start to complain upward. If you haven't already gotten buy-in, these user complaints will result in pressing questions from senior stakeholders about your strategy: Why are we funding this work when the current users aren't getting what they need? Why are they using technology X? Who signed off on this? Unless the new project is going perfectly (and when does that happen?), you can find your entire roadmap flipped over. To avoid this, you need to get the trust up front.

Seek Technical Stakeholder Buy-in for Trust of Rearchitectures

When rearchitecting, it's critical to spend time explaining to stakeholders what you're doing and why *before* you start the work. This is why in Chapter 8 we suggest a formal decision-making process to guide these investments, which generates a record that shows not just the justifications for the decision to fund the project, but that your teams are held to high standards for such justifications.

While management stakeholders might be satisfied with evidence that you have gone through a strict vetting of these investments, senior ICs (staff engineers and the like) will want to see more, particularly around technical decisions. That is why even if your company doesn't have a standard "design review" or RFC process, you should still produce a yearly project proposal, similar to what we discussed in Chapter 7. In the spirit of Amazon's "Have Backbone; Disagree and Commit" leadership principle, if you don't let senior engineers in customer teams give their feedback before you start, you should not expect them to "shut up and commit" when you later push for their teams' adoption.

Seek Executive Sponsorship for Trust of New Products

When proposing a new product, you have an opportunity to get more than baseline technical and investment buy-in. This is a chance to get executive sponsorship from more senior stakeholders who can bring a bigger-picture perspective of what might be most meaningful to the business. Platform leaders often get focused on the technical goals: can we scale, can we operate, can we reduce costs, and so on. They can end up focusing on these goals in a vacuum, forgetting that platforms are expensive to build and have a high opportunity cost for the business; after all, these engineers could be building other things for the company. Furthermore, sometimes platform engineers (and leaders) confuse the platform itself with the outcomes they're trying to drive—the existence of a new platform isn't an outcome.

Bringing in other leaders to hear about what matters to their areas of the business can help you avoid blind spots in the platform design. It's easy to assume that everyone cares about costs, or performance, or 24x7 availability, but often when you dig in you realize that the real problem is not what you thought. They can also provide guidance as to whether you're aligned to their technology strategy; you might think that a core application or architecture pattern is critical, while they are planning to cut that investment in favor of another area of business growth.

Maintain Old Systems to Retain Trust

Even with stakeholder buy-in, big investments are high-risk activities. Executive sponsorship lasts only so long; if you're working on a 12-month or longer project, you want to get out of the mindset that legacy improvements are pointless throwaway work, because your users won't see the new system for a long time yet. We don't just mean doing basic KTLO work here. You need to keep investing in system improvements until load on the old system is significantly falling. Further, as we discussed in Chapter 10, sometimes you need to add new features as well, either to accommodate urgent business needs or just to mollify your customers and their stakeholders.

No matter how confident you are in the big investments, others will have reasonable doubts; if you don't give some ground to maintaining their old systems in the meantime, you will lose their trust.

Gaining Trust Requires Flexibility on What Is "Right"

In the following example, we return to the time when Ian was working as a compute platform leader. One of his teams was in the process of digging themselves out of a lot of operational instability. While they had put the right leadership in place to improve the operational practices, there was still mistrust from important stakeholders—especially one of the most business-critical teams, which we'll call Icicle.

The Icicle team had a workload that was very sensitive to performance latency, and they had historically solved that problem by running their workload only on highly customized bare-metal servers. The problem with this was that these servers had low utilization and high cost. Their own business leadership wanted to improve their cost efficiency, but they trusted the judgment of their engineering team over that of the platform team. And the Icicle engineers saw that the current platform's approach to reducing costs (oversubscription of the servers) was causing unpredictable latency problems, which they were not willing to tolerate.

By treating this as a technical problem, the two teams had reached a stalemate over what was the "right" next step. The compute team wanted the Icicle engineers to provide "hard SLOs" that would allow the compute team to design and test a solution. The Icicle team wanted the compute engineers to build an extensive "stress test engine" to prove that their platform would perform under real-world conditions. The result of the stalemate was low trust, to the point that the Icicle engineers proposed to staff up their own shadow platform team to meet their special needs.

To resolve this stalemate, Ian and his leadership team changed not only their roadmap but also their product strategy. They put together a new offering that ripped out all of their platform's oversubscription features. Yes, the new offering was more expensive than the older offering, but it was still a substantial improvement over the bare metal the Icicle team was using.

Even with this concession, the Icicle engineering team was unconvinced it would be operated to their standards. As a result, the platform team first shipped it for data science users, delivering improved performance to a highly visible business group and building confidence in the system design through this effort. Only after six months of demonstrated operational success did they earn enough trust to get the Icicle engineering team to commit to moving to the platform.

By being flexible in finding a solution that would meet the needs of both technical and business stakeholders, and showing that they were committed to operating that solution to high standards, the team was able to move past a stalemate that was fundamentally about a lack of trust.

Trust to Prioritize Delivery

Finally, you need trust that your platform will not slow business delivery. It doesn't matter how much you manage complexity or make developers productive in the longer term; platforms that are a bottleneck to delivering business value clearly have questionable leverage in that moment. Even when the initiative is something understood to be difficult, like standing up your platforms on a new cloud vendor, people outside of the platform team tend to underestimate the complexity of the work. As the bottleneck drags on, they lose trust and start questioning every aspect of the platform team's decision making, sometimes even questioning the utility of the platform entirely.

In this section we bring together three activities that are critical to avoiding these bottlenecks: velocity of delivery, prioritization, and challenging assumptions of product scope.

Create a Culture of Velocity

When they hear complaints that the platform team is a bottleneck, it is common for stakeholders and your executives to blame a lack of planning. And it is true that if you have not done any of the planning work we discuss throughout this book, they may have a point. If you're prioritizing big rearchitectures or building new platforms when the business demands are not being met by your existing platforms, you may very well have a planning and prioritization problem to solve.

But in the face of an agile and dynamic business, it's a mistake to think that planning solves all trust issues. Circling back to Chapter 1, there is a reason Agile won over waterfall—there is enough uncertainty about the business value of most features that it is far higher-leverage to build something fast, get feedback, and make it better.

If that's a two-week iteration cycle for application teams, momentum is absolutely destroyed by a platform team saying "this needs to wait until next quarter's OKRs." That is why planning—by your team or by your customer teams—cannot be the only solution to delivery bottlenecks. Not only do you waste their time seeking clarity of value that the business cannot provide, but you also create a culture that insists that the business not providing perfect roadmap requirements is a fault, as opposed to a fact of life.

When Ian led a platform organization that often found itself crucial to an application organization's dynamic new feature needs, he shaped its culture to uphold the value of velocity: balancing the throughput that came with planning via a responsive, agile approach to unplanned application demands. There were two goals to this:

- To stress to his team that it was not acceptable to resist a new application team ask just because it wasn't in their earlier plans

- To remind his stakeholders that not telling his team early about their needs would result in higher costs, because the plan would have to change to accommodate the new work

Prioritize Projects to Free Up Team Capacity

We asked Diego Quiroga, a senior platform engineering leader, to describe his experience of turning around a team that was on the brink of becoming a bottleneck to the business. What follows is from Diego.

PLATFORM PERSPECTIVES

As I stepped into the engineering leader role for our platform team, I began to learn about our domain and look for interesting problems to solve. One team reporting to me was a small platform team with the critical responsibility of managing an array of foundational services powering an enterprise social network. Application teams relied on this platform's diverse capabilities to craft customer-facing features.

The platform team remained integral to the development of these features. During each quarterly planning cycle, application teams would articulate their requests for new capabilities or enhancements of existing ones. Due to the team's limited bandwidth, several of these asks inevitably fell below the line, and the backlog continued to grow.

While the organization valued our efforts, there was mounting concern over the team's ability to manage the growing backlog, especially as a delay in certain features would jeopardize the organization's objectives for business growth. Previously, in an attempt to tackle this dynamic above all others, the team had compromised their investment in operations, leading to not just an increased on-call burden, but also negative perceptions regarding the platform's operational stability.

With fixed headcount as a constraint, I worked with the team to understand the nature of our customers' requests, seeking patterns that might reveal opportunities for efficiencies elsewhere. Looking back over a year's worth of data, we identified several recurring requests, such as configuration changes across a complex chain of services required to establish new feeds. This presented an opportunity to package these requests in a self-service manner that would minimize future workload for the team.

In the face of being an active bottleneck, making the case for an investment in team efficiency presented challenges. Balancing the immediate value of tangible features against a promise of increased team throughput was a tough sell. To maintain the trust of leadership that allowed us to sustain the effort, it was critical for us to demonstrate the impact of the investments with clear visuals and metrics.

Following the completion of the project, we introduced this new "self-serve" capability to our portfolio. Customer requests that had previously demanded the undivided attention of a platform engineer for an entire month now required only a few consulting sessions, allowing us extra capacity to dedicate to other pieces of work. In a scenario where a long-term roadmap from the application teams was not available, relying on past trends for investment decisions was a calculated bet. This one paid off well and set a precedent for seeking out similar opportunities in subsequent planning cycles.

We adopted a similar strategy to enhance our team's response time to support requests. Application teams regularly sought the team's assistance for code reviews, guidance on utilizing platform capabilities, and resolving operational issues. As the engineering organization expanded, the team fielded an average of 30 weekly support requests. Despite having a dedicated engineer to manage triage, the pressure mounted for quicker responses, especially toward the end of each quarter. To address this, we allocated capacity to develop new troubleshooting dashboards and self-diagnosis tools, offloading noncritical workloads to the application teams. Implementing "canned responses" that directed users to documentation also was effective in reducing the volume of such requests.

With the bottlenecks addressed, the team's projects evolved into more interesting, impactful, and high-leverage work, increasing the engagement of the engineers. Customers benefited too—with the newfound surplus capacity, we were able to consistently address performance and reliability issues and establish a reputation for operational excellence. Overall, while the analysis was not cheap and the projects somewhat of a risk in returning value, they were absolutely critical in transitioning us from being a bottleneck for the business to being its trusted foundation instead.

Challenge Assumptions About Product Scope

Prioritizing delivery for platforms is a constant give and take; ideally, we build broadly useful offerings that meet the majority of our customers' needs, and we aren't under constant pressure to quickly add features as part of the critical path for an application team. But there are some cases where the key characteristics of the platform give it a scope that leads to inherent bottlenecks—namely:

1. The platform is trying to expose a large surface area of functionality.
2. The platform is trying to support a diverse set of applications.
3. The platform is developed in such a way that it cannot trust its own users to unblock themselves.

A classic example of this occurs at companies that put responsibility for all public cloud adoption on a centralized cloud enablement team, and charge them with ensuring not only that developers can get access to the cloud offerings they need quickly, but also that there is significant security vetting of the offerings and the way teams can use them. This case almost perfectly hits the three characteristics we just described:

1. The surface area of the public cloud offerings that developers might want to use is huge and, worse, changes pretty quickly.
2. Unless the company is very small, the team is going to be supporting a wide set of applications and developers who probably have many divergent opinions about which of the public cloud offerings they want to use for their applications.
3. The best way to resolve this would be to let application teams resolve it for themselves, but they can't trust these developers with the superuser access to do whatever they want for security reasons, so they are stuck trying to prioritize and negotiate what will be enabled, with new requests coming in all the time.

To reduce the bottleneck in situations like this, we have had some success with diminishing the scope, by supporting fewer application types and providing more curated, higher-level product offerings. Instead of unlocking cloud primitives for everyone, we built platforms that orchestrate compute and storage for major use cases, providing a smaller but focused surface area that allowed the platform team to make the right choices about the underlying management of the cloud infrastructure. This may seem like introducing an unnecessary middleman, but it allowed for a platform that integrated core company concepts around identity management and security, handled the complexity of the cloud on behalf of users, and drove major leverage for the company.

Even this solution was imperfect; for cases where teams wanted access to cloud products outside of those wrapped in the platform, there was still a bottleneck to evaluate, secure, and enable the new product. But limiting that to edge cases by building rich platforms for the common 80% meant that the team was able to clear these bottlenecks more quickly.

Where you are building platforms to enable your users without granting them too much trust, it's important to think about the platform features with an eye toward how you will manage or avoid these bottlenecks:

- Have you considered limiting the scope by supporting only certain types of applications?
- Have you iterated and identified the right abstraction that will support customers without exposing such a large surface area?
- Have you designed a system where users can contribute to unblocking themselves by limiting the control points that might require a security/compliance review?
- Have you included extensibility mechanisms for some platform features to be augmented by your users themselves?

You may need all four of these approaches to solve your biggest challenges: a limited scope with good abstractions to cover the common cases, and better practices for extensibility and user-driven contributions for the edges.

Tying It Together: The Case of the Overcoupled Platform

We'll call this story from our past "The Case of the Overcoupled Platform." The problems started with a two-year push to build platforms that were "batteries included." This was in reaction to a prior generation of platforms whose benevolent dictators were all thinking in silos as they built their individual platforms, and so nothing worked together. "Batteries included" was used to convey the vision of a heavily aligned approach to product strategy going forward. The vision painted was much less about platforms being "products" and more about platforms enabling "workflows," so customers would be able to use the platforms without having to build things themselves, and without being troubled by the operations of what was underneath. In many ways, this sounds like an ideal "glueless" platform—isn't this type of end-to-end focus the reason people love Apple products?

So what was the problem with applying it to these internal platforms? Unfortunately, the high bar of "batteries included" meant that the platform teams needed to design the end-to-end workflow impact for every use case before they could start writing code. This was hard enough that the initial offerings took shortcuts, and as new feature sets developed over time everything became deeply coupled. This deep coupling made rearchitectures especially hard, leading to the platform teams deciding they needed to rewrite everything into v2s that would deliver architectural improvements with feature innovations. Of course, these ambitious scopes caused massive delays and increasing customer frustration.

These platform teams were caught in their own swamp, offering end-to-end workflows that were always not quite done, not quite ready, not quite reliable, and not quite what the customers wanted. This meant that while "batteries included" had been a great trust unifier in the early days of close collaboration and progress, as the platform organization's delivery ground to a halt due to the coupling, and the solution was seemingly only to build v2s, trust had very much dissipated; more than one stakeholder gave the feedback that "your organization builds new platforms for the sake of building new platforms."

To correct for this, Camille needed to switch up the approach, and she knew she had to address not just the cultural aspect but the product side as well. Thus, she set forward an OKR objective of "building blocks, not batteries included" (as mentioned in Chapter 11). This metaphor was based on the following three concepts:

Treat building blocks as foundational.
In their efforts to quickly create the first version of the batteries-included workflows, the team had integrated different platforms at the component level, as opposed to using well-defined APIs. As workflow features grew, these components were often not operationally stable—poorly defined interfaces led to systems that were difficult to change, difficult to test, and difficult to monitor. To address this, the team paused on some of the workflow features to make sure the building blocks of those workflows were solid.

Blocks are composable.
Component-level coupling was not just a problem for stability, it was a problem for improving the "batteries included" workflows that crossed platforms. That coupling meant changes in one platform sometimes had unexpected side effects in other parts of the workflow, greatly slowing down feature delivery. Worse, fixating on platform use as workflows rather than abstractions completely precluded advanced customers unblocking themselves by building their own workflows. The building blocks approach recognized that, even while the team would still provide end-to-end wrappers for common workflows, they also needed individual platform abstractions to isolate side effects. This allowed platform teams to debug and manage their systems more easily, and it allowed trusted customers to "pierce" the workflow abstraction[1] and unblock themselves.

---

1 See Will Larson's article "Providing Pierceable Abstractions" (*https://oreil.ly/w-p3o*) for a larger writeup of this idea.

Blocks can be switched out incrementally.

As we mentioned in Chapter 11, the whole platform organization went through an alignment process that picked out some big initiatives to pause so that the team could focus on the most important ones and still have time to deliver solutions for more immediate demands. It was not enough to promise that a big v2 would revolutionize the platform and solve all the users' problems eventually; proposals were now evaluated based on (1) whether they could be delivered incrementally as rearchitectures, (2) their migration costs, and (3) executive support for the potential business value.

This approach meant that, in some places, the team backtracked on usability in order to stabilize, decouple, and remove bottlenecks. Camille built senior stakeholder support through incremental unblocking, including our earlier example of Ian's team delivering a better offering for the high-performance users. Going back to the Apple analogy, the platform offerings became a lot more like early Android devices—not as polished, but allowing a lot more options. You can argue your preference there, but we are confident that for internal engineering platforms the value of stability and future flexibility for platform customers cannot be sacrificed in the name of ideal usability.

Wrapping Up

Trust takes much longer to build than it does to destroy. Many events outside of your control can erode trust: black swan operational issues, major business changes that you can't keep up with, team turnover that leaves you unable to execute despite thorough planning. Knowing that these risks are ever-present, leaders must work hard to shore up trust through everything they do.

We see this as one of the most common ways that platform leaders fail their companies. Through their own hubris, they believe that they know better, they don't bother to communicate with adequate transparency, and they trust their teams to the exclusion of listening to their customers and stakeholders. When you accept that success in the job requires building and maintaining trust, you take the steps necessary to deliver trustworthy platforms that can keep up with business demands.

CHAPTER 13

Your Platforms Manage Complexity

We must design for the way people behave, not for how we would wish them to behave.
—Donald A. Norman, *Living with Complexity*

We started this book by describing the "why" behind platform engineering. What is the problem to be solved? The rapid increase of complexity in technology is slowing application engineering teams down, and the business is getting less value per developer over time. Why do we need platform engineering? Because it takes a holistic approach to the problem of complexity, allowing a team of software and systems experts to reduce the drag of complexity on the application teams.

This does not mean that platforms remove all complexity. Platforms generate leverage by effectively *managing* complexity, not eliminating it; as a leader of a platform team you must become very comfortable addressing complexity in everything you do.

In this chapter, we'll highlight four areas where complexity needs to be managed to ensure you are on a successful path:

- *Accidental complexity*, where attempts by a platform to address complexity in fact just move the problem somewhere else, often creating new work for humans

- *Shadow platforms*, which are a delicate game of letting application organizations be agile, without ending up with a complex outcome of many similar shadow platforms

- *Uncontrolled growth*, where the only way a platform organization manages complexity is under an assumption it can hire new engineers tomorrow to deal with the tech debt created today

- *Product discovery*, or understanding that, for some problems, it will take iterative attempts at delivery to discover the product that actually reduces complexity for both the customer and the platform team

As this chapter's introductory quote points out, we must be realistic about human behavior when designing solutions. A technology approach is necessary but not sufficient; leverage comes when we combine technology with an understanding of human and organizational dynamics to tackle all aspects of complexity.

A Success Red Herring: The Single Pane of Glass

The idea of bundling everything into a "single pane of glass" is a popular concept in tech UX these days. Many open source and vendor tools promise to give you a single UI to control your whole system, manage your whole development experience, or streamline all of your communication. Reducing cognitive load for users by providing one UI for everything seems like a smart way to remove unnecessary complexity, and many teams invest heavily in building unified UIs, betting that they will solve their UX problems. These initiatives usually start off strong and deliver value for some common use cases, but in our experience, this early success does not sustain itself over time.

Camille saw this firsthand when a DevEx platform team she managed decided that developers had too many different places to go to find information about their work: one for code reviews, one for build progress, one for tickets, one for code search, and, of course, their chosen editor for writing code and the command line for various other activities. To address this complexity, the team brought some of these activities together into a single pane of glass web UI to improve flow and protect people from context switching.

This seemed like a good idea at first, but over time the team realized that in order to keep everyone in their in-house interface, they would have to re-create all of the workflows from each of the underlying vendor tools they were using.[1] These vendors in turn were themselves each trying to become the single pane of glass by providing hooks and integrations with one another. Over time, the team realized that their "single pane of glass" was becoming either an extra stop between the developer and the UI they needed to get to or a worse version of the real thing.

They also hit another complication that's common when building tools and platforms for developers: the developers didn't want to use the interface. Developers are picky about the way they work. Many want nothing to do with UIs, and prefer to do as much as possible on the command line; others want everything integrated with their IDE; still others want ChatOps integrations (but only when they're on-call).

---

1 This is reminiscent of the challenges in wrapping vendor/OSS APIs for internal use, only arguably worse, as you not only have to keep up with API changes but also must keep up with UI/UX changes.

The platform's single pane of glass would only work for one persona; not only do different humans have different personas, but the same human may operate with the same tools as different personas depending on the role (support engineer, software developer, project manager) they are playing that day. The team ultimately realized that it was better to rely on the integrations available in GitHub, Slack, Jira, etc., and integrate their platform into these common offerings to account for the different personas and their demands.

As this example shows, the single pane of glass concept is often best generalized to something else. While we might build these experiences for certain scenarios, the goal is not so much the pane of glass itself but the ergonomics of a setup where everything a user needs is within reach. Recognizing that your systems will need to accommodate different personas using different tools at different times, the basic building block of your ergonomic environment is the API and the corresponding data model. By starting not with the single pane of glass but with the APIs that will power that interface, you leave yourself room to develop different experiences depending on the persona. You can create an easy UI for basic use cases, but allow developers who prefer the command line to integrate there (and rely on the existing UIs for your tools where possible as these are likely to be better than anything you can provide).

UIs are inherently complex and hard to build right, so if your goal is to reduce complexity, we recommend you start by ensuring your products have accessible, documented, coherent API access. Follow REST standards for your APIs, as closely as is possible. Name things consistently; do one thing per call and don't require stateful sequences of calls to do one thing; plan for backward-consistency and try not to change your APIs too often once they are released. From here, you can explore integrations with command-line tools, chatbot-type interfaces, IDE support, and yes, web interfaces. It's still hard to reduce the complexity of your API layer, but if you neglect that, it's unlikely a UI will solve the problem.

Managing the Accidental Complexity of Human Coordination

A key measure of success in managing complexity is evaluating how much glue application teams still need to build to work with your platforms. As introduced in Chapter 1, "glue" refers to the code, automation, configuration, and tools that these teams build to hold things together. Glue is a response to the complexity of managing the underlying systems, and platforms should aim to create abstractions that eliminate the need for each application team to build their own. Less overall glue is a sign that you have reduced the infrastructure complexity for application teams.

There is another type of glue that we didn't talk about in Chapter 1: human glue. This is the "glue work" that Tanya Reilly so eloquently describes in her talk and blog post "Being Glue" (*https://noidea.dog/glue*): all of the manual workarounds, documentation, and coordination needed to resolve gaps between the things a team needs to do and what they are actually doing. In a quest to limit the technical glue from Chapter 1, some platform teams end up creating a new "accidental" complexity by over-relying on human glue.

Imagine a platform that hasn't bothered with operational tooling for its application teams. It's like trying to drive an old car with the hood welded shut—you don't expect most drivers to know how to fix their engine, but they still need to know where the smoke is coming from. When an incident happens and the platform hasn't provided enough diagnostic tools, the application team is stuck. Instead of handling the issues themselves, they have to get on a call with the platform team to figure out if the platform is the culprit, which is frustrating for both teams. As we covered in Chapter 6, exposing platform metrics and using synthetic monitors is key to avoiding these escalations. Complex outages will still sneak up on you, but with proper tooling, you can stop using platform engineers and DevOps/SREs as human dashboards.

If you're looking for a rule of thumb to know whether you're doing enough to manage complexity, ask yourself how often you rely on "human glue" to resolve issues. Do you rely on manual processes to coordinate open source software upgrades, or to drive fixes for common application outages? As engineers, we believe that humans should be reserved for managing the truly complex scenarios, and we should apply software to resolve the merely complicated. In the following sidebar, we give an example for the case of migrations; in general, the less you need to rely on humans to coordinate programs across your platform and the application teams that use it, the better you are at removing complexity from your users' lives.

Managing Migration Complexity

We covered one of our migration success stories in Chapter 9: in the face of a major operating system version upgrade, Camille challenged her team to do everything they could to complete the migration without human project management support. The team responded by first writing a small piece of code that tracked each host, whether it needed to be upgraded, and by whom. This was run daily to produce a report that showed how the migration was progressing. The report was then fed into Jira, which automatically created and assigned tickets with details about what needed to be done to complete the migration.

Of course, this wasn't as simple as it sounds. A key element for success was the ownership metadata registry mentioned in Chapter 2, which provided tracking of which code belonged to which team. That data was used to bootstrap the process of figuring out where to assign the tickets. The team then wrote code to apply heuristics to various identifiers associated with the system resources in order to find the most likely person to assign the tickets to, and thus minimized the churn of incorrect assignments. This turned into a useful system for tracking and maintaining ownership data more broadly, which could then power other migrations.

This changed the way most migration exercises were approached across the company, reducing the complicated human-driven processes into more predictable machine-driven ones. Instead of defaulting to project managers tracking spreadsheets and endless status update meetings, the team spent time making the tool more powerful through more nuanced dependency mappings and smart reminders, and they put more time into automating common elements of the migrations so there was less migration work for the customer teams. Over time, the biggest challenge we had with this process was that too many groups wanted to use it to drive migrations before they had thought through the details of the migration process.

We did not completely eliminate the need for TPMs, but their role evolved from doing hand-to-hand combat with each team in the migration path to acting as overseers and ambassadors. They scaled to support more migrations because there was less manual work for them to track in each migration, and they could focus on the *weird* 20%. If, for example, we saw that to complete a migration we needed to get a big customer storage system upgraded and that work required a lot of coordination with the customer team, we could deploy TPM support at this point to enable the unblocking of another automatable tranche.

The goal of all of this is to treat TPMs as the rare specialists you bring in when you can't think of any other engineering-driven tricks that could make the migrations either automatic or self-service on the part of the customer. In our experience this will still mean you need to have folks with this skill set on staff, but they should be the few that you all admire for their discipline, attention to detail, and organizational savvy.

Managing the Complexity of Shadow Platforms

We discussed shadow platforms in Chapter 10, but as a reminder, they are the duplicative platforms that application engineering teams sometimes build for themselves. In general, shadow platforms increase the overall complexity of the company's software; however, they are usually built to reduce the complexity for a particular area. Because of this local view, there will always be some amount of platform work happening outside of your platform team. The goal is not to restrict all of it, but to be aware of it.

Trying to stop every application engineering team from ever building something that could be considered part of the platform remit is a fool's errand. At scale, it's impossible. Moreover, it's simply ill-advised to try to halt all platform-related experimentation and innovation happening in teams outside of your organization. These teams, as experts on their own needs, will take a pioneering mindset to knocking down their problems. When your platform fits their needs they will probably use it, but when there's an advantage for them to build their own thing, sometimes they will do just that. In doing so, they might build the first draft of the next valuable platform offering.

To wrangle those shadow platforms, you need to build on the trust that we discussed in the previous chapter—that's what keeps you in the loop. Being informed gives you the chance to prepare for whatever comes your way, whether by embedding one of your engineers into the project, getting regular updates from the team, or even setting up expectations about what would need to happen in the future if this team decided they wanted you to take over the project.

If and when you decide to take over a shadow platform, it's important to realize that you are inevitably going to create some new complexity in the process. After all, you're aiming to make it useful beyond the scope of its original team, which usually means expanding its surface area. The trick at this point is to reduce the pioneer-driven complexity while corralling the new complexity within your platform team, rather than letting it leak out to the users.

An Example of Managing a Shadow Platform

In our experience, a successfully dealt-with shadow platform looks more like a well-managed mess than a black-and-white picture of great execution. The following story illustrates just how iterative and messy success can turn out to be.

About six months after Ian took over the second of five in-house compute platforms, the CTO started pushing for AI for data science, giving significant headcount to one of the business-facing technology executives to execute this strategy. This executive then hired a leader for the initiative who was a type that platform engineering leaders often cross swords with: a pioneering visionary eager for radical change. This new leader believed that the barrier to AI innovation was the coupling to existing flawed (in his mind) in-house platforms, which hindered data scientists from quickly adopting cutting-edge public cloud and OSS systems. He aimed to create a platform where each data scientist could have their own cloud account, using whatever IaaS infrastructure primitives and OSS they wanted, like they were at a small startup.

In handling this, Ian's first mistake was assuming that everyone could see how complex this would be, and that the pioneer would get this feedback and quickly change course. After all, most of the data scientists could barely administer their own development workstations, so individual cloud environments were going to be a mess. Furthermore, most data scientists were going to need an incredible amount of platform integration for their existing workflows to be usable, and that was the work Ian's org already had planned. It was just going to take a while to do it "right" and avoid unnecessary glue.

The pioneer, however, remained stubbornly on course and hired a team to drive this effort, planning to build shadow platforms wherever Ian's team wouldn't cooperate with his vision. He justified this by pointing out that about 10% of the data scientists came from engineering backgrounds and could handle the complexity of administering their own environments and writing their own platform glue. Since this platform was only for experimental work, which would need a rewrite to go into production, both the pioneer's team and the early users believed it would be fine to deliver a system that didn't provide the same operational foundation as the broader ones Ian's team was providing. They figured they could deal with those architectural issues later.

Once Ian realized that the original plan was going to stick, he began holding regular meetings with the pioneer leader and his team. The goal was to get serious about what it would take to increase the coverage of this platform beyond the 10% of advanced users to include everyone else. These meetings exposed the places where the pioneering team was overlooking the complexity of scaling their offering. For example, they hadn't thought about how to migrate users off of existing systems (which would take hundreds of developer years), or how to manage the administration for the nontechnical users.

However, it was clear that the need to "make progress on AI" meant the effort had backers up to and including the CTO. So, Ian had a choice: he could let the pioneer team build a complex shadow platform without his support, or he could figure out a compromise that would let him influence the work to avoid some of the inevitable complexity.

The compromise he landed on was to shake up one of his teams' roadmaps, freeing up two developers to support this initiative. This was the upside of the CTO's attention—when other stakeholders questioned the changes, Ian could tell them this was coming from the CTO's priorities. The developers he chose were settler types, and he gave them a difficult remit: "Your job is to not slow this project down, but to find the places where you can build the right 'long-term' components and use the opportunity to build those earlier than we would have."

In practice, they succeeded about halfway; keeping the project moving quickly was always going to mean creating some amount of glue that wouldn't scale. But even the half success was a positive thing, especially because as the system became real, two things happened:

1. The 10% of data scientists who had previously been blocked could now successfully access the cloud for iterative experimentation.
2. Now that they had something real to play with, some of the remaining 90% of data scientists were able to try the system, and Ian's teams' earlier concerns around the complexity of operations, administration, and integration became obvious to everyone.

This didn't immediately solve the standoff, and it took a couple of years of reconciliation before the whole thing was sunset in favor of an integrated platform. Still, in those two years the company was able to benefit from a lot of innovation that otherwise would not have been possible. This became a case study to show how the platform organization could partner with application engineering teams without slowing them down, as opposed to always being left out of the "scrappy" part of the cycle. All told, it was a successful example of partnering to create a better (and more sustainable) product, as described in Chapter 5.

Managing Complexity by Controlling Growth

Growth is addictive. When you have scaled out a platform team from its early days to a stable organization, it can be tempting to think that the only way to accomplish more is by adding more people to the mix. How else will you ever close the gaps in the product offerings? You need a full set of engineers to cover both development and the on-call rotation, a product manager, and all of the supporting apparatus that a new team might need. The only way to provide all of that is to grow and grow and grow.

The danger in this mindset is that unchecked growth contributes to the complexity that you're trying to avoid by building a platform. First, it reduces appetite for managing complicated stuff: there's a strong temptation to throw bodies at problems instead of investing in automation or rethinking the work. This then creates the kind of work that software engineers don't want to do: tedious on-call rotations where you are constantly doing manual fixes, migrations that require human follow-up across the company, and provisioning requests that take dozens of steps to complete. The longer you go without investing in automation, the more likely you are to end up in situations where automation can't do enough to manage the complexity, and you're stuck in a nonscalable staffing model just to keep up with support.

Growth also encourages complexity by removing the pressure to be smart about what you build and where you invest. When engineers can justify any pet project, they will often build without regard to what the customers need. Managers and product managers in turn realize that it's easier to build their own empire rather than getting alignment with their peers on how to solve problems. Growth gives everyone an excuse for why things aren't quite going well: another person to point the finger at, a newcomer who doesn't yet know how things work around here. In the worst case, you end up with a sprawling portfolio of half-baked ideas and products that don't quite fit together well; a complex swamp of offerings for your customers to navigate. And frankly, we're not sold on platform teams being the originators of many new initiatives. As we said in Part I, we expect most innovation to come from the application teams building what they need, not the platform team itself.

Even considering all of this, those of you who have spent your careers in growing companies might think we're off base to suggest slowing growth when you aren't being forced to do so. Why would you even pretend to do new things when you're barely keeping up with the rapid growth and scaling of the company itself? And why would we push platform teams to reduce growth when application engineering teams are just as guilty of indulging in it?

Remember, though, that there is a difference between platform teams and application engineering teams: a platform team is more likely to be seen as a "cost center" and therefore an area where efficiency is expected, rather than a revenue-generating organization. Guiding a culture of smart efficiency is part of the mandate for leaders in this space, and complexity is the enemy of efficiency. The platform engineering mandate is not driving efficiency through any means (say, outsourcing to manage the cost of manual approaches). You achieve efficiency by strategically simplifying through software engineering and product discovery.

We know that there are times when you need to grow, and entering new product areas can be one of these times. If you have run your organization so efficiently that you cannot pull from existing teams to cover a new offering, you will need to grow. And of course, there are times of scaling and company growth where expansion is sensible. But good platform leaders understand that their platforms deliver leverage, and that means they shouldn't need to grow at the same rate as the overall engineering team, once that leverage point is established.

As a guardrail, we recommend this rule of thumb: most of the new work in established areas should be funded by existing people on those teams. This forces management to sharpen their focus; if their KTLO workload has gotten out of hand, can they find ways to reduce that cost? Do they have a strong sense of the most important areas to work on, and are they divesting from adding to features that either are "good enough" or, worse, haven't shown their promised value?

Managing complexity implies not only that your platforms can support far more users than the number of developers of the platform but also that, once you have achieved baseline coverage for a product area, you do not need to linearly scale the number of platform engineers for every new thing you want to do in that space. This doesn't mean you should cut yourself to the bone and have no slack in your organization. This is why the measurement of KTLO + mandates + operational improvements is so important: knowing the minimum number of people you need to handle that workload gives you the absolute bottom of your potential team size (which is probably that number + 20% so everyone doesn't immediately quit). Above that baseline, you can exercise discretion and think about investments. Being thoughtful about the next set of work, incorporating customer demand, team demand, and your own strategic insights, and getting the most out of the team you have before you go and ask for growth is a sign of mature platform planning and leadership.

Managing Complexity Through Product Discovery

Product discovery is the work of understanding customer demands and creating, in the words of Silicon Valley Product Group (*https://oreil.ly/N5Icw*), "a product solution to this problem that is usable, useful, and feasible." Product discovery is not just needed for the products you build from scratch; it is also an important exercise to go through when you are creating platforms that are based heavily on open source systems. If you want to create curated product offerings, discovery is key. Yet under constant pressure of new potential shadow platforms, many teams take customer demands literally, providing whichever open source system the customer asks for without taking the time to determine whether it is the right product solution for the overall platform.

This leads to a common predicament, where teams that have provided (or, more commonly, inherited) these open source systems are stuck with operational complexity that grows linearly with the number of users and use cases. You can reduce the coefficient of linearity with investments in automation, but from a design perspective, most major open source products have too wide a surface area exposed to the users. This is most evident in distributed OSS for data processing, such as RDBMSs (PostgreSQL, MySQL), Cassandra, MongoDB, and Kafka. These systems are highly complex by nature, and the OSS vendor model drives them to compete with one another by adding more and more features, which means they have very broad interfaces.

Some leaders immediately jump to the conclusion that they have to standardize and limit choices in order to manage this challenge. That's a great idea, but how do you do it? In our experience, while application developers on the whole may agree that fewer infrastructure choices would make their lives easier, they rarely agree on what the limited set of choices should be. If you're disciplined (and have senior leadership support), you may be able to establish standards early enough to avoid annoying your customers by taking away features they're already using and forcing migrations to reduce duplication. But this can backfire if it slows application teams down much, and it's politically unpopular. Most of the time standardization happens only when the platform team hits a breaking point, where the support burden of so many OSS offerings prompts the question of why you need so many in the first place.

There's an option in between "let a thousand flowers bloom, until you can't stand it anymore"[2] and "offer a strict platform that allows for very little variation," and, as you might have guessed, it involves your product culture. To do this, you need to take the time to understand your customers. Explore *why* teams are using their

---

2 See Peter Siebel's article "Let a 1,000 Flowers Bloom. Then Rip 999 of Them Out by the Roots" (*https://oreil.ly/slEdD*).

chosen tools, whether it's out of habit or for specific must-have features. Through an iterative process of product discovery, you can develop the insight needed to curate your offerings, reduce complexity, and better meet your customer needs. In our final story, we will walk through just such an exercise and the many iterations that led to success.

Tying It Together: Balancing Internal and External Complexity

In this story, Ian had a team of about 10 people who owned a collection of OSS systems (PostgreSQL, Kafka, and Cassandra). The team followed a data reliability engineering (DRE) approach,[3] which meant they offered a "platform" that provided all of the support and provisioning for these systems, with the team's proactive engineering spent on automation, particularly around resilience and autoscaling.

Burning Out on OSS Operations

As we predicted in Part I, this approach to platform delivery wasn't scaling. Each OSS system had a large feature surface area, and the complexity of operating that as a company foundation led to constant operational strain. Even with two pager rotations, the number of high-severity incidents a week was much closer to 50 than 5, and this was only somewhat ameliorated by the fact that rotations could follow the sun. The DRE team had reached the limits of efficiencies that could come from automation alone.

Unfortunately, the application teams weren't seeing this pain; indeed, they were happy with the flexibility provided by the OSS systems' extensive feature set. Their primary demand was that the DRE teams should expand their portfolio with more offerings. But when the DRE leaders tried to explain that they needed twice as many engineers to sustainably manage the existing workload before they could even think of adding more offerings, they were met with disbelief. The DRE team could continue to grow only by agreeing to support more systems and configurations, which they knew would quickly arrive at the same unsustainable scaling point.

Trying (and Failing) to Change the Game

This impasse prompted the team to make several attempts at reducing the complexity they had to manage. The first attempt to change the model was trying to get out of the game altogether and move to vendor "hosted open source" IaaS implementations, where application teams would own their own operations. In another company,

---

3 See *Database Reliability Engineering* by Laine Campbell and Charity Majors (O'Reilly).

putting the operational load on the vendor might have solved the problem. But due to the multicloud requirements of this company, the differences across vendors made it too hard for the application teams to operate themselves. This was only truly appreciated after the vendor offerings were rolled out, when the DRE team was still constantly being paged to handle acute operational issues because the application teams lacked the depth to debug them. At this point, they realized "get out of the game" really meant "stay in the game, but as an operations team."

The next tactic was to take a page from the SRE book (*https://oreil.ly/p5cFs*) and try to improve things through SLA documentation. The idea was to provide clear documentation of what the team could and could not support within its SLA; this would help application teams understand that their bespoke configurations couldn't be supported by the DRE team alone and lead to a shared operational model. The DRE team saw this as a rational compromise, balancing customers' needs for customization with their ability to manage these at scale. But it sounded like a lawyerly abdication of responsibility to those customers, who saw the team as using rules and processes to position themselves as advisors and evangelists rather than owners. Ian brokered a top-down handover for one of the biggest customers, forcing trade-offs on both sides, but it was clear that this approach wasn't going to be sustainable without constant conflict and politics.

The team turned next to a software-based approach: full encapsulation. We described this in Part I: creating a service API layer that fully encapsulates the open source APIs, which allows the platform team full control over what they support/operate. The users were not particularly interested in giving up their direct access to the data stores in favor of this option, but the team hit on the idea of tying this to a feature supporting multiregion reads and writes with simple (key, value) semantics. Early customers were satisfied, but as the platform team looked for the next tranche of potential customers, they realized that no one else was interested in the multiregion use cases in the short term, and instead they wanted a full SQL interface. So the team started creating a plan for adding secondary indices, with a view to eventually supporting SQL semantics. At this point Ian stepped in, noting that the idea of building their own in-house global SQL database was less thinking big and more of an impossible dream.

Shadow Platforms Force a Reset

During the time these three attempts were being made, frustrated application teams had started building shadow platforms to get the features they needed, such as MongoDB for document support and FoundationDB for transactional write semantics that could horizontally scale. These had the usual characteristics: when the application team was growing rapidly they were happy to own all the operations, but as the initial engineers moved on and the operational load kept growing, the application teams were eager to offload them onto the platform team. Adding more OSS to the portfolio was the opposite direction of where the team wanted to go, but there was something here that the company needed, and Ian challenged his team to figure out how to meet those needs.

At this point, the team did a reset by bringing in some managers who had experience building product-oriented infrastructure. These managers started by doing product discovery, looking across the collection of offerings and, using their prior experience to guide them, investigating what the application teams actually needed from these systems. That is, they attempted to discover what the teams specifically *required*, as opposed to just preferred, in Cassandra, MongoDB, PostgreSQL, Kafka, and FoundationDB. With this understanding, the platform team sought to identify a narrower surface area of common needs that could be used to remove one or two of the broader offerings. Through this effort, they found two major opportunities:

Simplification
> There was a lot of demand for a cross-application configuration platform for which (key, value) semantics were fine. Here, the team leveraged the shadow platform investment in FoundationDB to power a managed service focused only on solving this use case.

Coupling multiple primitives
> There was still a demand for something schema-aware, but product discovery revealed that this requirement was as much about caching and search as it was about ACID transactions. The team realized if they combined PostgreSQL with searchability and caching functionality, they could offer a more limited SQL system that would satisfy most customers.

They also realized that if they could succeed on these two projects, then both a platform (Cassandra) and a shadow platform (MongoDB) could be sunset.

Executing on the Reset

To create these new platforms, the team collaborated closely with application teams that had pressing demands for the offerings. The result was rapid development of platforms that, while scrappy, satisfied these customers and turned them into advocates for the work throughout the company. Thanks to the early successes, a long list of application teams signed up to onboard as the platforms matured.

In all, it took about four years of iteration to identify the right product offering that would meet the major application needs while limiting the complexity for the platform team, meaning their growth could be controlled without ceding all future feature development to shadow platforms.[4] You may be wondering whether a process

---

4 We would be remiss not to be honest about the cost of this change: at the time of writing, the team is in the second year of a five-year plan to fully deprecate the MongoDB and Cassandra offerings.

that involved three false starts and a multiyear migration is really a success. But this is the reality of delivering platforms that manage your company's unique complexity: they will evolve, trade-offs are hard, and sometimes the best solution isn't even viable at the time you identify the problem. Don't be afraid to keep iterating.

Wrapping Up

Alignment and trust are challenging but achievable goals for your platform team. Managing complexity, on the other hand, is a North Star that you'll use to guide your organization, but it's unlikely you will ever fully accomplish this task. There are things you can do to detect complexity, and practices you can use to help control it, but complexity will always be there. That doesn't mean you should throw your hands up and give up on the task entirely. When you find complexity in excessive human coordination or shadow platforms, see it as an opportunity to develop new ways to automate, simplify, and understand the needs of your customers. As your platform organization develops and matures, use this North Star to remind yourself that too much growth too fast can make it that much harder to keep complexity in check, and that the iterative process of product discovery is critical to finding the simplest scalable solution among the sea of more complex options. The more time you are able to spend thinking about and driving down complexity for your users, the more mature your platform will become.

CHAPTER 14

Your Platforms Are Loved

What's love got to do, got to do with it? What's love, but a second-hand emotion?
—Tina Turner

We know a head of platform product management who boils his key metrics down to "simpler, faster, cheaper, and your users *love* it." This usually prompts two questions. The first is what Tina Turner asks in this chapter's opening quote, which we think is a totally legitimate question: why should it be a goal for a system targeted at internal engineers to be done so well that users love using it? "Love" implies that you are appealing to your users' emotions. This is important for a company selling products and looking to establish brand affinity so users will keep buying them, but is it really something for an internal platform to aspire toward?

That ties into the second question: is winning platform users' love worth the cost? Massive tech companies can build bespoke internal tools that their employees rave about for years afterward (yes, we are talking about you, people from Google and Netflix), but few of us can spend that much effort and time optimizing for our users' needs—it just doesn't seem to make economic sense unless you're a massive technology business that has margins to match.

To answer both questions, it's worth reflecting on the everyday tools *you* love: things you use in the garage, kitchen, bathroom, etc. Rarely are they the most expensive tools on the market. Rarely are they the ones that try to be all things to all people. Instead, they are made with care for a specific purpose that matches your needs. You love them because they work well and bring pleasure to getting the job done. When we talk about platforms that inspire love, this is what we mean. For internal platforms, "love" is a good proxy for improving productivity.

Why not just talk about productivity? Well, for one thing, we have yet to find a good way to objectively measure engineering productivity that fits even most circumstances, let alone all of them. When we instead end up focusing on simplistic metrics like "adoption" or "efficiency," we start to see our job as eliminating complexity, as opposed to managing it, and this almost always leads to building systems that are easier for the platform teams to control, instead of systems that application teams love to use. Oscar Wilde once said a cynic is someone who "knows the price of everything but the value of nothing," and so we emphasize "love" to remind you that success is not as simple as improving a number.

Luckily, our experience is that inspiring love by building tools that are enjoyable to use is something that every team can strive for. In this chapter, we'll share some examples of platforms that we have seen be loved and why we think they succeeded. We'll also discuss why you have to be careful with simplistic metrics when trying to capture love.

A Success Red Herring: Lies, Damn Lies, and CSAT Scores

Many platform teams run customer satisfaction surveys as one of their key metrics-gathering exercises. One common metric in these surveys is the customer satisfaction score. With that as a target, you might think you have the ultimate tool for determining how much your platforms are loved, and thus successful, in the sense that people who are satisfied feel they have a good tool for the job.

We've run these surveys across our platforms, and we've found that they've provided some interesting baseline information, and some red herrings. So, before you go out with a CSAT survey, consider:

Are you getting a good sample population?
> Nothing will cause you to lose trust faster than bragging about your customer satisfaction survey results when you had a very low response rate. If you want to run this kind of survey, you need to ensure you are getting a good response rate from your target audience, not just relying on the few people who bother to fill it out. Surveys can fail by being attractive to the least satisfied and most vocal target group, or by getting such a low response rate that your own organization can skew the results. Don't lie through virtue of your sample population. If you have a small user base, do everything in your power to get the highest response rate possible. If you have a large user base, aim to get representative responses from each major user group, whether that is determined by their area of the organization, type of role, frequency of use, or what have you. When you share your survey results, be honest about the response rates, where they came from, and any gaps you might have in your survey coverage.

Would you change your work based on the survey results?
> If you ask people in a survey which products they are least satisfied with, what areas they would like to see investment in, or other types of questions that lead them to believe that you might actually change your focus based on their responses, make sure you are actually willing to do that. Filling out a survey year after year where they complain about the same system or ask for the same feature and see no action is likely to make your customers feel even worse about your team than they did before the survey.

Did you try to manipulate responders, or are you actually interested in their feedback?
> Presenting users with a biased survey that makes your pet project sound like the best way forward is a tactic you could use, but we beg you not to do that. This survey should be used to figure out what people actually want, not to manipulate them into providing cover for your pre-canned decisions.

Is there realistically something you can deliver based on the responses?
> Similarly, if you give people a bunch of options that all sound good, and they respond with enthusiasm to all of your ideas, could you actually deliver all of those things? Again, be realistic. Instead of asking people whether they would like each of a long list of good things, ask for rankings.

Now, with all of that said, a good customer survey can provide a lot of valuable insights and support. Sometimes, a survey will express just how frustrated a large part of your customer population is with a system. We've seen surveys that made platform teams realize that the instability they thought was a bit of a problem was actually a really big problem that many people were painfully aware of. It's one thing to know you are having some stability and performance issues, and another thing to have overwhelming responses from people who were not otherwise complaining, making it clear you are causing them pain! And on the flip side, surveys can point out the offerings that people love and that need to be protected.

Surveys can also provide cover for making big changes that may cause short-term pain. In one instance, we saw regular complaints about our code review process, providing a clear signal that users were dissatisfied with the tool we had to offer. Changing the tool required a large migration effort, but through a combination of planning, communication, and the backing evidence of the pain reported in surveys, we were able to show users that we were doing this work exactly in response to their complaints about the old system.

Surveys (and similar qualitative data) are a valid part of your toolkit, but one you should deploy as rigorously as possible. Plan your questions thoughtfully, get a good sample size, and think about what changes you might realistically make based on the results. If you misuse your surveys, they will lose all of their value, as people will stop responding to them or ignore their results. No one is interested in a survey that changes nothing, is used to cover up bad experiences they know are happening, or generally doesn't seem to reflect their view of reality.

Love Just Works

Ian's most-loved platform from his 11 years as a hands-on engineer was the deployment platform at Amazon, called Apollo. Amazon is, of course, a massive tech company, so you might think we're cheating with this example. However, the Apollo system was built relatively early in the company's history, around 2004, and Ian started using it in 2006. Apollo predated containers, but in essence it was doing similar things to modern container-based deployment systems—laying down binaries on the filesystem, then starting and terminating processes to make the binaries run.

While it wasn't perfect, the overwhelming experience was that it just worked. The elements that made it work at Amazon's then 5,000-engineer scale were:

Great UI and automation interfaces
It was very clear that the UI was not an afterthought that had been tacked onto the underlying entity or system model, and the users never questioned whether the UI was actually showing the true state of the underlying system. Everything that the system was capable of doing could also be done through the API and be observed by the API. Apollo dated back before the "automation as configuration" movement, so all the automation came from rich command-line scripting, but the team had put in the work so it was very easy to script multiple actions and avoid the "clickops" trap.

Strong opinionation
Apollo had strong "paved path" opinionation on what a release looked like for files laid down on the host machine, and on what a release process looked like. These choices did cause issues for the tail 20% of systems with special needs, but for the other 80%, they "just worked." It was very easy to set up a release for a new application, and the processes were the same from one team to the next even when their application structures were totally different (say, an offline batch process versus an online service).

Pierceable opinionation
To support the remaining 20%, the platform did offer one significant point to "pierce" the abstraction. When a release was started, it had a workflow that allowed users to execute arbitrary scripts on the deployed host. This meant that when you had an application with special needs (for example, Ian had a service that had to do a ~10-minute handover of state between old and new processes, which was not ideal and also not something he could reengineer quickly) you could develop Linux scripts to make it work. So, while you sometimes hit these edges of opinionation and had to write glue, you never felt trapped with no options.

Ian loved using this tool and used it for over seven years, across a wide variety of software. It earned its place as his favorite platform because it took complicated needs and built the interfaces to make things just work.

Love Can Look Like a Hack

The product that Ian's platform team developed that was most loved by users was one of the five competing compute platforms we referred to in Chapter 11, called Waiter. Waiter was a classic pioneer offering, built alongside the application teams who built tools for data scientists. Thanks to this close collaboration with the users, Waiter was beloved because it was tailored to give them exactly what they wanted, even when the implementation details used to get there sometimes looked like hacks to other platform engineers.

The main reason Waiter was successful was its focus on eliminating user friction. The pioneer builders cared about productivity not only for the application developers, but also for the data scientists calling into the applications as they iteratively developed their code. The major innovation was a "run as" feature—the workload would run as the same Unix account as its caller, inheriting access and entitlements. Technically, this required a complex and somewhat hacky coupling of the load balancer (to intercept incoming application calls) to an orchestrator that could spin up application processes with the right account. But it meant that the callers of those applications could very simply reason about what downstream resources the application would have access to. This was hugely important for applications targeting data scientists, because the application teams could give them access to the application and not have to worry about managing the permissions for the data, since the application would run as the human caller and only have access to whatever that human was supposed to see. It also eliminated the massive pain of debugging cases where it worked on someone's developer workstation but not in the production environment.

Eventually, the pioneer team handed the system off to a platform team of settlers, who kept the core culture of "productivity first" as they evolved it to be more scalable. Any time they found a gap between development and production experience, their mission was to make this user friction go away, even if it meant more "hacky" complexity in their implementation. Harking back to the last chapter, they saw their mission as managing complexity on behalf of their users, not eliminating it.

Beyond Waiter, some other beloved hack systems we've seen include a service library that would spin up an in-process instance of the remote system if it couldn't find one running (terrifying and brilliant!) and a command-line process that would run any binary built by a monorepo whether or not it had been deployed to that machine, pulling down artifacts on demand to support starting the necessary process. They had pioneer fingerprints all over them: systems built by people looking to power through a problem and make something easier for everyone, but not necessarily thinking about what this would all mean at larger scale. While these systems had many ugly edge cases, they all had a shared quality of brilliance; they took a problem that most users didn't want to have to think about at all and made it go away.

When you find yourself inheriting these kinds of systems, it can be tempting to decide you need to get rid of them or change them completely due to their deficiencies and the pain they cause the platform team itself. We get it, but we recommend that you first try to understand which of the weird inherited systems people love (through, among other things, customer satisfaction surveys) and why they love them before you plan major changes.

Love Can Be Obvious

One of the most-loved platforms Camille's organization developed and launched was an internal version of S3. Yes, you read that right—something as simple as an internal blob store was loved. This company was mostly on-prem at the time, and while they had several good internal storage offerings, there was no S3-compatible object store. No one was demanding such an offering, but the product manager for the storage team had a strong belief that they just needed to make this available and everyone would start using it. He saw the widespread external value of S3, particularly among engineers in the data science space, and was confident that it would provide significant value to the user population. And he was right! It was a wildly popular offering, with massive adoption soon after launch.

This probably seems like an obvious outcome; after all, S3 is one of the most successful innovations from AWS. But just because some technology is popular in the larger world doesn't mean it will be embraced in your organization—sometimes popular tech flops when brought into a company. When weighing whether to bring something in, how can you most accurately predict whether it's likely to be a success or a failure? It comes down to a few underlying factors that are important in building products that people love, and that you can't just take for granted even when you're following a trend:

Awareness

When people not only know about a product but know how to use the product, you're in good shape. That's the advantage with something like S3: many of the developers had experience using it either in college or at other companies, so there was no need to explain the value proposition to them. The platform team also did a good job of getting the word out about the product through the customer teams, so they knew when it was available.

Compatibility

In this case, S3 had another advantage: it was already supported by many of the tools in use by engineers and data scientists, so most of the implementation work was wrapping the internal authentication protocol and making efficiency tweaks, rather than having to think through every possible client implementation. A common pitfall of introducing popular external technology into a company ecosystem is that the work it takes to actually integrate that technology with the existing software outweighs the incremental value of the new technology. In this case, the team anticipated and avoided that pitfall by investing in the integrations early and delivering a good user experience out of the box.

Engineering quality

Reiterating a common theme of this book, if this product had been unstable when it was launched, it might not have gotten the immediate wide adoption it did. People love things that just work, especially when they're using them for critical production workloads. Since this platform was built on top of production-hardened components, it was much easier to get to a stable offering.

Time to market

Some of the love this product generated came from the fact that it went from product insight to launch much faster than most major offerings—in this case, there was less than a year between the product manager starting research and an alpha release that included most client integrations. This was thanks to the fact that the platform was built on top of existing components, it didn't require anyone to do a big migration to start using it, and it didn't need a lot of new documentation, integration, or customer tooling. Drafting off the success and popularity that Amazon had created meant less product work, and reusing internal components meant much less engineering complexity. As we mentioned in Chapter 13, people will forget the pain of late delivery when you deliver something great, but it still feels very good to deliver something that is both great and ships quickly.

This may not sound like a piece of brilliant product management, but few have the sense to perceive the confluence of awareness, compatibility, and engineering foundation that can be turned into a fast, high-value product win. When it all comes together like this, love is quick to follow.

Tying It Together: Love Makes Your Users Awesome

Smruti Patel, VP of engineering at Apollo GraphQL, has built platforms for 20+ years. We asked her to share a story of building a platform that users love, and key strategies for making users awesome and autonomous. What follows is from Smruti.

The Problem

We had a monolith with undesirable dependencies due to years of accrued tech debt. In our developer productivity surveys, we would routinely have users sharing concerns around not being able to confidently know what changes were running in production. We also saw how this would then manifest in incidents due to accidentally rolling out breaking changes to production.

So, we decided to build a service delivery platform. We were clear about our purpose: make the product engineering teams a lot more productive (reduce the lead times for feature delivery by over 50%) and make change management safer.

The Approach

We intentionally brought a product mindset to the platform, defining our user personas and their jobs to be done. Here, I've routinely found it most valuable to focus on 10 super-delighted users, versus 1,000 who are partially satisfied with what we have to offer.

Building delightful user experiences and making users awesome requires us to deeply understand their workflows and the toolkit we can offer in addition to the platform. *What are the gardened/paved paths? What are the guardrails baked into the platform? What escape hatches do we need to provide?* The goal is for the users to find it easy to do what is right, and hard to do what is wrong.

When we've done this user analysis correctly and understand our personas' skill sets, strengths, and pain points, then using the platform feels like wielding a Swiss army knife with a variety of tools at hand specific to the need, the occasion, and the gradual maturity of the user. For the last, I think about it in terms of progressive disclosure or looking at the solution in terms of layers. Platforms are for developers, and as you're abstracting away some complexity, you will always have some developer who is curious enough to peel the onion, look under the hood, and tinker around to suit their own unique needs. A successful platform should offer programmable and composable building blocks for that class of developers.

A year in, we had less than 5% of production traffic on our platform. Not only that, we now had the dual cost of maintaining two delivery platforms: the new one, which was not yet at feature parity, and the old one, which continued to see scaled usage. Net-net, we were far worse off than when we'd started 18 months ago!

We realized that we had left the adoption of the platform to a "build it and they'll come" mindset. We had not been intentional about how our platform would get adopted and the level of investment we were expecting the organization to take on once the platform was shipped. Consequently, we couldn't land the impact we sought —our work wasn't "done" once the platform was built out.

To fix this, we built a detailed migration strategy, accounting for the off-ramp from the old platform and the on-ramp onto the new platform. We found that we had to build out an A/B testing tool so that our developers could incrementally dial up the traffic from the old to the new platform, while promising ~zero downtime throughout the migration.

About a year later, 100% of our services had migrated over, and every new service started onboarding directly onto this platform. Our average lead times for feature delivery reduced not just by 50%, but by 65%, and we saw far fewer breaking changes in production.

Key Takeaways

The highest leverage a successful platform can provide to an organization is by driving velocity for its users, bringing delight to its users, and making its users *awesome at what they do*. This not only requires bringing a product mindset to building a platform, but also shifting away from the "build it and they'll come" mindset to a more intentional, focused objective around day zero adoption.

Wrapping Up: What Is Love? Baby Don't Hurt Me

Joking aside, love is hard. Most of the time we're lucky to have products that fade into the background, where people may not express love, but they don't express constant pain and frustration either. Smruti Patel once gave a talk where she advised that a good platform was a multitool, boring but useful, not a mystery mushroom where you think you'll have fun using it, but you're always a little nervous that you might have a bad to deadly experience. Most of our platforms will be boring but useful; they might not be fun, but users can trust them to do what they expect.

One of the most overall successful platforms we've seen was a distributed job scheduler, built in the early days of a company. The platform had evolved and grown as the company had evolved and grown, doing what it needed to do, making incremental improvements and occasionally getting serious investment to ensure it could deliver the reliability guarantees of such a critical system. Over the years, many people looked at this ugly legacy system and proposed replacing it with something newer, fancier, more full-featured—Airflow, Luigi, or whatever the flavor of the day might be. These attempts were well-meaning but never got adoption outside of a few specialty systems. In the meantime, the job scheduler chugged on, often with only a skeleton crew for support. That's another lesson of platforms; even the best are sometimes underappreciated.

If you want to replace a successful but neglected platform with something you believe will go beyond acceptance and get to love, don't neglect the hard work we discussed in Chapters 7, 8, and 9. Be sure you have a plan to know what features of the existing system are in use, either rearchitect to decouple some of the tight integrations or reimplement them in the replacement system, dual-write to ensure you're at least meeting feature compatibility, and plan a careful migration. If it seems strange to end a chapter on love with a bunch of reminders about details, planning, and diligence, remember that this is platform engineering, and love in this world requires a strong baseline of trust before it can fully take hold.

Concluding Remarks

A question we asked ourselves before writing this book was whether platform engineering is just a fad, like many others[1] that have swept the industry over the last 25 years. And while we hope that the ~100,000 words we've written on the subject have convinced you otherwise, we still see a real risk of platform engineering falling victim to the tech hype cycle. With vendors pushing specific implementation details and consultants writing checklists, we're in danger of losing all nuance in favor of some metrics for an executive's dashboard.

That's why we spent so much time in Part I talking about the inflection point of complexity that the industry is facing today. While the cloud, vendor, and OSS ecosystems have accelerated technical innovation where it's demanded by the business (in 2024, it's anything related to AI), they haven't made software systems any simpler than they were in the '90s with servers as pets and proprietary vendor platforms. The frustration has shifted from dealing with data center engineers to grappling with the copy-and-paste nature of Terraform "codebases," but the complexity remains. In fact, with the continual push for innovation and the need to integrate legacy systems, the overall complexity has grown, leading to the over-generalized swamp we discussed back in Chapter 1.

---

1 Not naming names.

The industry needs to move past seeing platforms as either hype cycle implementation details (such as IDPs[2]) or the ad hoc glue that today's hot application team uses to stick together their vendor and OSS systems without considering future costs. Getting past these expedient approaches (and convincing application teams to come along) requires balancing the things we covered in Part II, like:

- Creating teams of engineers with a mix of software and systems focus and specialties
- Mixing product, engineering, and operational perspectives in answering the question of what the right thing for the team to work on is
- Delivering by combining an Agile approach with more rigorous planning as needed
- Spending much more engineering time rearchitecting and migrating from old systems than just building new ones

Managing this balance is not easy. Potential failure is around every corner, and even your successes will constantly be critiqued, by your team, your peers, your stakeholders, even your leadership—all of whom have only a partial view of what you are keeping in balance. We showed some examples of what success looks like in Part III, and as you saw, even the successes had plenty of moments of frustration along the path. But then, we became engineers to solve hard problems, and solving hard problems is inherently frustrating—otherwise, they wouldn't be hard problems. We try to remember that frustrations bring opportunities for humility and growth.

And that brings us back to why we, Ian and Camille, keep doing this, despite all of the challenges. Firstly, it's just an honest love of technology at the nuts and bolts level, and of the power of using software to solve big problems. There's also the love of understanding complex systems, be they technical or human, and using that knowledge to improve them. And finally, we believe that the industry can do better, should do better, and must do better at wrangling complexity and making it easier for engineers to get their jobs done.

Everyone who has read this far shares these qualities, too. Use them to become better platform engineering leaders, and bring together people with diverse skills and perspectives from inside and outside your teams to build the platforms that your company needs—even when they're fighting against you. The true mark of a platform leader is the ability to turn friction into opportunity, forging ahead to create systems that are greater than the sum of their parts. Lead with resilience, empathy, and vision, and you'll transform skeptics into believers.

---

2 Yes, this is a dig. Why are so many of the top 10 search results for platform engineering talking about an implementation detail? We're not sure, but we're pretty sure that's just a fad.

Index

About the Authors

Camille Fournier is a technology executive with leadership experience ranging from early-stage startups to Fortune 50 corporations. She was a founding member of the CNCF Technical Oversight Committee and currently serves on the board of *ACM Queue*. She has published two other books with O'Reilly, *The Manager's Path: A Guide for Tech Leaders Navigating Growth and Change* and *97 Things Every Engineering Manager Should Know*.

Ian Nowland has been in the software industry for 25 years, most recently spending 4 years at Datadog, where he was the SVP of core engineering. Prior to this, he was at AWS in their early days (2008–2016), where he was the lead engineer on the launch of Amazon EMR and the leader of the first five years of the EC2 Nitro project. He is currently a cofounder at a stealth mode startup.

Colophon

The animal on the cover of *Platform Engineering* is a marbled newt (*Triturus marmoratus*), a striking amphibian native to Western Europe, specifically France and the Iberian peninsula. Its name is derived from its distinctive appearance: its dark brown or black body is adorned with irregular, marbled patterns of green. This coloration provides excellent camouflage in the newt's natural habitat of woodlands and meadows. Female marbled newts also have an orange stripe running along their back. While females are larger, these newts range from about 5 to 6.5 inches long.

The marbled newt's diet consists mainly of insects, worms, and other small invertebrates, which it hunts both on land and in water. Though this animal is primarily terrestrial, as an amphibian it requires access to water for breeding and tends to remain in ponds during colder times of year. During breeding season each February, males develop a striking, feathery crest on their back and attract mates by spreading pheromones through a tail-lashing motion. Female newts deposit eggs individually, first smelling and inspecting the leaves of aquatic plants before selecting a leaf to wrap around the egg. Scientists have determined that marbled newts rely on celestial clues such as geomagnetic fields and constellations to locate familiar breeding ponds.

The marbled newt is listed as vulnerable by the IUCN due to habitat loss. Many of the animals on O'Reilly covers are endangered; all of them are important to the world.

The cover illustration is by Jose Marzan, based on a black-and-white engraving from *Lydekker's Natural History*. The series design is by Edie Freedman, Ellie Volckhausen, and Karen Montgomery. The cover fonts are Gilroy Semibold and Guardian Sans. The text font is Adobe Minion Pro and the heading font is Adobe Myriad Condensed.

Milton Keynes UK
Ingram Content Group UK Ltd.
UKHW052134301024
450441UK00002B/5